Gender and Archaeology

The study of gender in past societies has emerged over the last two decades, and has transformed the work of archaeologists. *Gender and Archaeology* is the first volume to critically review the development of this now crucial topic internationally, across a range of periods and material culture.

Roberta Gilchrist explores the significance of the feminist critique of archaeology and feminist epistemologies. She shows the unique perspective that gender archaeology can bring to bear on issues such as the division of labour and the life course. She examines issues of sexuality, and the embodiment of gender identity. A substantial case study of gender, space and metaphor in the medieval English castle is used to draw together and illustrate these strands.

Gender and Archaeology is a comprehensive, accessible and original survey of this key area. Through its lucid discussion of masculinity, sexuality, multiple genders, queer theory and the lifecycle, it will further debate, whilst also becoming the standard introduction to gender archaeology.

Roberta Gilchrist is Professor of Archaeology at the University of Reading, and Archaeologist to Norwich Cathedral. She has published extensively on both gender and medieval archaeology, including *Gender and Material Culture: The Archaeology of Religious Women* (Routledge 1994).

Gender and Archaeology

Contesting the past

Roberta Gilchrist

London and New York

First published 1999
by Routledge
11 New Fetter Lane, London EC4P 4EE

Simultaneously published in the USA and Canada
by Routledge
29 West 35th Street, New York, NY 10001

Routledge is an imprint of the Taylor & Francis Group

Transferred to Digital Printing 2003

© 1999 Roberta Gilchrist

Typeset in Garamond by Routledge

British Library Cataloguing in Publication Data
A catalogue record for this book is available
from the British Library

Library of Congress Cataloging in Publication Data
Gilchrist, Roberta.
  Gender and archaeology: Contesting the past /
Roberta Gilchrist.
  Includes bibliographical references and index.
  1. Feminist Archaeology. 2. Sex role – History –
Philosophy.
  I. Title.
  CC72.4.G55 1999   99–28835
  930. 1'082–dc21   CIP

ISBN 0–415–21599–4 (hbk)
ISBN 0–415–21600–1 (pbk)

For my mother, Gail

Contents

List of illustrations

Preface

> That laugh of hers was the kind of laugh you imagine women having long ago, before they realised they were an oppressed category of people.
>
> Rose Tremain, *The Way I Found Her* (London: Vintage, 1998)

This book critically reviews the progression of gender archaeology over the last fifteen years. It considers the major themes, common concerns and problems of method that have arisen through the study of gender in a broad range of chronological periods and material culture. The structure of the book is both thematic and sequential: after placing gender archaeology within the intellectual context of feminism and social theory, subsequent chapters trace phases in the development of the subject, including: the significance of the feminist critique of science; study of gender roles and the sexual division of labour; consideration of sexuality and the embodiment of gender identity; and the experience of gender through the lifecourse.

In these pages gender is revealed as a metaphor for relations between men and women: gender is an expression of social practice and beliefs about sexual difference. The act of contesting the past serves as a central image of the book, one addressing the tensions between gender and archaeology. The contested past symbolises an intellectual space in which certainties, fixed categories and rigid boundaries have been collapsed, and where the connections between sex, gender and sexuality will remain contingent. Our readings of the past are contested in order to challenge universal and essentialist gender stereotypes, most familiar among them being woman the gatherer, horticulturalist and gardener. In the medieval case study (Chapter 6) the contested space is a garden, one perceived equivocally: the garden is a place of female segregation, but equally a creative female preserve;

simultaneously a symbol of chastity and purity, but also a stage for deception and sexual encounter. The contested past, and more poignantly, 'the contested garden', is a place where binary distinctions are dissolved: nature becomes culture, public becomes private, and the meanings of gender are ambivalent and contradictory. Like the garden, gender is a threshold between oppositions, and its archaeology provides a gateway to a finer textured, interpretative archaeology.

Inevitably, this study has been influenced by own background in medieval European archaeology, but an attempt has been made to represent international trends in the gender archaeology of all periods. Theory and practice are brought together in the final chapter, where a new case study explores gender metaphors and perceptual experience in the medieval castle. The sub-discipline of medieval archaeology has seldom engaged with wider theoretical discourse. Through my case study of the medieval castle and its garden, in addition to my shorter vignettes on medieval weaving and gender identity, and time, space and the lifecourse in relation to medieval parish churches (in Chapters 3 and 5), I hope to bring the audiences of medieval and theoretical archaeology into closer contact.

Acknowledgements

In writing this book I have been fortunate enough to receive the support of many friends, colleagues and students. Much of the book's structure and emphasis results from my experience of teaching gender archaeology to undergraduate and postgraduate students at the University of Reading since 1996. My colleagues at Reading have been generous with their intellectual and practical assistance, variously lending books, reading draft chapters and drawing my attention to debates outside my own purview, most especially Grenville Astill, Richard Bradley, Bob Chapman, Michael Fulford, Heinrich Härke and Steven Mithen. The case study on the medieval castle was first discussed at the Women's History Group at the University of East Anglia. I still value the encouragement that I received from this group over several years, and the specific insights on medieval women offered in particular by Carole Rawcliffe and Veronica Sekules. Subsequently, my castle case study benefited from the comments of seminar groups at the Universities of London, Oxford and York, Dumbarton Oaks (Washington) and the Centre for British Studies at Boulder, Colorado.

The impetus behind the book owes much to my commissioning editor at Routledge, Vicky Peters, who has not only helped to shape the book, but was convinced for some years before I was that I should write it, and that it would be for Routledge. I am especially indebted to the friends who have encouraged this project, notably Lynn Meskell, Jez Reeve and Nyree Finlay.

I am grateful to Steve Allen for his excellent drawings that accompany the text, and to Rosemary Joyce, Lynn Meskell, Geoff Egan, Diane Lyons and East Anglian Archaeology, for permission to reproduce figures.

Glossary

age There are three measures of age: chronological age, which is measured by accepted calendaric means; social age, which reflects the normative behaviour that is culturally imposed on particular age groups; and physiological age, a medical construct that estimates levels of functional ability or impairment (Ginn and Arber 1995: 5).

agency The potential for individual or collective social actors to engage in social practice, and to bring about innovation or social transformations.

analogy To argue from analogy is to reason from similarities between two cases, and to infer further correspondences between unexamined aspects (see Wylie 1985).

anchoress A female recluse who took vows of permanent enclosure and was walled up in a cell attached to a parish or monastic church. This religious vocation was prevalent particularly in northwestern Europe in the later middle ages.

androcentrism A term describing the tendency to privilege male-biased, or male-centred, values and assumptions.

attribution (gender) An archaeological approach that attempts to link specific activities, artefacts or spaces with men or women, often involving the proposal of particular material-correlates for male and female labour (such as Janet Spector's 'task differentiation' method: Spector 1983).

binary Two terms that represent opposite attributes, with the first term usually seen as superior in relation to the second, for example: clean/dirty; light/dark.

Cartesian   Referring to the philosophy of René Descartes (1596–1650), and particularly to his theory of dualism, which proposes that there are just two substances or principles: mind (thinking) and matter (extension).

contextualism   A school of archaeological interpretation that emphasises both the spatial relationships in which artefacts/sites occur, and their wider cultural place and significance. Associated first with the archaeologist Ian Hodder (e.g. Hodder 1987), this approach aspires to the 'thick description' advocated for anthropological interpretation by Clifford Geertz (e.g. Geertz 1988).

diachronic   The study of change in phenomena over time.

difference   'Difference' is used in several respects in relation to gender (as opposed to use of the term by Jacques Derrida, for example). It refers to the alternative positions that have challenged the essentialising tendencies of second wave feminism and its theories about global female experience. *Différence* also carries the connotations of French feminist deconstruction, for example the work of Luce Irigaray (Irigaray 1985), who argues that gender difference does not result from essential biology, but from the experiences of culture, sexuality and gender that make men and women distinctive. Within feminist anthropology, gender difference may be understood as the social and symbolic metaphors that create the complementarity between men and women that is necessary for the functioning of a particular society (e.g. Strathern 1988; Moore 1994).

epistemology   A theory of knowledge concerning the justification of knowledge claims, and encompassing methodologies and means of validation.

ethnography   A branch of anthropology concerned with the study of contemporary cultures through direct observation.

essentialism   A term used in discussion of gender to represent the belief that gender differences are based on natural male and female essences, rather than on experience or social practice.

eunuch   A man or boy castrated by removal of the testes or external genitalia.

feminism   The political conviction to challenge existing power relations between men and women. It has been proposed that feminist thought has developed in three waves (see pp. 2–4). Distinct and often contradictory principles are put forward by different branches of feminist thought, including Marxist, socialist, radical, liberal, standpoint and poststructuralist feminism. For detailed definitions see Brooks 1997; Humm 1995; Tong 1989; Weedon 1987.

gender The cultural interpretation of sexual difference that results in the categorisation of individuals, artefacts, spaces and bodies.

gender identity The private, individual experience of gender, which is also conveyed outwardly through physical and material expressions.

gender relations Culturally specific social relationships that inform attitudes toward, and relations between, different genders.

gender roles The activities and statuses that are associated with specific genders in each society.

gerontology The study of elderly people, and in particular the effects of ageing on the body.

gerontophobia The expression of anxiety or fear towards elderly people.

gynocentricism A term describing the tendency to privilege female-biased, or woman-centred, values and assumptions.

habitus A practical logic and sense of order that is learned unconsciously through the enactment and repetition of everyday life (Bourdieu 1977).

hegemony The domination of one social group or set of cultural values (e.g. of masculinity or femininity) over others that may prevail in the same society (counter-hegemonies).

hermaphrodism A term describing an intersex individual with a congenital condition of ambiguity of the genitalia, recalling the Greek name for the god that combined Hermes and Aphrodite.

hermeneutic Concerning interpretation; a term used in archaeology to convey the reflexive process that is necessary for an archaeologist in the present to make sense of the material culture of past societies.

humour A term deriving from classical humoral theory, and linked particularly with the works of Galen (129–199 AD). It was believed that the human body was made up of four basic elements, which also made up the universe: fire, water, earth and air. The dominance of a particular element in an individual's complexion created the corresponding humours: choleric, phlegmatic, melancholy and sanguine.

kinship Relationships of family and inheritance based on culturally sanctioned rights and taboos.

matriarchy An apparently mythological form of society characterised by female rule, wherein mothers are political leaders and descent is through their line.

matrilineal Inheritance through the line of the mother, rather than the father.

matrilocality The practice whereby, following marriage, a man moves to his wife's place of residence.

menarche A young woman's first menstrual period.

menopause The cessation of menstruation that occurs when women cease to be reproductively fertile.

metonymy The process whereby an attribute or association comes to be used in place of the subject of reference: for example, where phalluses or weapons come to represent masculinity.

misogyny A term describing a deep-rooted hatred of women.

ontology Concerning the nature of existence or being; and the means by which we address issues established epistemologically.

oriel A bay window projecting out from an upper storey.

paradigm The term put forward by Thomas Kuhn to represent the perspective, or problem-solving exemplar, shared by a scientific community. Shifts in paradigms are indicative of scientific revolutions (Kuhn 1962).

patriarchy Power relations that systematically oppress women through structural mechanisms of male authority over social, political and economic institutions.

patristic Referring to the church fathers or their writings.

patrilocality The practice whereby, following marriage, a woman moves to her husband's place of residence.

performance A term linked with the philosophy and queer theory of Judith Butler (Butler 1990; 1993). Through 'performance', the repetition of cultural acts associated with gender, difference is emphasised.

phallocentric A term describing the tendency to define masculine attributes as the norm, and referring to phallic symbols of power and desire.

phenomenology The examination of the intentions or experience of conscious existence, or being. Phenomenological approaches are varied, and include those of the philosophers Heidegger (1962) [1927], Merleau-Ponty (1962) [1945] and Butler (1990; 1993). The existential phenomenology of Maurice Merleau-Ponty (1908–61), for example, emphasised the importance of the body to experience, and sought descriptions of bodily perception at particular points in time and space. In archaeology, it is associated particularly with the work of British prehistorians Christopher Tilley (1994) and Julian Thomas (1996).

postfeminism A term having two divergent meanings. It has been used derogatively to imply that the feminist movement is redundant following women's achievement of legal equality. Conversely, it has sometimes been adopted to represent the tradition of postmodernist or third wave feminists (e.g. Brooks 1997).

postcolonialism The study of the experience of a culture that has been shaped by imperialism, even after independence.

postmodernism A late twentieth-century movement prevalent in the arts, architecture and philosophy, that is characterised by the rejection of single philosophies or explanations of culture.

postprocessualism A term encompassing many different approaches to archaeological interpretation (such as critical theory, contextualism, structuralism, neo-Marxism), all of which reject the mono-causal, functional reasoning of traditional processualism (see Hodder 1986).

poststructuralism An intellectual movement representing the rejection of fixed and unitary cultural identities in favour of more pluralistic readings of cultural representations. An exponent was Michel Foucault, whose discourse analysis examined power structures and the assumptions behind social practices and institutions.

primatology The study of primate behaviour.

primogeniture Right of inheritance by the eldest son.

processualism A school of archaeological thought that emphasises the dynamic relationship between social and economic elements of culture and environment in examining the processes of change.

psalter   A book containing a collection of psalms used for personal devotion.

purdah   The seclusion of women from public view among contemporary Muslims and some Hindus.

queer theory   A term representing the diverse body of theory that takes as its starting point the definition of queer as an identity that acquires meaning from its opposition to the norm. Homophobic categories are reversed to represent heterosexuality as a constructed 'political fiction' or 'other'. 'Queer' is also used to represent alternative positions to age difference, sexuality, etc.

relativism   The assumption that there is no absolute measure or value of true or false, and therefore no reasonable standards for choosing between competing interpretations.

sex   General use of this term refers to classification by means of observable biological differences between men, women and intersex individuals, based on appearance of genitalia, chromosomes and hormones. However, perceptions of sex are to a great extent socially contructed (Laqueur 1990).

sociobiology   A science that assumes that the basis of social behaviour is biological or genetic.

structuralism   The study of symbolic and linguistic structures (independent of cultural context) as systematic patterns that can be measured and described.

sumptuary   Laws intended to regulate consumption, for example through prescriptions on the types of clothing that are considered to be appropriate to different social classes.

transsexualism   A condition describing contemporary individuals who possess the physical characteristics of one sex, and the emotional and psychological identity of the other.

Chapter 1

Gender archaeology
Beyond the manifesto

Gender may be understood as the cultural interpretation of sexual difference: its qualities can be conflicting, mutable and cumulative, contingent upon personal and historical circumstances. The archaeological study of gender in past societies has emerged over the last fifteen years, until today distinctive traditions can be discerned in the practice of gender archaeology. This book aims to assess the place of gender studies within archaeology, charting the changing definitions, concerns and methods of gender archaeology, and its impact on the wider discipline. Such a survey requires a critical consideration of the study of gender within the intellectual histories of both archaeology and feminist theory. While not all gender archaeology is allied with feminism (or conducted by feminists, or even by women), it has evolved symbiotically with feminist thinking. Together with many of the social sciences, archaeology is experiencing a paradigm shift that has resulted from feminism. This transition may be traced from the ungendered (or male-biased) narratives that characterised most archaeology up to the 1970s, through the greater concern for visibility of women in publications of the 1980s and early 1990s, to today's focus on the feminine and masculine. Attention to equality of recognition, and representation of women and men in the past, is being replaced by an interest in gender differences between, and among, men and women.

This chapter examines the catalysis from equality to difference that is taking place in gender archaeology, and sets it within the much wider expansion of perspectives from 'second' to 'third' wave feminisms. Changing definitions of gender are examined, with particular reference to debates on the biological *versus* social construction of gender, and the challenges to prevailing perceptions that have resulted from critiques as diverse as cognitive science and queer theory.

Feminism and gender archaeology: making waves

In common with feminism, gender archaeology is represented by a plethora of approaches. Broad parallels can be traced, however, between the evolution of gender studies in archaeology and the progression of feminism. Here, the background to feminist theory is outlined briefly in order to place gender archaeology within a wider intellectual framework. Its origins can be located in the concerns of what has been termed 'second wave' feminism, while its present aims correspond more closely with those of the 'third wave'. Further, gender studies can be seen to have diverged within the discipline, with particular philosophical aims more typical of Americanist *versus* European gender archaeology.

All feminism is characterised by a political commitment to change existing power relations between men and women, but feminist thought is perceived as having advanced in three separate waves. There is some disagreement amongst feminists as to the precise breakdown of these stages; one common definition is outlined here (after Humm 1995; Brooks 1997). 'First wave' refers to the suffrage movements, between roughly 1880 and 1920, through which women achieved public emancipation and greater rights in the realms of politics, education and employment. The late 1960s saw the emergence of 'second wave' feminism, which focused more on personal issues of equality in relation to sexuality, reproduction, and fulfilment in public and private spheres (Deckard 1975). The intellectual movements that grew out of the second wave were concerned with identifying the root causes of women's oppression: in particular, the theory of patriarchy provided a universal, explanatory framework. 'Third wave' feminism has emerged over the last decade, as feminist theorists have embraced elements of postmodernist thought and shifted their interests to more cultural and symbolic approaches. Significantly, the universalist meta-narratives of second wave feminism have been replaced by greater pluralism, while the emphasis on addressing inequality between men and women has been superseded by the imperative to understand gender 'difference' (Brooks 1997).

Second wave feminists were united by the theory of patriarchy: power relations which structure the subordination of women, through institutions such as the family, education, religion and government. Patriarchal relations are assumed to be structural, operating at an institutional level, rather than resulting from personal intentions. Particular schools of feminist thought emerged that promoted their own universal explanations for patriarchy (see Gunew 1991; Tong 1989). Among the most prominent is socialist feminism, which perceives gender as socially produced and historically changing. In contrast, radical feminism generally proposes a trans-historical definition of gender, in which patriarchy operates through the medium of the family as a social institution that oppresses women. Radical feminists focus more on the biological differences between women and men, and are frequently criticised for promoting an essentialist view of womanhood, in which all women share similar identities and experiences, despite differences in class, race or cultural situation. Marxist feminism, eminating from Engel's assertion that the oppression of women was rooted in the origins of private property (Engels 1884), has also viewed women as a single class, united by the appropriation of their labour and sexuality by capitalist systems of production. More epistemologically based is standpoint feminism, which attempts to construct theories informed by the perspectives of women's lives (Harding 1986, 1991). As part of the second wave, feminist scholars examined the way in which inequalities and male bias had impacted on their own disciplines, with critiques of androcentrism – male bias – in the study of history, anthropology, primatology and the natural sciences (Kelly-Gadol 1976; Rosaldo and Lamphere 1974; Haraway 1989; Keller 1984).

The third wave, sometimes referred to as postmodernist feminism, or even postfeminism, has been influenced by poststructuralism and postcolonialism (Weedon 1987; Brooks 1997). This body of thought rejects the idea of an essential character or experience which typifies men or women. Here the emphasis is on difference: the differences between men and women, or among men and women of contrasting sexualities, ethnicities or social classes. Postmodernist feminism is concerned broadly with examining the creation of subjectivity, through approaches such as psychoanalysis, discourse analysis or deconstruction. Influenced particularly by the works of Michel Foucault, postmodernists contend that each human agent or subject draws meaning and experience from competing, multiple discourses, and that this complex constitution of the subject develops continuously throughout the lifetime. Postmodernist and standpoint feminisms reject universal laws of human experience: their perspectives are characterised by cultural relativism, the assertion that a reasonable observation of one society's tendencies cannot be projected onto another. The contrasting concerns of second and third wave feminism have been identified as a 'paradigm shift' within feminism, as the major objective has moved from a concern with equality to one of difference (Barrett and Phillips 1992).

Archaeological historiography has begun recently to explore the impact of the first wave of feminism on our own discipline. Prominent women, such as Hannah Rydh in Sweden, and Amelia Edwards and Margaret Murray in Britain, can be highlighted for their concern with both the emancipation of their female contemporaries and the archaeological recognition of women in the past (Díaz-Andreu and Sørensen 1998). Second wave feminism took at least a decade to cause scholastic ripples in the deep waters of archaeology. Although by the 1970s a small number of female archaeologists in Scandinavia had begun to consider the more active role that women had played in prehistory (Bertelsen *et al.* 1987; Dommasnes 1992), the first feminist critique of male bias in archaeology was not published until 1984. In a groundbreaking article, American archaeologists Margaret Conkey and Janet Spector argued that archaeology was perpetuating a 'gender mythology' by employing gender stereotypes uncritically. Despite their claims of objectivity, archaeologists were failing to consider historical variations and cultural diversities in gender relations.

> When archaeologists employ a set of stereotypic assumptions about gender, how it is structured, and what it means – what might be called a gender paradigm – a temporal continuity of these features is implied. Even when this paradigm is 'merely' a cultural backdrop for the discussion of other archaeological subjects (e.g. what an artefact was used for), there is a strong presentist flavour to archaeological inquiry: presentist in the sense that the past is viewed with the intent of elucidating features that can be linked with the present.
>
> (Conkey and Spector 1984)

By drawing implicitly on contemporary gender stereotypes, archaeologists were implying a long-standing cultural continuity of gender roles, a linear evolution connected intrinsically with the biological functions of women and men.

The women's movement had demonstrated that it was possible for transitions in gender relations to occur within a very brief timespan; moreover, historians and anthropologists were providing insights to the cultural specificity of gender, the way in which relations between men and women, divisions of labour, and attitudes to sexuality, all varied between cultures. Thus, feminist archaeologists sought a more explicit study of gender in past societies.

> We argue that the archaeological 'invisibility' of females is more the result of a false notion of objectivity and of the gender paradigms

archaeologists employ, than of an inherent invisibility of such data.

(Conkey and Spector 1984)

In order to accomplish this, however, it was necessary to identify and remedy the mechanisms by which biases were introduced to archaeological enquiry. Eventually, the second wave of feminism heralded attention to issues of equity in archaeological employment (Nelson *et al.* 1994; du Cross and Smith 1993), a critique of gender bias in the presentation of the past to the public (Figure 1.1) (Jones and Pay 1990; Moser 1993; Gifford-Gonzalez 1993; Hurcombe 1995), and a concern with exploring women's contributions through more critical historiographies of archaeology (Claassen 1994; Díaz-Andreu and Sørensen 1998). These distinct strands share some of the goals of gender archaeology. They are not concerned specifically with the interpretation of archaeological evidence, however, and therefore fall outside the parameters of this book.

Figure 1.1. 'Flint chipping in Upper Palaeolithic times'. Despite the gender stereotyping of many contemporary reconstructions of prehistoric life (see Moser 1993), the eminent prehistorian Abbé Breuil published a series of vivid colour drawings showing both men and women engaged in hunting and stone tool production, in addition to a more representative picture of age ranges, including the older woman shown here making a spear. His illustrations anticipated the feminist critique by four decades, and were inspired by a sojourn in South Africa during the Second World War. They were dedicated to 'the children, to the adolescents' (Breuil 1949: 16).

Source: Breuil 1949: scene 10, 54. Copyright retained by Gawthorn Press.

Feminist critiques in archaeology have developed from merely identifying male bias, to examining the processes by which knowledge
becomes gendered (see Chapter 2). Here, second wave feminism has
joined with postmodernist themes to challenge claims about knowledge, objectivity and truth – issues crucial to the development of the
whole discipline of archaeology. The study of gender in past societies
has been influenced in turn by the second and third waves. Today their
impact may be felt more as a deluge, with at least 500 articles and an
increasing number of books devoted to the subject. It has been argued
that gender archaeology has not been allied expressly to feminism, but
results from a more grassroots movement that is concerned with
reclaiming the past for women, and highlighting their contributions
and visibility, in a discipline that has previously focused on the male
(Hanen and Kelley 1992: 98). In contrast, I would argue that the
impact of the two waves can be detected very clearly in the aims and
methods of gender archaeology.

Traditions of anthropology and archaeology have been influenced
overtly by second wave feminism, and in particular the search for
universals to explain women's subordination. The work of anthropologists Sherry Ortner and Michelle Rosaldo, for example, stimulated a
persistent interest in supposedly universal binary oppositions of
culture/nature, public/private and male/female (Ortner 1974; Rosaldo
1974; for discussion see pp. 32–5). Within American gender archaeology this tendency has prompted a strong motivation to explore the
sexual division of labour in specific historical contexts, and to examine
the connection between reproductive and gender roles (Chapter 3).
This concern with labour roles has been personified by a search for
universals (such as the inherent proposition that women gathered,
cooked, potted and wove), in addition to an interest in female agency
and women's contributions to innovation and change (e.g. Gero and
Conkey 1991; Wright 1996; Claassen and Joyce 1997; Kent 1998).
Such approaches are consistent with the second wave's concern with
equality and with the aim of producing explanatory meta-narratives.
They have also achieved the integration of a wider range of evidence in
American gender archaeology, including environmental sources and
osteology. Although exceptions may be cited, of course, this type of
gender archaeology has predominated in North America, and has fitted
comfortably with the objectives of both processual archaeology and a
more 'grassroots' movement.

European gender archaeology has focused more generally on the
symbolic and cultural manifestations of gender, with lesser regard for

gender roles and the sexual division of labour (e.g. Moore and Scott 1997). It is marked by a greater concern for the individual, manifested through study of gender identity, sexuality and the body, and with the representation of gender through forms of signification such as art, space and grave goods (Chapters 4 and 5). European gender archaeology has largely omitted the broader corpus of environmental evidence that has been harnessed by American studies. The examination of gender in European archaeology has been represented to date predominantly by British and Scandinavian approaches. Alternative perspectives include Marxist feminist work in Spain (Colomer *et al.* 1994), while other regions are more characterised by their complete absence of gender archaeology. In Italy and Greece, for example, national traditions have been empirically driven and lacking in more theoretical concerns that might have encouraged work on gender (Vida 1998: 15; Nikolaidou and Kokkinidou 1998: 253). A similar lacuna in French archaeology has been attributed to the supposed reluctance of French feminists to isolate women as a category for analysis (Coudart 1998: 61).

The distinctions between American and European traditions result from several factors, including the greater impact of second wave feminism on the American academy. The explicitly political objectives of feminism have been explored more determinedly in American archaeology, resulting in a marked concern for cultivating feminist networks and programmes of research and teaching, a tendency shared with feminist archaeology in Scandinavia and Australia (see, for example, the journal *Kvinner i Arkeologi i Norge* ['Women in Archaeology in Norway'] and publications of the series of Australian conferences on women in archaeology: du Cross and Smith 1993; Balme and Beck 1995). At the same time, European archaeologists have been more dissipated in their political objectives, but more receptive to structuralist and symbolic anthropology, such as that of Mary Douglas (Douglas 1966, 1970), and to poststructuralist, largely Foucauldian approaches (Foucault 1981). Thus the advent of structuralist, contextual and postprocessual archaeology (Hodder 1982, 1987; Shanks and Tilley 1987) has fostered in gender archaeology the greater plurality that is associated with the third wave. These contrasting traditions are teased out in the chapters that follow, with the case studies in Chapters 2 and 3 dominated by the work of American archaeologists, and those in Chapters 4 and 5 predominantly European. Although parallel concerns are increasingly evident, it seems that contrasting epistemological traditions of gender archaeology have emerged.

Recent feminist work in many disciplines is embodied by an interest in 'difference', although this term is used inconsistently. Generally, the acknowledgement of difference has resulted from critiques of second wave feminism by Third World feminists, women of colour and lesbians (Brooks 1997: 16). In this sense, 'difference' refers to the alternative positions that have challenged the essentialising tendencies of second wave feminism and its theories about global female experience. '*Différence*' also carries the connotations of French feminist deconstruction, for example the work of Luce Irigaray, who argues that philosophy and language are phallocentric discourses that mask the positive qualities of difference that emerge from the sexualised female body (Irigaray 1985). This type of gender difference does not result from essential biology, but from the experiences of culture, sexuality and gender that make men and women distinctive.

'Difference' is also promoted by queer theory, especially by Judith Butler, who has confounded the concept of gender identity and the notion of fixed categories of gender and sexuality (Butler 1990, 1993). In some respects Butler is the new orthodoxy: she is an American feminist philosopher and the doyenne of queer theory, to the extent that a fan magazine, *Judy!*, has been devoted to her. She aims to destabilise the apparent coherence and centrality of heterosexual gender identities by examining the processes by which such identities are created. She suggests that through 'performance', the repetition of cultural acts associated with gender, difference is emphasised (see pp. 13–14, 82). Yet for archaeology, the most important considerations of 'difference' may be those emanating from feminist anthropology. A shift of focus has occurred in anthropology, from considerations of hierarchical power and differential prestige between men and women (e.g. Ortner and Whitehead 1981), towards attention to gender difference. In this context, gender difference may be understood as the social and symbolic metaphors that create the complementarity between men and women that is necessary for the functioning of a particular society (e.g. Strathern 1988; Moore 1994).

Consistent with the plurality and 'difference' of the third wave is an emergent masculinist perspective in archaeology, one which perhaps reacts against the woman-centred tendency of much existing gender archaeology. Ironically, the masculinist outlook may prove vital in achieving the ultimate aims of gender archaeology, and should not be rejected by feminists on the grounds of gut reaction. 'Gender mythology' in archaeology has masked the contributions and experiences of both women and men in the past. Masculinist theory challenges nomothetic, essentialist views of the male; for instance that men in all societies are aggressive, uninterested in nurturing children, or highly competitive (Connell 1995). The concept of masculinity itself is being re-examined as a multi-dimensional quality that is selectively adopted by men, and sometimes women (Cornwall and Lindisfarne 1994; see Chapter 4). This perspective is slowly permeating archaeology (e.g. Yates 1993), with masculinity considered as a relational construct, one which is divergent and constantly changing (Knapp 1998: 368; Meskell 1996: 5).

Culture *versus* nature: is gender made, born or lived?

> Sexual difference is one of the important questions of our age, if not in fact the burning issue.
>
> (Irigaray 1984, cited in Moi 1987).

Second wave feminists in all disciplines have emphasised the distinction between sex and gender, viewing sex as a stable biological category, and gender as a socially created and changing set of values. The social sciences have been dominated by this perception of gender, termed 'social constructionist', but the coherence of this position is now challenged by contrasting insights, such as those offered by cognitive science and queer theory. Until very recently, a social constructionist definition of gender was adopted unanimously within archaeology. Gender has been described as a social construct (Sørensen 1988, 1991), social agency (Dobres 1995), socially constructed male and female categories (Hastorf 1991), a cultural construction (Hodder 1992: 258), and so on.

Social constructionists argue that sex and gender are distinct: one is biological, the other cultural. Gender is not taken to reflect biological givens of maleness and femaleness, but rather the symbolic investment in biological difference that varies between cultural traditions (Ortner and Whitehead 1981). Gender is understood to be learned behaviour, resulting from historically specific processes of socialisation. This position developed from the views of early feminists, such as Simone de Beauvoir, epitomised in her much quoted phrase, 'one is not born a woman but rather becomes a woman' ([1949] 1972: 295). This view is also consistent with the basic premise of socialist feminism that sexual inequalities are socially, rather than biologically produced (Gatens 1991). The social constructionist position was further solidified by debates surrounding sexual orientation, in particular whether homosexuality is culturally or biologically created (Caplan 1987; Stein 1990). Polar, fundamentalist opinions have been established, with constructionists viewing gender as environmentally induced, and essentialists (including radical feminists) regarding gender as intrinsic and universal. This schism has perpetuated through thirty years of feminism, despite the growing body of evidence that suggests that some aspects of gender may be constructed, or highly influenced by, biology. To what extent is gender made or born?

Sociobiologists believe that behaviour is genetically controlled, and that human choices are ultimately motivated by the unconscious desire to pass one's genes to the next generation. This view, popularised in works such as Richard Dawkins' *The Selfish Gene* (1976), proposes that social structures and behaviour develop to increase the 'fitness' of individuals, thus maximising their chances of contributing genes to future generations. Sociobiologists would argue that divergent social behaviour in men and women results from the evolutionary need for reproductive fitness: males had to be more aggressive, territorial and promiscuous, while it paid females to be more altruistic, passive and sexually loyal (e.g. Lovejoy 1981). Such approaches can be criticised for reducing human behaviour to a single cause, with gender determined by male and female hormonal differences. Field studies of non-human primates have indicated the relative independence of sexual behaviour from strictly hormonal control, while an anthropological perspective reveals that the human hormonal and lifecycle is highly sensitive to cultural differences (Sperling and Beyene 1997: 142, 144).

More recent Darwinian studies have proposed a link between female reproductive strategies and the emergence of sexual symbolism as a 'set of deceptive sexual signals aimed by female kin coalitions at their mates to secure increased male reproductive investment' (Power and Aiello 1997: 154). It is argued that menstruation was recognised as signalling impending fertility, and that women developed strategies such as 'sex strikes' and sham menstruation to hold on to their mates (Knight 1991). While this perspective claims to introduce female agency to evolutionary studies, it retains the proposed primacy of reproductive strategies, and reduces gender difference to essential biology. These studies continue to serve sexist aims, and it seems no coincidence that sociobiology gathered momentum just as the women's movement challenged the validity of a 'natural' female link with motherhood and the home. Sociobiology is inherently political: witness Kingsley Browne's recent, popular thesis linking the modern workplace with evolutionary gender differences (Browne 1998). He argues that the 'glass ceiling and the gender gap is the product of basic biological sex differences' that 'have resulted from different reproductive strategies followed by the two sexes during the course of human evolution' (Browne 1998: 5). In particular, he asserts that 'men are more competitive, more driven towards acquisition of status and resources, and more inclined to take risks ... women are more nurturing, risk averse, less greedy and less single-minded' (*ibid.*). In short, he concludes that due to the evolution of their temperaments, today's men will be frustrated if forced to make a greater domestic contribution, while women will suffer undue stress or will underperform if given managerial responsibility (*ibid.*: 59).

More penetrating studies of sexual difference have been put forward by cognitive science. There is some evidence to suggest that men and women differ in the physical structuring of the brain, and that specialised brain functioning has developed in the male and female. Dean Falk has summarised the sexual disparities in the human brain (Falk 1997: 116–23). The female brain is on average only 90 per cent of the size of the male's, while female neuronal densities are higher. Sexual dimorphism exists in three separate pathways that connect the right and left sides of the brain, resulting in dissimilarities in average performances for certain abilities in men and women. Women process certain types of information in both hemispheres of the brain, while men rely on only one hemisphere. The sexes age incongruously, with men three times more likely to suffer aphasia. It seems that the brains of modern men and women are 'wired differently' (*ibid.*: 119). But how do such discords in 'hardware' affect social behaviour?

There seem to be consistent differences in the average performances of men and women in cognitive skills, across populations and situations (Halpern 1992; Silverman and Eals 1992). There is a wide overlap in male and female performances, however, and the sexual odds in mean performance are statistically significant but very subtle (Falk 1993: 216). Men have more highly developed visuo-spatial skills (such as map-reading), particularly in relation to three-dimensional space, and perform better in mathematics and musical composition. Women possess greater fine motor skills and are generally better communicators: they have higher verbal abilities, excel at reading and writing, and 'are subtly biased for certain emotional skills such as understanding non-verbal body language' (Falk 1997: 122). Some of these tendencies relate from brain lateralisation, the different use of right and left hemispheres of the brain by men and women, in addition to hormonal fluctuations in both sexes that affect spatial abilities (Silverman and Eals 1992: 533).

Given the documented sexual differences in the human brain, it has been widely speculated that such dimorphism is evolutionary, and connected with reproductive strategies (although it should be stressed that the influence of environmental and hormonal factors on such differences has not been fully explored). Dean Falk has proposed that early human males required more precisely honed visuo-spatial skills in order to travel across larger territories to increase mating opportunities. She reasoned that female verbal skills evolved from the mother-infant relationship, and the need for vocal communication to ensure survival (Falk 1997: 126). Silverman and Eals, in contrast, have argued that there is a female advantage in spatial visualisation. Further, they suggest that selection for spatial dimorphism resulted from an early sexual division of labour: the female gathering and male hunting that is postulated for early hominid groups (see pp. 19–21). Their experiments with modern men and women indicated *specialisation* in spatial abilities, rather than the superior performance of men in visuo-spatial tests. This comprised a male aptitude for spatial and mental rotations, *versus* a female ability for remembering selections and placements of objects. They concluded that such divergences resulted from the particular requirements of men to track and kill animals, and women to recall plant locations over wide regions and time spans.

These cognitive studies of gender difference are problematic in a number of respects. First, the observed differences in cognitive abilities between men and women are based on averages between the sexes, and considerable overlap exists between individuals. Indeed, these proposed cognitive differences may be exaggerated. In addition, experiments on modern males and females have not taken cultural and environmental factors into sufficient account. Further, the evolutionary explanation of gender difference is not fully convincing. It assumes that cognitive differences observed in modern men and women may be traced to evolutionary strategies that began to emerge two to three million years ago. Little consideration is given to the impact that cultural constructions of gender have had on brain development in the intervening millions of years, and particularly over the last 100,000.

Moreover, reproductive fitness does not explain the variety of historically attested human sexual preferences, including homosexuality and cross-generational sex. True Darwinians might dismiss such choices as 'deviant', but historical and ethnographic studies have emphasised the social and historical character of homosexuality (e.g. Herdt 1994). It was a controversial moment, therefore, when Simon LeVay, a gay neuroscientist, proposed in the early 1990s that homosexuality was biologically determined. LeVay argued that there were differences between heterosexual and homosexual men in the size of part of the brain (one of the interstitial nuclei of the anterior hypothalamus), with this region in gay men's brains being closer to that of women's (LeVay 1993). Lynda Birke has commented that the receptivity of this theory in some circles was due to the moral pressure placed on gay men, particularly in the United States: if one is born gay, it cannot be morally reprehensible to be so (Birke 1994). In common with sociobiological theories of sexual difference, the 'gay gene' promotes a single, biological mechanism behind sexuality.

Whether gender, social cognition or sexuality are dependent fully on biology *or* culture is no longer the issue. The interesting questions are how biological and/or cognitive difference is interpreted culturally, how this varies between societies, and how the mind and body may evolve in response to cultural definitions of gender. Differences in male and female cognitive abilities are slight, and cannot explain the diversity of gender roles and identities. Study of the interaction between genes and culture has the potential to examine human choices and gendered experience, for instance the relationship between chromosomal sex, physical appearance and social gender (see pp. 56–8). Surely the variety and distinctiveness of the human condition cannot be explained simply by a constant, unconscious drive to transmit one's genes?

Conversely, social constructionists cannot afford to dismiss evidence for cognitive differences out of hand. Refusal to engage with such evidence may lead to the misapplication or popularisation of bogus theories (as frequently happens with sociobiology). Exploration of the cognitive differences between men and women may even be compatible with certain elements of postmodernist feminism, in particular the pyschoanalytic approaches of French feminists such as Luce Irigaray, Hélène Cixous and Julia Kristeva, who concentrate on the distinctive ways that men and women use language, speech and writing (Moi 1987). In light of such debates, can gender archaeologists continue to assert that 'nothing about gender is genetically inherited' (Nelson 1997: 15)?

The sex/gender dichotomy has been rocked furthered by queer theorists and historians of the body, who contend that sex and gender are equally constructed categories (see Chapter 4). The social constructionist separation of sex and gender is viewed as an artificial distinction between the body and mind, a binary gender construct which assumes that the body is a fixed reference point onto which cultural elements of gender are inscribed. The work of Judith Butler has been particularly influential in this respect, destabilising sex and gender categories to create 'gender trouble' (Butler 1990, 1993). She argues that hetero-sexual norms are constructed political fictions, and that the disunity of sex and gender categories precludes a full understanding of the personal experience of *living* in a gendered body. She contends that gender and sexual identities are 'performances' that take on coherent meanings through their constant repetition: 'Gender is the repeated stylization of the body, a set of repeated acts within a highly rigid regu-latory frame that congeal over time to produce the appearance of substance, of a natural sort of being' (Butler 1990: 33). In this way gender takes on the appearance of something natural, such as woman and man; it is not just constructed, but a binary effect which is illu-sionary or artifical. Butler argues that our contemporary gendered categories are created by us and lived by us. This rejection of prede-fined categories in favour of self-embodiment is a challenge to conventional social and biological definitions. For archaeology this collapsing of categories remains problematic, since our interrogations frequently begin with biological sexing of human skeletons, without the benefit of direct observation or engagement with embodied indi-viduals. In applying a queer perspective to the past, however, we may detect inconsistencies and mutabilities in orthodox sex and gender categories.

Is this recent concern with self, and body-consciousness, symp-tomatic only of our own society's gendered preoccupations? The anthropologist Henrietta Moore has cautioned that the idea that 'gender is in the body' may not be universal to all cultures (1994: 36). Within gender archaeology these debates have led to a reconsideration of sex, gender and sexuality (Meskell 1996, 1998), including attention to changing definitions of biological sex (Nordbladh and Yates 1990), contextual emphasis on body imagery (Kampen 1996; Moore and Scott 1997; Koloski-Ostrow and Lyons 1997; Montserrat 1998) and the experiential qualities of gender lived through the body and lifecycle (Chapter 5). Beyond the manifesto, gender archaeology is making waves: it offers a more comparative perspective to modern theorists, probing the interstices of nature and culture, sex and gender, across societies, through lives and time.

Gender and archaeology: an illustrated history

It is beyond the scope of any single book on gender archaeology to provide a comprehensive summary of the approaches used in the study of gender in all geographical regions, chronological periods and categories of material culture. Instead, it is the intention here to critically evaluate the major themes and common strands that run through the diversity of gender archaeology. Epistemological issues are raised that may be common concerns, such as the use of ethnographic analogy in prehistoric studies (pp. 37–9), or source criticism in historical archaeology (pp. 110), and the controversial issue of 'attribution' in studying the activities, artefacts or spaces of men and women in the past (pp. 41–3, 128–9). This history of gender archaeology is illustrated by case studies that have been selected for their clear or innovative approaches to important themes, or for their explicit attention to methodology. These case studies have been selected also to provide an insight to the variety of different media encompassed in gender archaeology, ranging from Palaeolithic art to nineteenth-century ceramics, and everything in between. They include the examination of gender through artefacts, buildings and space, visual representations, environmental data, human skeletons, or cases which integrate multiple sources of evidence. The unfolding of gender archaeology, and the particular studies that have contributed to its emergence, are appraised critically. This discipline is ripe for such an assessment from within, one which questions the rigour of much earlier work and its woman-centred zeal (e.g. Nelson 1997).

This book is structured thematically, but also in order to provide a sense of the intellectual maturing of gender archaeology. Chapter 2 examines the impact of the feminist critique on archaeology, largely in the 1980s, and the development of feminist epistemologies as part of an ascending gender archaeology. The third chapter explores gender roles, with particular attention to female agency and the sexual division of labour. American case studies predominate, and reflect the first concerns of gender archaeology as it was informed by second wave feminism and processualism. An increasing dissatisfaction with universal explanations can be detected in recent work on this topic, a theme picked up in Chapter 4. Chapters 4 and 5 reflect the concerns of third wave feminism, and postmodernist influences such as the work of Foucault: European case studies are paramount. Chapter 4 examines the archaeology of gender identity, and the way in which the subject is constituted through sexuality and the body. The instability of categories of sex and sexuality is emphasised, for instance through changing historical definitions of sex, and the incidence of multiple genders; archaeological approaches to masculinity are reviewed. Chapter 5 examines the cumulative properties of gender as it takes on different meanings through the course of a lifetime, and gender and age are interrogated in relation to time and space. More phenomenological approaches are introduced, which focus on the experience of gender as everyday perceptions and performances, themes which unite recent work in both American and European gender archaeology. The final chapter offers a new case study, drawing together issues raised in the preceding chapters and employing multiple sources of evidence. The archaeology of the medieval castle is used to explore themes which include the meaning of gender segregation and female seclusion; body metaphors in gendered discourse; the interaction of gender, age and class; and a phenomenology of gender difference, with the aim of recapturing the sensations of being a man or woman in a particular historical context.

Chapter 2

Strange bedfellows
Feminism and archaeology

To what extent is archaeological knowledge gendered? Do men and women carry out different kinds of archaeology, or think about the past differently? Two decades of feminist critique have revealed inequalities in the language, visual representation and practice of archaeology (e.g. Conkey and Spector 1984; Moser 1993; Nelson *et al.* 1994). Have such discrepancies also affected the interpretation of archaeological evidence? How have the tensions and predispositions of our time influenced how archaeologists comment on gender relations in past societies? Within the social sciences gender is considered to be socially constituted, a term embodying the cultural values that result from perceptions of sexual difference between, and among, men and women. This chapter reviews the emergence of gender archaeology through the feminist critique of science, and examines the relationship between feminism and archaeological theory, postulating the development of a feminist epistemology in some branches of gender archaeology.

The feminist critique of science: all about Eve

The emergence of processual archaeology in the late 1960s and 1970s witnessed a new concern with the evolution of social structures and ranking within communities. Yet, where social differences between men and women were considered, it remained standard practice to simply invoke contemporary gender stereotypes. David Clarke, for example, in his influential study of living spaces at the Iron Age village of Glastonbury, proposed a fundamental division in settlement layout based on a distinction between major houses, representing family and male activities, and minor houses, in which female concerns were rooted. He argued that the minor houses were largely female, domestic areas

on the basis of artefacts found in association with them, including beads
and bracelets, querns, combs, and tools for spinning, leather and fur
working, in addition to human bones found beneath the floor that were
'in some cases certainly female' (Clarke 1972: 815, 817). He conjectured
that associated baking huts were warm, dry environments, in which the
women were 'gossiping pleasurably' (*ibid*.: 821). His interpretation of
spatial patterning has been criticised on the grounds of post-deposition
(Barrett 1987; Coles and Minnitt 1995), but the message conveyed of
gender relations at Iron Age Glastonbury was more invidious. In this
regard Clarke employed neither ethnographic analogy nor contextual
evidence. His assertion of a gendered division of houses in the compounds
rested purely on his own assumptions: the notion that women were
somehow *naturally* associated with domestic work such as food preparation and production of clothing. This case is typical of the implicit bias
which underpinned many 'ungendered' interpretations that predated the
feminist critique of archaeology. Such narratives frequently assumed that
female activities were confined to the domestic sphere, and further,
judged them by the standards of the 1970s as minor, peripheral and
unimportant. By failing to consider the gender roles at Glastonbury
explicitly, Clarke, like many others before and after him, fostered a
perception of gender as natural and timeless, in which female labour was
devalued and women's subordination somehow inevitable.

The 'new' archaeology of the 1960s had striven to ally itself with
the sciences. Organic analogies were adopted in the conceptualisation
of human 'systems', more rigorous methodologies were developed for
observing and recording archaeological evidence and formation
processes, and research was conducted through the generation of a
series of hyphotheses that could be tested. Processual archaeology
emerged as a discipline that claimed the potential for more scientific
and objective comment on the past, by isolating the different processes
or systems that operated within a society. Despite its aims, this revi-
talised archaeology was no less biased with regard to gender.

Once they had become sensitised to the existence of androcentrism,
feminists soon recognised substantial bias within the sciences (Harding
1983, 1986; Bleier 1984). Feminist scepticism emerged as it was
shown that scientific method did not guarantee the objectivity of results.
But how could disciplines that had evolved from the Enlightenment
tradition of rationalism, which valued the meticulous recording of
detail and the repeatability of experiments, be riddled with inherent
bias? Despite the inscrutable image that science presents, feminists
contend that there is no neutral position in the construction of know-

ledge. Today this viewpoint is shared by many, including postmodernists, environmental activists, anti-imperialists and postprocessual archaeologists. A facade of hard objectivity had been perpetuated, yet science lacked the capacity for self-reflection that is required to question the motives and agendas behind scientific research.

The natural and applied sciences were scrutinised by feminist philosophers on several levels. Their concerns included the extent to which women had been marginalised in scientific practice, or their contributions made invisible in the histories of science; the ways in which science and technology had been used to serve sexist, racist or homophobic aims; how androcentrism skewed the definition of topics chosen for study and the methods selected to pursue them; and how sexual metaphors and language had been used to make sexual stereotypes appear natural (Harding 1991: 19). Finally, and perhaps most significantly, feminists questioned the androcentrism of prevailing epistemologies. They asked how the absence of women in the practice of science affected the construction of knowledge, and they proposed alternative, feminist epistemologies.

Nowhere was the feminist critique more effective than in the study of human evolution: the emotive narrative that proposes the origins of gender inequalities. Within anthropology and primatology, approaches to human evolution changed dramatically in the 1970s and 1980s. Apparently this transformation was not the result of a specific feminist programme (Haraway 1989; Zihlman 1997; Fedigan 1997); instead, a radical rethinking of human origins was stimulated by the work of women primatologists studying female non-human primates.

The belief that humans evolved gradually, as a result of adaptive change, became fashionable in the second half of the nineteenth century, following the landmark publication of Charles Darwin's *The Origin of Species* (1859). Darwin's key concept of 'selection', in which populations reproduced selectively to improve features that would complement their environment, left the issue of human sexual difference unexplained. In *The Descent of Man, and Selection in Relation to Sex* (1871), Darwin pursued the problem of secondary sexual characteristics in humans, such as greater size and armament in males and enlarged breasts and buttocks in females. He argued that secondary sexual characteristics in all animals are unnecessary for reproduction, and therefore must have developed in relation to sexual selection. He observed that males are larger and more aggressive than females and juveniles, and reasoned that sexual characteristics had progressed in order to determine competition between males, and to provide an element of sexual choice for females. While in this scenario females are credited with choosing larger, more successful mates, evolution was understood to be biased towards the male. Darwin argued that secondary sexual characteristics evolved through selection in the male, with females evolving only 'on their coat-tails'.

> Thus man has ultimately become superior to woman. It is fortunate that the law of equal transmission of characters to both sexes prevails with mammals. Otherwise it is probable that man would have become as superior in mental endowment to woman as the peacock is in ornamental plumage to the peahen.
>
> (Darwin 1871: 874, quoted in Fedigan 1986: 29).

The cultural bias of Darwin's model has been commented on, in particular the characterisation of the male as 'active and ardent' and the female as 'passive and reclusive', gendered traits that were especially valued by Darwin and his Victorian contemporaries (Fedigan 1986; Hager 1997).

Darwin's model of human evolution was bound up with one of the increasing regulations of human sexual behaviour, that assumed a linear trajectory of evolution from polygamous groups to monogamous marriage. In the twentieth century, anthropological fieldwork cast doubt on such social evolutionary models (Fedigan 1986). Concern with human evolution was rekindled in the 1960s, however, when the impetus behind human development was explained by the 'Man the hunter' model. It was proposed that sexual difference emerged some 2.5 million years ago, when our human ancestors survived by foraging in the African savannah. Men engaged competitively in food procurement through hunting, and protected the mate and offspring for whom they provided. Women traded sexual favours and reproductive capacities in return for this food and protection (Washburn and Lancaster 1968; Lee and Devore 1968). For some, this model renewed the Darwinian precept that males could be credited with all evolutionary innovations, including bipedalism, the invention of tools, social cooperation and symbolic systems. It has been suggested that this version of human evolution appealed especially to post-war audiences: this creation of the 1960s was based on 1950s values, which hoped to see men returning from war to the workplace, and women retreating from public life back into the home (Hager 1997: 5). The aggressive, meat-seeking male and the passive, home-bound female were well suited to suburban America, where barbeques and Darwinism reigned supreme.

The 'Man the hunter' model was based on observations of non-human primates, in particular baboons, who exhibit male-bonding and hierarchies that were thought to explain the invention of weapons and hunting (Devore and Washburn 1968). Yet chimpanzees are the primates closest to humans, and the essence of their social life is not the male hierarchy, but rather the mother-offspring bond. This relationship stimulates the use of simple tools by chimpanzees to locate food, such as termite sticks and pounding stones (Fedigan 1986: 40–1). The observation of this behaviour initiated an alternative model of human evolution: 'Woman the gatherer' (Dahlberg 1981). Sally Linton proposed that the intense bond between mother and infant in primates, and the need for early female hominids to feed their young, would have led to the gathering, carrying and sharing of food. She suggested that females would have developed containers to hold gathered foodstuffs and young infants (Linton 1971). Adrienne Zihlman postulated the invention of tools by early female hominids, to assist in gathering plant foods, and carrying devices that would allow them to walk with their young for long distances in the open savannah (Zihlman 1978). The significance of the 'Woman the gatherer' model was supported by ethnographic evidence on hunter-gatherers, such as Richard Lee's study of fifty-eight foraging societies, which revealed that on average hunted food provided only 35 per cent of the diet, with half sustained by gathered foods collected predominantly by women (Lee 1968). In these communities women were shown to be active, productive and independent in achieving their subsistence (Lee 1979). The caricature of the immobile, passive female, trading sex for meat, could not be sustained. More recent models of human evolution credit both male and female hominids with active contributions.

It is significant that primatologists were the prime movers in placing women in models of human evolution. Primatology has been called an 'equal opportunities science', which enjoys a greater proportion of women practitioners, accords them equal influence, and as a discipline, values the careful observation of social life at which women frequently excel (Fedigan 1992: xii). Although primatology has been praised highly by feminists, Linda Fedigan has suggested that this is 'an unrequited love affair': primatology has fostered no feminist agenda, but instead has been receptive to female-centred models that are well grounded in empirical evidence (Fedigan 1997: 58).

The gendering of archaeological knowledge: keeping the house in order

How does the discipline of archaeology compare with such euphemistic developments in anthropology and primatology? In considering the construction of archaeological knowledge, two aspects of the feminist critique will be reviewed briefly: first, the feminist reinterpretation of androcentric narratives of the past; and second, the way in which knowledge is gendered by archaeological practice.

Feminist critiques of androcentrism in archaeology have focused on interpretations which present ungrounded stereotypes of women's lives, or render the female contribution invisible. While the 'Woman the gatherer' model was successful in highlighting the female role in early foraging societies, women are seldom credited with innovation in sedentary communities. The invention of agriculture, for example, is frequently perceived to be 'co-evolutionary', in other words plants are thought to have gradually domesticated themselves alongside human settlements. Even where a female connection with plant gathering is acknowledged, co-evolutionary models assume no active role for women in the development of horticulture. This supposition has been challenged by Patty Jo Watson and Mary Kennedy, who have reconsidered theories surrounding the development of horticulture in the Eastern Woodlands of North America. On the basis of ethnographically documented associations between women and horticulture, they proposed that plants were domesticated by the intentional disturbance of soil and the repeated introduction of seeds by women (Watson and Kennedy 1991). In particular, they suggested that this process would have accompanied everyday female activities, such as plant processing.

In the region under consideration, gourd-like cucurbits and bottle gourds appeared about 7,000 years ago. It has been proposed that this resulted from a deliberate introduction through trade with tropical areas, and further, that such an intentional act of domestication can only take place when introduced by a person of high status, such as a specialist or shaman (Prentice 1986). Thus a link was postulated between gourd domestication and trade and ceremony, assumed to be male domains. When viewed as a high-status act of innovation, rather than a passive, co-evolutionary process, Watson and Kennedy observed that any connection between plant domestication and women was denied. Two further phases of horticultural development were considered: native cultigens appeared approximately 3,500 years ago in the Eastern Woodlands, and maize was cultivated purposefully in the region's inhospitable climates by 800–900 AD. Watson and Kennedy inferred the deliberate acclimatisation of maize as a new species, introduced by women gardeners who had been responsible for the earlier development of native cultigens.

Watson and Kennedy concluded that some, if not all, species would have required deliberate treatment to convert them to garden crops, and, on the basis of ethnographic comparisons, suggested that plant domestication was carried out by women acting intentionally and drawing from an accumulated body of knowledge. Their account is no more provable in absolute terms than the androcentric interpretations that they challenged. But, in contrast to androcentric models, Watson and Kennedy were explicit in their assumptions concerning the sexual division of labour, and clear on the ethnographic sources of analogy on which they based their conclusions. Their study confronted androcentric perceptions by attributing a major cultural transformation to the deliberate and strategic activities of women. In common with many feminist approaches, they were concerned to emphasise the role of female *agency*: actions or changes created by the choices made by individual women, or resulting from the impact of female networks.

Archaeological knowledge may become gendered according to the different questions that men and women ask of the past, just as anthropologists are gendered in the way in which they select informants in their field research, formulate questions and analyse the accounts gathered (Strasser and Kronsteiner 1993: 166). Women generally make up the minority of professional archaeologists: in England and Australia approximately 35 per cent of archaeologists are female (Morris 1994; Beck 1994), in the United States the figure is estimated at 20 per cent (Gero 1991: 97), and even in Norway only 49 per cent of archaeologists are female, despite the exceptional position which women occupy with regard to the nation's archaeology (Engelstad *et al.* 1994: 142; Dommasnes *et al.* 1998: 105). Does this imbalance in the numbers of men and women affect the nature of archaeological knowledge? Would archaeology be a very different discipline if there were equal numbers and opportunities for women and men? As Joan Gero has asked, do women produce a different kind of knowledge, or construct knowledge by different processes? (Gero 1991: 98).

To address this issue, Gero reviewed the contrasting approaches that male and female archaeologists have adopted in the study of lithics. For example, experimental flint-knapping has been conducted exclusively by men, while the analysis of how tasks are carried out has been dominated by women (*ibid.*). Even the types of tools chosen for study differ: women study flake tools and nutting stones; men study arrow heads, splay points, axes and adzes – artefacts that are associated with hunting or warfare, and that require extensive retouching. In turning to the subject of palaeobotany, Gero observed a different kind of division. Men were writing synthetic, theoretical papers, while women were concentrating on the basic identification of plant material. In palaeozoology, men dominated the large mammal studies, indicating a consistent tendency across archaeology's subdisciplines for men to emphasise the role of hunting. Gero concluded that women's work in archaeology is painstaking, labour intensive and methodologically explicit. Although this work may be perceived as worthwhile, it is not considered to be amongst the highest status concerns in archaeology.

Elsewhere, Gero has proposed that men are more closely associated with archaeological fieldwork, while women are recognised for excelling in the specialised analysis of archaeological materials (Gero 1985: 344). Although Gero's premise is itself essentialist, assuming that archaeologists in all social and cultural contexts will follow the same gendered patterns, her observations are largely consistent with the way in which the construction of archaeological knowledge has been gendered throughout the discipline's history (Claassen 1994; Díaz-Andreu and Sørensen 1998). The general socialisation of women seems to have left them more reticent to engage in synthetic or highly theoretical studies, a reluctance that has masked their contributions in the long term. They have been less likely to tackle high-profile field projects, a situation which may result from cultural attitudes towards women's practical competence. Moreover, the gendering of the educational process may inhibit the confidence of female archaeologists, while the possibility of conducting fieldwork is sometimes precluded by the imbalance of domestic and family responsibilities that continues to fall on women.

Beyond a sexual division of labour in archaeological work, it may be possible to glimpse a more deeply rooted, gendered epistemology. Historically, female archaeologists are said to have pursued topics traditionally linked with domesticity and decoration, such as the study of textiles, jewellery, pottery and art (Díaz-Andreu and Sørensen 1998: 10). There has been a clear tendency for them to specialise in chronological periods in which women are more visible, or potentially more powerful, such as later prehistoric Europe (Dommasnes et al. 1998: 119) or its early medieval period, where women are well represented through abundant grave goods. But have women archaeologists developed distinctively female approaches, a gendered theory of knowledge?

In some cases a profusion of female imagery in ancient contexts has prompted women archaeologists to postulate an early period of matriarchy, a golden age in which women were prominent ritually and politically. Such alternative narratives were posited for Minoan Crete by Jane Ellen Harrison in the 1920s (Picazo 1998: 209), by Margaret Murray in 1934 (Talalay 1994), and more recently by Marija Gimbutas, in her celebrated vision of Neolithic Europe. Gimbutas interpreted female figurines as a direct reflection of a goddess cult that was egalitarian, matrilinear, peaceful, art-loving and woman-centred (Gimbutas 1989). Her work attracted notoriety outside archaeology, where her view of Old Europe as a gynocentric utopia was embraced by New Age and eco-feminist groups (Figure 2.1). Her interpretations were certainly a different way of viewing the past, and influenced by her position as a woman (Chapman 1998), but they have been criticised justly for their remarkable essentialism. Gimbutas interpreted all female figurines from any period or region as having been linked with the same fundamental beliefs about women and the goddess; further, her work is now recognised as having been flawed on the grounds of archaeological context, dating and typologies (Meskell 1995).

Figure 2.1 The image of the Goddess? Marija Gimbutas interpreted the symbolism of Neolithic Europe as 'the pictorial script for the religion of the Old European Great Goddess' (1989: xv). She considered even abstract images to represent the Goddess, such as the egg, seen as the symbol of birth, rebirth and regeneration, depicted on a bowl from Karanovo, Bulgaria (4500–4300 BC).

Source: Drawing by Steve Allen, after Gimbutas 1989: fig. 338, 218.

Feminist epistemologies: a different way of doing

Why has it taken so long for feminism to result in a more tangible gender archaeology – some twenty years after it regenerated certain other disciplines? Alison Wylie, a feminist philosopher of science, has observed that archaeology has matured through a similar three-phase process to that postulated by philosopher Sandra Harding for other sciences (Harding 1983): initial critiques of androcentrism, followed by 'remedial' research focusing on women, and finally broader reconceptualisations of existing subject fields which consider gender together with other structuring factors (Wylie 1991: 31–2). Elsewhere I have argued that this slow growth stems from two further factors that are specific to archaeology (Gilchrist 1994: 3–4). First, the social definition of gender was resisted for some time in archaeological circles, with favour given to the study of a biological notion of gender. Broad male and female associations could be extrapolated from grave goods found in conjunction with skeletons excavated from prehistoric burials. From such evidence generalisations were made about gender that suited the processual and structuralist preference for universal generalisations. Second, the positivist character of archaeology, devoted to the empirical testing of data, has over-emphasised the significance of methodologies, and mitigated against the study of more abstract, social issues such as gender. Because gender is not immediately visible as a feature in the archaeological record, it has been ignored by archaeologists (Wylie 1991b: 18).

It is perhaps not surprising that initially the diversity of feminist perspectives on gender was not viewed sympathetically by processualism, which sought generalisations and regularities in human societies. The relatively recent interest in a more holistic gender archaeology has been fuelled by postprocessualism, a broad church which embraces structuralist (Hodder 1982), contextual (Hodder 1987) and critical approaches (Shanks and Tilley 1987a). Structuralist archaeology stimulated a new interest in symbols and ideology; contextualism rejuvenated historical specificity; and critical archaeology examined the subjective nature of archaeological knowledge. Like third wave feminism, postprocessualism is eclectic: feminists and postprocessualists share concerns with the social, an interest in power relations and an emphasis on the potential of individual agency. Feminism and critical archaeology have both been allied to cultural relativism, and assert that the construction of knowledge is subjective (Engelstad 1991). Michael

Shanks and Christopher Tilley, for example, the postprocessualists *par excellence*, introduced the notion of the 'hermeneutic circle' to archaeology, whereby the past can only be understood in relation to the present, and interpretations are formulated only on the basis of our own experiences in the contemporary world. The process of interpretation demands subjectivity, with the past understood as 'other', a foreign culture, our perceptions of which are mediated through relations of the past and present (Shanks and Tilley 1987a).

Because of its political nature, feminist archaeology has resisted the extreme epistemological relativism of some brands of both feminism and postprocessualism, which denies the possibility of any reasonable standards for choosing between competing interpretations. As Alison Wylie has observed, a relativist position would remove grounds for adjudicating between feminist and androcentric archaeologies (Wylie 1991, 1992b). Is it possible instead to develop a feminist epistemology – a theory of knowledge based on feminism? Sandra Harding has proposed that within the sciences a feminist knowledge, rooted in the experiences of women's lives, would enhance the possibilities for objectivity (Harding 1991). While the relationship between the political project of feminism and the objective aims of science may seem contentious, Harding argues that the feminist critique of androcentrism demands a more self-critical and socially situated programme. She has characterised three feminist approaches: feminist empiricism, which aims to produce a less-biased, more rigorous science within existing structures; feminist standpoint theory, which attempts to construct scientific knowledge from the perspective of women's lives; and feminist postmodernism, which opposes essentialism and seeks plurality of knowledge. She has been influenced herself by postmodernist feminist debates in the 1990s, concluding that the generation of feminist knowledge, even standpoint feminist knowledge, is not restricted to women (Harding 1993).

Ultimately, Harding contends that a feminist standpoint epistemology can produce empirically more accurate data (Harding 1991: 119). She proposes that the socialisation of women (or other particular groups) provides them with different insights; their position slightly outside the scientific mainstream gives them a more analytical perspective, and distances them from establishment interests. Many women's greater concern with everyday life may prompt different questions and scales of analysis, and their experiences are based less on the reified structures that inform 'abstract masculinity' (Harding 1991: 119–31). Harding's standpoint feminism does not advocate any intuitive female qualities, and it rejects female essentialism, stressing instead the contrasting subjectivities of women drawn from different classes, races, sexualities and global positions. More recently Harding has extended her definition of standpoint feminism to include contradictory identities, arguing that it is not 'experience' itself that produces knowledge, but thinking from a contradictory position (i.e. outside the mainstream). In this framework, feminist knowledge can be produced not just by women, or oppressed women, but by men or particular social groups (e.g. defined ethnically, socially or sexually) (Harding 1993: 156).

Alison Wylie has suggested that much gender and feminist archaeology to date has been carried out within the tradition of empirical feminism (e.g. Gero and Conkey 1991), which aims to unmask bias and to identify the errors and inconsistencies of the 'bad science' that is conducted under the auspices of androcentrism (Wylie 1992b). Further, she argues that through its methodological rigour, feminism has the potential to enhance the conceptual and empirical integrity – the objectivity – of archaeology. Its political motivation leads to more critical use of ethnographic analogies and the more careful formulation of analyses. Wylie attempts to reconcile feminist archaeology and the strongly positivist line of processualism. Indeed, she argues that the feminist study of asymmetrical relations of power is processual, in that power is examined as the outcome of dynamic (rather than fixed) processes, and as the result of social structures rather than individual agency (Wylie 1992a: 62).

Feminist empiricism has scrutinised archaeological method as well as interpretation. In all disciplines, the feminist critique has opened up 'the method question', in which the conflict or continuum between method and theory are explored (Keller 1984). It is clear that no simple technique will unlock the complexities of gender, but some have argued that we must emphasise the way in which gender can be revealed through the archaeological record (Claassen 1992). In contrast, Joan Gero and Margaret Conkey proposed that such attempts at 'gender attribution' (for discussion see pp. 40–3), pinning male and female categories to material evidence, reduces the scope of gender archaeology to merely making women visible:

> Why is there a 'need' to 'find' females and not the same 'need' to 'find' males, who are, by implication, already present, active, and the primary contributors to the archaeological record and the human past?

> (Gero and Conkey 1991: 12)

They have argued that gender archaeology has no responsibility to be more 'testable' than the study of other abstract qualities, for example the emergence of elites or religions. As Wylie noted, however, the political convictions of feminist archaeology do carry responsibilities for methodological rigour. Moreover, archaeologists must resist epistemological relativism if they are to say anything at all meaningful about the past. In moving towards a distinctive epistemology, feminists have experimented with new archaeological methods.

The first studies in gender archaeology hoped to create cross-cultural frameworks for examining gender, such as Janet Spector's 'task differentiation' method which aimed to identify broad artefact-correlates for gender based on ethnographic models (Conkey and Spector 1984; see pp. 41–3). The definition of gender that is now adopted is more historically specific, so that cross-cultural generalisations are considered largely inappropriate. Prevailing methodologies have been challenged by feminist approaches that are more sensitive to gendered nuances. Anne Yentsch, for example, critiqued the artefact pattern analysis of American historical archaeology, which quantifies artefacts principally according to a description of their materials, and proposed an alternative based on the functions of artefacts as they relate to men's and women's activities (Yentsch 1991). Marcia-Anne Dobres developed a new, more contextual approach for examining bone and antler technologies of the French Upper Palaeolithic (Dobres 1995). She considered the tools within their spatial context, eventually recording ninety specific technological attributes for six classes of artefact at eight sites. On this basis she argued that it was possible to discern local strategies, technical abilities and social statuses that included gender relations.

This concern with the careful recording of detail, and micro-scale analysis, is consistent with the gendered approach to archaeological knowledge that Gero characterised as female (Gero 1991). Is it possible that some women are asking different questions of the past, and developing methods better suited to their aims? These feminist approaches, as Wylie has commented, share a focus on local, empirical detail (1992a). Especially within Americanist gender archaeology, a feminist epistemology seems to have emerged that concentrates on the small-scale, on everyday occurrences and relations between people, on subtle shifts in power and relations of production. While strongly rooted in the empirical tradition, feminist archaeology shares some qualities with Harding's standpoint epistemology. Drawing on their own perspectives, some feminists are creating an archaeology concerned less with hierarchies and meta-narratives, and more with the observation of detail, complexities, and local or personal experience.

To what extent has the discipline of archaeology been receptive to this feminist perspective? Up to the late 1980s, commentaries on archaeological thought failed to credit a feminist contribution (Trigger 1989), or considered it under-developed (Shanks and Tilley 1987b: 191). A minority dismissed gender and feminist archaeology as 'political correctness': Paul Bahn ridiculed gender archaeology as a feminist racket with little substance – 'the empress's lack of clothes' (Bahn 1992: 321). More constructively, Ian Hodder emphasised the positive outcome of the feminist critique of androcentrism, which resulted in reconsiderations of models of the sexual division of labour and more critical assessments of 'dominant' male activities (Hodder 1991: 168–70). Yet in 1992, it was possible for Marie Louise Stig Sørensen, herself a feminist archaeologist, to suggest that gender archaeology had failed, in that it had not shed substantial light on the past, or on gender relations (Sørensen 1992). It was certainly true that the majority of published work at that date had concentrated on critique, with few case studies that applied feminist theory to archaeological evidence. Sørensen also decried the quality of some feminist archaeology, rightly proposing that it was time for an internal critique of gender archaeology. While today some 'bad science' masquerades as feminist or gender archaeology, I would argue that in the intervening years gender archaeology has indeed progressed archaeology's outlook.

Gender archaeology is not necessarily a feminist or postprocessual project; it is concerned equally with processualism, and with masculinist studies by men, or of men. Gender archaeology will prove to be no more than a chimera, however, if it merely reorders the dominant subject as female to a silent, male 'other'. It owes a legacy to feminism in its promotion of a largely social and cultural definition of gender, its rejection of essentialist perspectives of what it means to be a woman or man, and its willingness to explore new methods and theories of knowledge. The following chapters will examine major contributions to our understanding of the gender relations of production, gender identity, representation and experience, as well as the impact of new concerns arising from the studies of the body, sexuality and the gendered lifecourse.

Chapter 3

Gendered hierarchies?

Labour, 'prestige' and production

For some time, archaeologists have been concerned with the ways in which subsistence and production activities were allocated in past societies according to sex. Universal tendencies have been sought in the ethnographic record to attribute specific tasks to male and female (e.g. Binford 1978), and in archaeological contexts material correlates for such tasks have been given gendered interpretations (e.g. Flannery and Winter 1976). The 'materialist' basis of archaeology has promoted an interest in productive roles that may have over-simplified the relation between gender and the sexual division of labour. Indeed, attempts to make gender more visible in the archaeological record have proceeded on the assumption that an exclusive sexual division of labour was present (Conkey and Spector 1984). A conflation of sex and gender, labour and production has resulted, with the common assumption that 'the function of gender is to organise labor' (Claassen 1992: 3). Archaeological approaches have been influenced by debates in anthropology, especially the concern with kinship, and the linking of productive roles with a gendered hierarchy that consistently devalues the female. Such issues have dominated gender archaeology particularly in North America (e.g. Gero and Conkey 1991), with its more anthropological and processual roots, in contrast to the greater concern with gender identity and its cultural construction within European archaeology (e.g. Moore and Scott 1997).

Gender is not necessarily reflected by a sexual divison of labour, but gendered values are embedded in the relations and processes of production. This chapter will outline the classic works of feminist anthropology that crystallised the link between male and female prestige and the sexual division of labour. Archaeological approaches to gender and production are reviewed, including the use of universal and evolutionary models, and methods such as 'gender attribution'.

Archaeological case studies are raised in a discussion of the theoretical and methodological implications of a gendered archaeology of production, one which challenges essentialist constructs of hierarchy and prestige.

'Female is to male': universals, binaries and the anthropology of gender

Anthropology's heritage has been one concerned with variability in sex roles, conjugality and the family, stretching back to nineteenth-century studies by Spencer, Morgan, Marx and Engels, that sought origins and explanations for social structures (Moore 1988: 46–8; Peacock 1991: 342). Nearly three decades of feminist anthropology have been devoted to scrutinising the sexual division of labour, prompted by a number of key contributions that asserted the universality of female subordination. Is sexual asymmetry universal, and if so, how can it be explained?

Sherry Ortner first addressed the apparent dichotomy of women's universal subordination, despite the cultural diversity and variation shown in their symbolic representations. In 'Is female to male as nature is to culture?' she explored the ways in which women's roles, symbols, work and products are diminished by culturally defined value systems that attribute higher prestige to the male (Ortner 1974). She proposed that there is a universal tendency in every culture to associate women with something that is devalued. In particular women are seen as closer to nature – physiologically, socially and psychically; while men are associated with higher orders of culture. The male/female, culture/nature opposition, she argued, is maintained through concepts of purity and pollution. Although Ortner conceded that the culture/nature axis was culturally constructed, her model proposed global female subordination which arose from women's reproductive role. Equally influential was Michelle Rosaldo's assertion that women were universally associated with a private, domestic sphere that was less prestigious than the public, male domain. A second opposition was proposed of male/female, public/private; again, the subordination of the female was traced to her role in biological reproduction, and also to her more domestic responsibilities within the sexual division of labour (Rosaldo 1974).

Thus two sets of binary oppositions emerged, linking male/female with public/private and culture/nature, that were applied cross-culturally to examine and explain gendered difference. Further, it was proposed by Judith Brown that the division of labour by sex is universal, and that compared with men, there is a relatively limited range of subsistence activities in which women make a substantial contribution.

This perspective also returned to biology, arguing that the sexual division of labour was due to women's role in childbearing and childcare, and from the innate physical and psychological differences between men and women (Brown 1970). Subsequent scholarship frequently built upon, or rallied against, these claims.

The 'prestige-oriented' character of gender relations was examined, exploring the means by which prestige was gained and conveyed through kinship and marriage. It was proposed that there is a general cultural tendency to define men in terms of their status and role categories, such as warrior, hunter or elder, while women are defined almost entirely in terms relational to men, such as wife, mother or sister (Ortner and Whitehead 1981: 8). It was clear, therefore, that considerations of gender roles in production could not be divorced from kinship: social networks that structure marriage, reproduction and inheritance (see Moore 1988: 49–56). Kinship systems were viewed as observable and empirical forms of sex/gender systems (Rubin 1975: 169). Following the work of Claude Lévi-Strauss (1969), it was argued that in patriarchal societies social reproduction was structured through marriage patterns that required an exchange of women (a theme taken up by Claude Meillassoux [1981]). In this way male power was established over women, and male prestige could be built partly upon wifely production, labour, and kinship links to trading partners and property rights (Ortner and Whitehead 1981: 16).

Inevitably, crucial flaws were identified in these unifying models, both by observers and by the original proponents themselves. The universality of female subordination was questioned: egalitarian societies could be cited in opposition to the theory (although no examples were forthcoming of matriarchal ones). The notion of global models essentialised the categories of man and woman, reducing them to a-historical types without the fine texturing of age or social context. The concept of the exchange of women through marriage rendered them passive objects, negating any degree of female agency or female roles in social and economic networks. Rosaldo (1980) concluded that her proposed public/private dichotomy emphasised the differences between men and women, but did not explain or illuminate the relationships between them. She stressed that gender could only be understood in relation to other social markers (such as class).

The binaries proposed by Ortner and Rosaldo have been challenged on various grounds. The culture/nature and public/private oppositions may be more apparent than real, perhaps the result of the general western intellectual tendency to seek Cartesian dualities, or the specific influence of structuralism within anthropology. The formulation of public and private domains is now regarded to be a postindustrial construct, frequently inappropriate for application to non-capitalist societies. Where the domestic domain is present, its lower status may be an ethnocentric perception on the part of western viewers, rather than an estimation of real value accorded within a particular social context. Finally, the very concept of a male/female dichotomy assumes a binary gender structure in all societies, precluding the possibility of multiple genders or fluidity in gender metaphors.

Ethnographic studies have challenged the universal applicability of these binary gender structures. For example in her study of the Iñupiat of the North Slope of Alaska, Barbara Boderhorn has debunked the assumption that a sexual division of labour results in the gendering of space; and further, that where a distinction exists between public and private, this will necessarily be gendered (Boderhorn 1993). Among the Iñupiat labour is gendered, in that men are linked more directly with ritual and hunting, and women with sewing and butchering. Yet it is believed that both sexes are needed for successful hunting and main-tenance of relations with animals: animals are said to give themselves to men whose wives are generous and skilful (*ibid.*: 187). There is no domestic sphere as such; houses are not units of production, but symbolic of the cohabitation of marriage, which is fluid and easily dissolved. The spaces in which work is carried out are not gendered – the tundra, ice, domestic and communal spaces in the town. In work, space and cosmology, Iñupiat men and women share an interdepen-dence that defies the public/private dichotomy (*ibid.*: 198).

Recently, Sherry Ortner has revisited the debates that she sparked, observing that imbalances in male and female prestige are universal, but that there are differences in the pervasiveness of male dominance (in relation to female autonomy) and the degree of female power present (Ortner 1996: 139). She now contends that prestige structures and power systems cannot be considered separately (*contra* Ortner and Whitehead 1981), but rather that a study of hegemony and counter-hegemony is needed, because 'no society or culture is entirely consistent' (Ortner 1996: 146). Thus universals have been discredited not just across cultures, but within them. As an example she considers the Andaman Islanders, whose leadership unit is the older couple, who share a considerable degree of equality and a complementarity of religious roles. Age and generational status are more important than gender in defining prestige; there is no exchange of women, but instead there is exchange of children; and the public/private opposition is not articulated. Ortner concludes that male domination can no longer be considered a universal, but instead that some societies are 'hegemonically egalitarian' (*ibid*.: 172). In many contexts she believes that male dominance is fragmentary, not hegemonic, but she remains concerned with the reasons behind its emergence. She argues that male dominance must have been realised intentionally, through 'some sort of "will to power" emerging from a "natural" aggressiveness' (*ibid*.: 176). Here we see a return to evolutionary essentials, the sexual division of labour and reproductive roles. Ortner proposes that male dominance emerges because male domestic responsibilities (such as hunting) are more episodic, allowing greater time for male congregation. She cites Jane Collier and Michelle Rosaldo's view that male power relations are grounded in violence (1981) and Peggy Sanday's cross-cultural evidence for male aggressiveness (1981). This is another assertion of universals, a gauntlet which must be addressed by masculinist studies (for discussion see pp. 64–71).

Investigation of the sexual division of labour, and in particular the female contribution to subsistence, has been furthered by new ethnographic field methods that closely record the tasks and activities of each member of a social group (Peacock 1991; Hawkes *et al.* 1997). It is now possible to test the hypothesis that the sexual division of labour is determined by logistic constraints on female work, created by childbearing and childcare. It had been proposed that women's contribution to subsistence would be low unless early weaning was introduced and carers alternative to the mother were employed. Nadine Peacock has challenged these assumptions in her study of the Efe of northeastern Zaire, foragers who maintain a symbiotic relationship with the neighbouring Lese, who are village-living horticulturalists. The Efe exchange hunted or gathered food, or their own labour, in return for the Lese's agricultural produce. The Efe men hunt, collect honey, make and repair their tools, while the women forage, process food, collect firewood and water, and work in the gardens of the Lese. There is a sexual division of labour, yet this is flexible, and men who are seen doing women's work are not emasculated. Women contribute substantially to subsistence, but they do not participate in potentially life-threatening activities (such as hunting and honey collecting) that would place children at risk. Pregnant or nursing women continue to engage in energy-intensive tasks, such as carrying heavy loads, although they do so with less frequency than usual. The Efe women practise late weaning of infants, yet they make a high contribution to subsistence, including tasks which do not seem highly compatible with childcare. This apparent contradiction is facilitated by the women's sharing of childcare, including nursing, comprising an 'intricate and varied pattern of co-operative work and mutual caretaking among women' (Peacock 1991: 354). Thus, in response to supposedly universal limitations created by women's reproductive role, it seems that local variations and solutions are devised.

Assumptions can no longer be made concerning the universal subordination of women or the dominance of men. Feminist debates in anthropology have resulted in the re-examination of notions of relational prestige, sexual difference and duality. The central gender relation may not be limited to pairings of husband and wife, in which the woman's prestige is relational to the man's, but in the case of Samoa, for example, also a mutual relation and status defined through brothers and sisters (Tcherkezoff 1993), or amongst the Iñupiat of the North Slope of Alaska, a cooperative interdependence between men and women (Boderhorn 1993). The connection between gender and the sexual division of labour is continually redefined. As Henrietta Moore has observed, perhaps 'one of the more notable failures of gender anthropology has been the inability to think about difference without implying hierarchy' (Moore 1993: 194). The necessity to examine gender as difference is a lesson that archaeology would do well to learn.

Gendering the machine: the archaeology of labour, production and technology

In considering the gendering of labour from an archaeological perspective, archaeologists have been faced with stark choices. Generalisations might be proposed from tool kits associated with burials containing sexed skeletons, for instance, or extrapolations may be made from broad ethnographic evidence concerning the sexual division of labour. Both approaches have their problems. Apparently utilitarian artefacts in graves do not necessarily reflect the subsistence activities of its occupant, but rather may represent symbolic items or mementoes placed by mourners; nor does the linking of biological male and female sex with specific tools further our understanding of the relationship between production and the social processes of gender. Conversely, where implements found in association with sexed skeletons may contradict received opinion on gendered patterns of labour, the context of the evidence is disregarded. An example of this has been discussed by Anne Stalsberg, who has questioned previous interpretations of scales and weighing equipment in the graves of Viking women in Russia and Norway as reflecting the women's status as merchants' wives, or instances where a wife coincidentally died while acting as a trader on behalf of her absent husband. On no account had it been considered that the women in these graves were themselves 'tradeswomen', who were represented in death by the objects of their profession (Stalsberg 1991: 77). While the use of ethnography might be expected to act as a check on our own modern assumptions concerning the sexual division of labour, the use of ethnographic analogy for explanatory purposes is contentious (see below); further, much of the existing ethnographic record is biased towards male activities. Given these limitations, archaeologists have developed their own frameworks for the use of ethnographic sources, and divergent approaches to the archaeological study of subsistence, production and technology.

The discipline of archaeology has borrowed from anthropology to construct its own set of universals. There is frequently the assumption that male and female labour were accorded differential prestige, both within their own contemporary context, and by the commentaries of archaeologists or ethnographers. Hence there has been a concern with rescuing 'feminine technologies' from their degraded status (Wright 1996; Gero 1991). There has been an assumption in favour of the general existence in past societies of an absolute sexual division of labour (Costin 1996; Sassaman 1992), and an impetus to recognise activities or tasks that can be associated with men or women cross-culturally. For archaeology, the lure of such universals can be irresistible, as they would enable the identification of artefact correlates for men's and women's labour in archaeological contexts. Use has been made of the cross-cultural files developed by Murdock (1937) and studied by Murdock and Provost (1973), who considered fifty technological activities in a sample of 185 societies, ranked in descending order according to the degree of male participation. Further, archaeologists have adopted evolutionary models that explicitly connect enhanced levels of social complexity with an increased emphasis on the sexual divison of labour, and the tendency cross-culturally for particular tasks to be carried out by men or women.

In their discussions of early foraging societies, for example, archaeologists assume that women gather plant foods and men hunt; while in horticultural, sedentary societies it is proposed that women do the majority of garden labour, planting, weeding, preparation of food, cooking, collecting wood and transporting water (Watson and Kennedy 1991; Bentley 1996: 37). Although some have challenged the notion that the production of stone tools was solely the preserve of men (Gero 1991), it continues to be asserted that pottery production should be attributed to women (Arnold 1985; Wright 1991; Sassaman 1992). In relation to craft specialisation generally, Cathy Costin has argued that even where men and women work in the same general range of activity, their labour is gendered by subtasks, resulting in 'a remarkably consistent ideal of keeping men's and women labor distinct' (Costin 1996: 123). Increasing social complexity is considered to structure a gendered labour pattern beyond the domestic unit, with full-time craft specialisation dominated by men. It has been argued that cross-culturally, state societies reproduce the sexual divison of labour in the family through the imposition of taxes and wage controls that effectively limit female labour to the domestic sphere. Female labour loses prestige while a more prestigious, male public domain emerges to legitimise such oppression through political and ritual elites. Through such mechanisms the control of women by the state has been viewed as a means of controlling kinship-based households (Silverblatt 1987; Wright 1996: 80; Brumfiel 1996: 146). Strictly evolutionary approaches have been adopted for much gender archaeology, in which universals are drawn for levels of social complexity, modes of production and the gendering of labour. This rather 'vulgar' materialist approach constrains the study of gender as an historical process, one potential means by which transformations in technologies and labour relations may be realised.

Even explicit studies of change have been based on the unproblematic use of ethnographic analogy. For instance, Kenneth Sassaman has commented on the sexual divison of labour that is likely to have accompanied the transition from mobile to sedentary societies. He argues that in prehistoric eastern North America this transformation is characterised by a shift in the dominant artefacts, from formal lithic technologies (hafted bifaces) to pottery and stone tools produced by expedient core reduction (Sassaman 1992). His proposal that this shift should be considered in terms of gendered labour relies solely on the assumption that women are universally linked with early pottery production, and with the incipient horticulture and collection of shell-fish that would have prompted expedient technologies. Should the use of analogy be used more critically in assigning the sexual division of labour in past societies?

The issue of analogy has been well debated in archaeology, particularly with regard to using ethnoarchaeology to seek universals in human behaviour or technological responses (e.g. Gould 1980; Binford

1985; Wylie 1985). To argue from analogy is to reason from the similarities between two cases, and to infer further correspondences between unexamined aspects. The use of ethnographic analogy to provide cross-cultural explanation has lost favour in archaeology, given the proved diversity in cultural experience, and the extent to which ethnographic data have been biased by the contact of subject groups with anthropologists (Trigger 1989: 336). Attempts have been made to place limitations on deductions drawn from analogy, and to distinguish contexts in which such inferences may be more appropriate. For example, the use of relational analogies has been proposed in which suitable ethnographic analogues for archaeological evidence are sought between societies which share similar environments (even when separated by space and time), or levels of technological skill. Direct historic analogies have been viewed as less problematic; for example, where folklore or ethnohistoric sources are used to assist in the interpretation of archaeological contexts which are linked with the same culture, but are non-contemporaneous. Such direct historic approaches assume long-term continuities in cultural and technological traditions, while relational ones frequently fail to consider the causal and functional connections that may be shared by the source analogue and the subject. Even such controlled use of analogy has remained controversial when used to predict or explain archaeological patterns, as opposed to generating interpretative possibilities. More rigorous use of analogy would consider both similarities and differences between analogues, and develop a more creative use of multi-source analogy in interpretation (Wylie 1985). While more recent epistemological trends in archaeology have favoured contextual over analogic approaches, the very specific interests of gender archaeology have used ethnographic analogy in a way which continues to emphasise universal and evolutionary assumptions. The parameters for the use of analogy, whether relational or directly historic, are seldom elaborated. Both ethnographic and historical sources are used to predict or explain the sexual division of labour, with little or no consideration of the circle of inference that has been employed.

Increasingly, the fine detail of ethnography and its applicability to archaeological problems is being questioned. The widely influential model of the !Kung, for instance, in which plant foods gathered by women represent the majority of the !Kung diet (Lee 1979), has been cited for evidence of women's substantial contribution to subsistence. It is now realised that the !Kung's foraging region is depleted of game resources, so that their diet is unusually dependent on women's gathering (Claassen 1997: 86). Further, the standard 'Woman the gatherer' model does not illuminate the sexual divison of labour in arctic or subarctic regions where plant foods are minimal. In a study of the Chipewyan and Cree of Saskatchewan (Canada), for example, it has been shown that women concentrate on the acquisition and processing of food resources, but that this includes hunting of small mammals (Brumbach and Jarvenpa 1997). A sexual division of labour can be observed, but this relates to the size of hunted animals and the differential distances travelled by men and women from the home village, rather than a rigid division between plants gathered by women and animals hunted by men. It is clear that in preference to universals extracted from ethnography, archaeological studies of gender and subsistence must emphasise particular ecologies and site catchment analysis of food resources.

Approaches to gender and production have begun to focus on technology as a set of social relations, rather than as a suite of disembodied, mechanistic actions. Our own perceptions of technology have been tinged by industrialisation: technological processes appear devoid of human creativity and social relations, and technology seems a self-powering force divorced from human enterprise. Yet, even production of the simplest artefact requires negotation between people or cooperation among groups, frequently with a breakdown of specific subtasks. Production of stone tools, for instance, demands skill, biological strength, and access to raw materials, including the time and mobility required to collect them (Gero 1991: 171). Such tasks must be scheduled in relation to other activities, such as childcare, or established in association with arrangements for the sharing of tasks (see above; Peacock 1991). Rather than one sex being responsible for production of all stone tools, both sexes are likely to have fashioned implements most suited to their needs, with specialisation emerging. Different groups or individuals may have been responsible for different stages in the sequence of production, for example quarrying and transporting of raw materials for stone tools or pottery, before completion by more skilled workers. In her discussion of pottery production in the Indus Harappan civilisation (6000–1800 BC), Rita Wright observes that even where the potter may have been male, the tasks of procuring clay, collecting wood, loading kilns and finishing vessels may have been carried out by women (Wright 1991: 198–9). How important is it for us to be able to attribute specific tasks to men and women in the archaeological past?

Margaret Conkey and Joan Gero, among others, have challenged the notion that gender archaeology should be confined to the 'attribution' as male or female particular types of artefact (such as spindle whorls or flint flakes) or feature (such as hearths, butchering sites or workshops) (Conkey and Gero 1991: 11–12). This sort of approach proceeds from the basis that gender needs to be made visible and concrete within the archaeological record. In this way consideration of gender is sometimes reduced to a methodology for rendering male and female activities visible, or at least a version of them based on our assumptions regarding the sexual division of labour. Marcia-Anne Dobres has sought a broader approach to gender and technology through the consideration of social relations that could have structured the production of Palaeolithic stone tools, such as kin, clan, moieties and tribe (Dobres 1995). Despite a detailed and explicit methodology which aims to identify cultural attitudes to technology, she considers it unnecessary 'to attribute specific genders to artifacts and technical strategies' (*ibid.*: 42). In direct contrast, Cathy Costin has argued that gender attribution is essential in order to examine more closely the specifics of the sexual division of labour and changing social relations of production (Costin 1996: 112). She contends that gender attribution is essential to provide the detail of men's and women's lives in the past; otherwise 'we create a "genderless" gender theory' (*ibid.*: 116). It may be that through more abstract approaches to gender (e.g. Dobres 1995; Barrett 1989) we lose the more personal or human quality of the past – the faces which gender archaeologists hoped would replace the 'faceless blobs' of prehistory (Tringham 1991: 94).

Attempts to assign artefact correlates for men's and women's work have been influenced predominantly by Janet Spector's 'task-differentiation framework' (Conkey and Spector 1984; Spector 1983). Spector begins with the premise that the sexual division of labour is not fixed or absolute. Her framework is not an archaeological methodology, but rather a means of organising ethnographic data to consider tasks: segments of activity which can be assigned to specific social units of a group, for which season, frequency and duration can be estimated, location of task performance pinpointed, and the materials required for artefacts, structures and facilities identified. This approach has been used to facilitate a more discerning use of direct historic analogy, employing ethnohistorical or historical sources. In Spector's study of the Hidatsa, for instance, a Native American group who occupied earth lodge villages in the Great Plains, she sought evidence for task differentiation in early twentieth-century accounts of nineteenth-century Hidatsa life (Spector 1993). Despite the limitations of early ethnography, she was able to identify significant patterns in the setting, timing and units of labour for men's and women's work. Women, with the exception of killing animals, collected and processed all food and natural resources, including processing skins, constructing and maintaining structures. The unit of female labour consisted of sisters, mothers and daughters drawn from individual households; in contrast the unit of male labour drew men from several households with labour divided by age. During summer buffalo hunts, younger men scouted and tended horses, older men planned and carried out ritual acts, and those remaining killed and butchered animals, and policed the hunting camps. Women conducted their work primarily in gardens, lodge interiors and areas adjacent, up to one mile, and their work involved a greater number of stationary storage facilities; men were more likely to work beyond the village boundaries, although both men and women travelled considerable distances during buffalo hunts. Women's tasks were sometimes seasonal (such as garden work), but there was a daily routine of chores throughout the year. Men, in contrast, had few activities scheduled on a daily basis, and while hunting spent periods of days away from the villages. Spector's use of Hidatsa ethnography throws up important spatial and temporal dimensions that accompany a sexual division of labour. The potential of ethnography is limited, however, in addressing her aim to consider gender in relation to change, stability and adaptation. We are presented with a snapshot of Hidatsa life, one selectively constructed through the lens of early twentieth-century ethnographers.

In their study of the Chipewyan and Cree of modern Saskatchewan, Hetty Jo Brumbach and Robert Jarvenpa adopted Spector's 'task differentiation' framework to order ethnographic data, but also used the interviewing techniques of oral history to gather further information, particularly on elements of change over time and during the lifecycle (Brumbach and Jarvenpa 1997). The 'task differentiation' approach has also been used to organise historical sources, with the more direct aim of identifying material correlates for men's and women's work, that too frequently results in attempts to verify the *presence* of women (e.g. Gibb and King 1991; McEwan 1991). For example, Elizabeth Scott used Spector's framework in a study of the eighteenth-century fur trading settlement at Michilimackinac (Michigan) (Scott 1991). In an attempt to 'predict' archaeological assemblages, she classified historical evidence for divisions in labour by sex, class and ethnicity and attributed specific foods and artefacts with a particular gender in different ethnic groups. When excavated evidence for subsistence activities in three households was compared with documented details of their occupants, it became clear that artefact correlates for women's work did not reflect the actual *presence* of women. In frontier communities it is not surprising to find that the gendering of labour is fluid, and that men take on tasks generally associated with women in their broader cultural milieu. The need for a more diachronic emphasis is acute, and one which confronts the implications of variability resulting from transformations such as urbanism, immigration, colonialism and acculturation.

How has the sexual division of labour been tackled in contexts which do not benefit from direct historical or ethnohistorical sources? There is potential in a bioarchaeological approach that examines the impact of men's and women's work and lifestyles on their own bodies. Through study of excavated skeletons it is possible to view gender through sexual difference in diet, lifecourse events, incidence of disease, physiological stress and injury (Grauer and Stuart-Macadam 1998; Larsen 1997). For example, sex differences have been observed in patterns of toothwear, in some instances suggesting women's involvement in the mastication of plant fibres for basket-weaving, or hides for the making of clothing or structures (Larsen 1997: 257). Because this approach generally conflates sex and gender categories, it has been left largely undeveloped by feminist archaeology. However, it does offer the possibility of considering changes in the sexual division of labour through time, differences between cultural groups, and the consequences on the human body of gendered work patterns throughout the lifecycle. Such an approach subverts certain universals, but may neglect the problematic relationship between biological sex and the cultural construction of gender identities.

Osteological studies have their own problems of methodology, requiring adequate sample sizes and comparative populations from which to draw inferences relating to sex and age. Certain methods are still experimental: for instance, attempts to compare male and female diets through stable carbon isotope analysis assume identical bone chemistry in men and women, which remains unproved (Bumsted *et al.* 1990). Specific pathologies may not be fully understood, and it remains problematic to link particular traumas and degenerative diseases with occupations during life. Where it is possible to compare ethnohistorical and osteological sources, contradictions may be apparent. In Sandra Hollimon's study of health consequences of the sexual divison of labour among the Arikara of the Northern Plains, for instance, she found that Arikaran men were three times more likely to suffer degenerative joint disease, despite the ethnographic evidence that women performed much more physically demanding, repetitive tasks (Hollimon 1992: 84). Here some caution may be required, however, since sexual dimorphism has been observed in osteoarthritis cross-culturally, with a greater general prevalence among men (Larsen 1997: 177).

Bioarchaeological evidence has been used particularly to infer a sexual division of labour that is thought to have resulted from the transition from foraging to agriculture. For example, bones from the Neolithic site of Abu Hureyra (Syria) showed distinctive differences between an early pre-agricultural phase and a subsequent period in which domestic cereals were cultivated (11500–8500 BP). It was proposed that individuals of both sexes, and especially young adolescents, showed signs of excessive strains from carrying heavy loads (Molleson 1994: 60). There were repeated bone deformities, predominantly among women, that included collapsed vertebrae (the upper dorsal) and grossly arthritic big toes. It was concluded that these bone changes resulted from the long hours that women spent kneeling in order to pound and grind cereal grains using mortars and saddle querns (*ibid.*: 62–3). While this interpretation appears plausible, it is rather self-fulfilling: an exclusive sexual division of labour is expected, with men postulated as cultivating crops and women preparing cereals for consumption. Other explanations for the bone pathologies are not explored, and the possibility of more flexible, seasonal, and perhaps age-based divisions of labour are not considered.

The transition from archaic foraging to Mississippian agriculture in the southeastern United States was studied by Patricia Bridges, who concluded that women were closely involved with early cultivation. She proposed that the shift to agriculture would have necessitated greater physical exertion, resulting in remodelling of bone from increased strain. She examined the length of longbones, diaphyseal diameters and circumference, and cross-sectional diaphyseal structure. She was able to conclude that Mississippian agriculturalists had thicker, stronger longbone diaphyses than their archaic predecessors, and that during this transformation women experienced more general diaphyseal remodelling than men, perhaps reflecting their closer link with agriculture (Bridges 1989). Clearly, future studies would benefit from considerations of the experiential qualities of gender on men's and women's bodies. We must be cautious, however, that bioarchaeological evidence is not used merely to confirm existing essentialist suppositions regarding the sexual division of labour.

Americanist gender archaeology has been dominated by the concern to determine how subsistence, production and technology become gendered. Individual studies have employed either processual models (e.g. Gero 1992) or more contextual analyses (e.g. Dobres 1995). Here, case studies are summarised which bring together evidence for gendered concerns in the spheres of subsistence and ritual. Crucial issues are raised, such as how change in gendered relations of production may be recognised, how certain tasks become inextricably linked with masculine and feminine identities, and how the gender relations of production are interwoven with broader ideological values.

Food, cloth and pots: spectres at the feast

Within the community or household, arrangements for the acquisition, storage, preparation and consumption of food are essential in establishing gendered relations. Food is not merely a basic for subsistence; practices governing its preparation and consumption may become highly ritualised and socially embedded (Caplan 1997). Food taboos sometimes structure differences between genders; feasts bind social groups, and gendered food practices consolidate gendered identities. In medieval Europe, for example, woman's responsibility in the preparation of food for her family was extended to a wider nurturing role that frequently involved the distribution of food to the poor as a charitable act. Women who chose to break with social convention by following a religious vocation, often signalled their defiance through food asceticism: the denial of social and physical demands through deliberate starvation of their own bodies. Medieval women were linked with all aspects of food, excepting the eucharist, the ritual consumption of the body of Christ as bread and wine. This highly bounded aspect of food consumption was controlled entirely by a male priesthood (Bynum 1987).

Food may be taken as the starting point for examining the symbolism of gender or specific divisions of labour surrounding its processing (Counihan and Van Esterik 1997). It may also provide insights to power relations, and contestation regarding control of food production and storage, and preparation and disposal. Christine Hastorf has taken this approach to gender and food in a study of the pre-Hispanic Sausa of Peru. Hastorf's framework does not emphasise gender attribution of particular tasks, but is concerned rather with 'gaining evidence of differential control in how the activities are performed' (Hastorf 1991: 134). She begins by reviewing modern ethnography and ethnohistorical sources for gender relations in Andean society, noting that significant changes must have been effected by the Inkan and Spanish conquests of the region. A complementarity exists today in which bilateral inheritance provides each sex with material resources and membership of their same-sex parent's territorial political unit, the *ayllu*. There is a reciprocity in cosmological and domestic spheres, and a sexual divison of labour exists but is flexible, particularly in relation to agricultural tasks. Women sow and plant seeds, while men plough and load pack animals; women are sometimes responsible for processing and storing the harvest, and they control the kitchen and domestic storage areas. Crops indigenous to the area include legumes, potatoes, quinona and maize, the last of which had a documented ritual importance through its consumption as *chicha*, maize beer.

Hastorf uses ethnographic and ethnohistorical sources to suggest a gendered division of labour. While her analysis does not rely on material correlates for women, she is able to suggest women's domains according to their expected connection with food processing in the home. She uses two complementary approaches to examining the connections between food and gender in later pre-Hispanic Sausa compounds (Figure 3.1), comparing the pre-Inka, Wanka II (1300–1460 AD) site of Tunánmarca with the post-Inka Wanka III (1460–1532 AD) site of Marca. Both compounds are well preserved and dated, with evidence of only a single phase of occupation. First, she examined the spatial distribution of charred plant remains in relation to spatial features, reflecting processing, consumption and disposal, either at refuse dumps or in activity areas. Second, she considered food consumption and access to reserved food stuffs through isotope values in bone collagen extracted from excavated male and female skeletons.

Pre-Hispanic Sausa compounds consisted of one or more circular structures entering onto a curved, walled courtyard area, with internal divisions indicative of specialised areas. The first compound, of the Wanka II period (1300–1460 AD), indicates a more diverse and greater density of charred plant remains in structures than in patio areas. This distribution reflects the position of hearths in structures, which were used for cooking, eating, sleeping, and storage of food and fuel, suggesting that these were primarily women's domains. The distribution of maize tended toward patio areas, possibly suggesting that the wider social group cooperated in processing this higher-status crop in an area also used for tool manufacture, metal production and midden deposits. The second compound, of the Wanka III period (1460–1532 AD), showed lower plant diversity and density. More

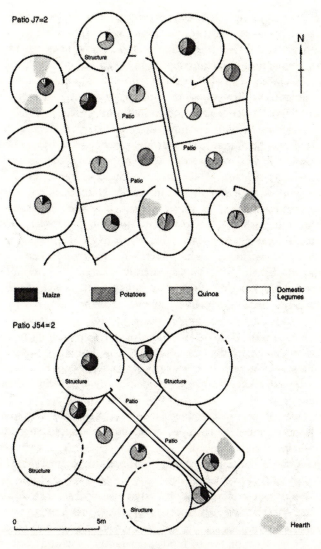

Figure 3.1 The distribution of charred plant remains in pre-Hispanic Sausa compounds at Tunánmarca (1300–1460 AD) and Marca (1460–1532 AD). The earlier compound (above) shows a greater plant diversity and density within structures, with maize concentrated in patios. The later compound (below) shows lower plant diversity and density, an increase in maize, and processing near a hearth in the patio.

Source: Drawing by Steve Allen, after Hastorf 1991: figs 5.1, 5.3.

maize was processed, whereas the potato, the Andean staple, was reduced in presence. Activities were concentrated toward a hearth area in the patio, which Hastorf suggests reflects a greater degree of specialisation, regulation and intensification of female processing labour (Figure 3.1).

Stable isotopic analysis was used to compare sexed skeletons of the Wanka II and III periods in order to build up a picture of cumulative food consumption and any indication of dietary difference by sex. Extracted bone collagen from individual skeletons was examined and compared with ideal isotopic values for major food types assessed from modern regional plants. This study was hindered by the small sample groups and the experimental nature of the method, often subject to modern contamination. However, in a sample of seven Wanka II skeletons no difference was found in any food group between men and women. In a sample of twenty-three Wanka III skeletons, 50 per cent of the men were found to have diets significantly enriched in maize beyond the female diets. This apparently differential consumption of maize is interpreted by Hastorf as indicating that only Sausa men attended the ritual and political functions of the Inka, where maize beer was served, while women's position outside the home became more restricted under Inka rule. She concludes that during the period of the Inka state, gender was constructed by the symbolism of maize and differential access to it. While women participated in intensified levels of production, they were excluded from more public ceremonial consumption.

Rosemary Joyce has examined labour organisation in Classic Mayan society, contrasting information from ethnohistorical sources with a study of male and female imagery in stone sculpture, ceramics and figurines from the area of modern Mexico, Guatemala and Belize (250–800 AD) (Joyce 1992). Joyce argues for complementary gender roles, both from iconographic and ethnohistorical sources. She examines the sixteenth-century account of Diego de Landa, bishop of Yucatan, who emphasised the role of men in warfare and ritual, and women's connection with food preparation, weaving and rituals surrounding childbirth. Agricultural land was held commonly by married couples; women gardened, raised animals and spun and wove in cooperative groups, subsequently marketing their products. Complementary ritual roles are indicated, with men's rituals linked with the temple, and women's with the house, although older women danced in temple ceremonies. Both men and women were connected with feasting, which conjoined men's agricultural products with women's labour in cooking. During the feasts, textiles and pottery vessels were distributed, and in the rituals women were specifically responsible for offering presents of cotton stuffs, and offerings of food and drink.

Joyce argues that gender imagery was conveyed through the public medium of anthropomorphic sculpture, in which the body and face are sexless, with male and female represented through the use of distinctive costumes (Figure 3.2). She has proposed that female and male figures were regularly paired, with their costumes representing contrasting elements of the Mayan cosmology, the horizontal world space and the vertical world tree, respectively. The distribution of the paired male and female figures divided the space of the Classic Maya centres into two halves, bisected from front to back, outer and inner, right and left, north and south, up and down: pairings which Joyce argues represented complementary rather than oppositional gender constructs. In some cases there are gendered patterns in the costumes worn and implements held by the images, for example in net-skirted, costumed pairs, the female offers a ceramic vessel, perhaps containing ritual tools or maize. In less public sculptural images, such as figures shown on lintels inside the temple at Yaxchilan, male figures hold ritual staffs, weapons or sceptres, while women are shown holding a bowl or a tied cloth bundle.

Figure 3.2 Reconstructions of male and female figures from stelae possibly from Calakmul, Campeche, Mexico.

Source: Drawing by Susan A. M. Shumaker. Reproduced by kind permission of Rosemary Joyce.

Joyce interprets these gestures as referring to 'exclusively female labor in a system of ideologically exclusive and complementary, gender-specific productive roles' (Joyce 1992: 66). She discerns gender complementarity in the very processes of production, with raw materials linked with male labour, and their transformation into cultural products, such as ceramic bowls and cloth bundles, linked with female labour. She traces this labour system through images on pottery vessels and figurines, which also show gendered, supernatural beings, but occur in less exclusive contexts than the sculptures, including burials, hoards within houses and domestic middens. Men are shown as hunters, warriors and participants in ritual, and women are depicted weaving and grinding corn or preparing food in pots. Joyce argues that these small-scale images 'directly represent women's productive labor in the stereotyped roles of weaver and cook', while the larger-scale sculptural images indirectly refer to women's ideological roles in their offerings of cloth bundles and ceramic vessels. Further, arguing from the sexual characteristics sometimes depicted on pottery vessels, she proposes that the complementarity in the domestic sphere is sexualised, in contrast to the more reified complementarity of the ritual sphere. Joyce presents evidence for gender complementarity from ethnohistorical and archaeological sources, including ritual space and the iconography of sculpture, pottery and figurines. The central theme of this complementarity is the significance of women's labour in transforming the raw materials produced by men into 'useful products crucial to social, ritual, and political process'. She concludes that the linking of domestic and ideological gender roles was politically motivated, since the control of specialised products must have been crucial to the struggle between ruling families for political power (Joyce 1992: 69).

Weaving has been linked with women's domestic production in many societies, although this is by no means an exclusive, universal phenomenon. I would argue that in some instances this connection may be used to demonstrate how female labour becomes a crucial means of both constructing femininity, and in defining female roles ideologically. Within the context of medieval England, changes in gendered labour and values can be traced in tandem with technological innovations (500–1200 AD). From linguistic and literary evidence it has been argued that among the Anglo-Saxons there were sharply delineated roles for women as clothmakers and men as warriors or hunters (Fell 1984: 40). Evidence of grave goods from Anglo-Saxon burials suggests a correlation between spindles, woolcombs, weaving swords, thread-boxes and needlecases with female skeletons, while weapons are found almost exclusively with males. Women worked in pairs, weaving on warp-weighted looms up to two metres wide, evidenced by clay loom weights and post-holes in Anglo-Saxon houses (Pritchard 1996: 112).

By the eleventh century, we see a change in technology from the warp-weighted vertical loom to beam-tensioned horizontal looms. This required a greater specialisation and intensification of labour that took weaving out of the domestic domain, and shifted cloth production from rural homes to urban workshops. Such technological specialisation resulted in full-time, professional weaving in the Low Countries (Belgium, Holland) and southern England by the twelfth century. Cloth from these regions became a prized commodity, and weaving, dyeing and finishing of cloth became highly regulated male occupations. These crafts were increasingly controlled by guilds that were predominantly male in composition, although female membership was in some cities open to single or widowed women. Spinning remained a female occupation, along with certain finishing processes and particular crafts such as braid-making. Female labour was not automatically accorded lower prestige, although there were attempts to confine it to a non-professional, domestic context, and to limit its financial rewards. Fine embroidery remained a female skill, one associated especially with women of the highest status, who produced sumptuous church vestments and rich wall-hangings for castles and palaces.

Anglo-Saxon women conveyed their femininity through artefacts of spinning and weaving that accompanied them to the grave, while later medieval women were represented by shears depicted on their coffin lids, in both cases attributes exclusive to women. It has been argued that threadboxes in the graves of Anglo-Saxon women possessed some sort of magical quality, linked with women's role in healing (Meaney 1981). In medieval art women were represented by the distaff, the cleft stick that held wool or flax for hand-spinning, and the 'distaff side' came to represent the female branch of the family in heraldry and genealogy. Medieval Christianity provided women with images of the Virgin Mary, as both a role model and as the feminine element of a masculine pantheon. Mary's singularity was signalled through the Annunciation, the moment at which she learned of her immaculate conception. It seems significant that the conventional depiction of the Annunciation in medieval art showed Mary seated in a domestic context, most often spinning, when the archangel Gabriel appeared to her. The ideological link between women and textiles persisted when their connection with cloth production was largely severed. The association between women and textiles may have originated with the female contribution in domestic production, but extended to construct femininity and convey social and religious roles.

Toppling hierarchies: deconstructing universals

In contrast with early feminist anthropology and archaeology, gendered approaches have begun to dismantle universal and evolutionary models of the sexual division of labour. Studies of the relationship between gender and production have revealed that men's and women's roles cannot be reduced to a simple equation of prestige: value is relative and socially created. Instead, their respective social and economic roles will change in relation to political or technological transformations, and gendered identities may be experienced differently within specific spheres or social levels. The very concept of relative male and female prestige may be inappropriate to many contexts, where notions such as gender complementarity outweigh those of hierarchy. In some cases the individual male or female actor may be unimportant, with significance placed alternatively on pairings of older couples, brothers and sisters, or groups of men or women (see above). Social reproduction may be powered through gender complementarity or cooperation among same-sex groups, rather than differential prestige, as Joyce has recently observed in relation to Native American traditions of the Hopi, the Andean Aymara and the Tzotzil Maya (Joyce 1996: 180). Conversely, we should not anticipate complementarity in every context: extreme male domination has been a feature of many societies, although we have yet to explore the counter-hegemonies that this may engender. A more satisfactory consideration of gender and production requires its placement within broader social frameworks, including family, household and community, with patterns of men's and women's work delineated according to gender and the lifecycle (see Chapter 5).

For the most part, studies of gender and production have continued to emphasise gender attribution, in other words the assignment of specific tasks or roles to men and women. Discussion of gender has remained limited to arguments based on analogy, employing either relational or direct historic ethnographic analogies, or using historical or iconographic sources as forms of analogic reasoning. The uncritical use of analogy sets up gender categories that are a-historical, reinforcing the essentialism of androcentric and early feminist assumptions. More refined approaches develop multiple sources of analogy, exploring differences and similarities between comparative contexts (Wylie 1985). The analogues themselves should also be scrutinised carefully, considering the potential bias of ethnography or the particular circumstances in which historical sources were produced (see Hill's critique of Brumfiel 1991 in Hill 1998). As Spector has shown, direct historic analogy can significantly expand our appreciation of gendered labour in its spatial and temporal dimensions (Spector 1983). However, a more contextual framework is required to trace change in the relationship between gender and production, one which selects and compares archaeological evidence from contrasting chronological contexts and source types.

The most convincing and nuanced readings of gender have been developed from multiple lines of evidence, for example Hastorf's use of spatial and skeletal data in the study of food practices, and Joyce's comparison of gendered images in public and private media (Hastorf 1991; Joyce 1992). The inclusion of biological or iconographic sources also promotes consideration of categories based on gender and/or sex. Further, the study of several different categories of archaeological evidence may allow us to recognise tension and contradiction. In a study of Aztec figurines, Elizabeth Brumfiel has contrasted the representations of women in different media, including the images of mutilated women shown on monumental sculpture; the smaller sculptures that show women carrying out daily tasks, such as weaving and grinding maize; and the androgynous female figures shown in manuscript paintings. She has proposed that in different contexts it is possible to recognise official *versus* popular imagery, the latter perhaps indicating resistance to Aztec domination (Brumfiel 1996: 155–7).

From the examination of parallel lines of evidence, it seems possible to pursue the fragmentary nature of past gender relations through concepts of gendered hegemonies and counter-hegemonies. Understanding of production must be disentangled from the simplistic notion of the sexual division of labour, particularly as our perceptions of gender move beyond binary constructs of male and female, reconsidering sex and gender and posing the question of multiplicity. At last, models of hierarchy and universal subordination may be assuaged by the concept of gender as difference.

Chapter 4

Experiencing gender
Identity, sexuality and the body

Gender identity is a private experience: the intensity with which one inhabits one's own gendered body, feels desire, and expresses oneself physically and materially. In the modern West, gender identity and self-perception are deeply enmeshed with sexuality and the inherently public constructs of binary masculinity and femininity. The dominant cultural view is one of fixed categories of biological sex and orthodox sexualities. From the perspectives of history and anthropology, however, the categories of sex, gender and sexuality appear unstable. This chapter probes sex and gender categories, and challenges the social constructionist view that gender is socially created, while sex is fixed and biologically determined. The relationship between gender and sexuality is questioned, an issue which is very recent to archaeological dialogues, and in which the focus of study has been on sexed or sexualised bodies: burial evidence and visual representations. The potential of multiple gender categories is explored through cross-gender types which possess social, physical and archaeological presences. The nature of gender identity is considered through the prism of masculinity, and archaeological approaches to the gendered body are reviewed.

Unstable categories

Just as Darwin's views have permeated perceptions of sex and gender roles, understanding of sexuality has been dominated until recently by the thinking of Sigmund Freud. His 'libido theory' postulated the notion of an independent, disobedient sex drive which could be repressed or liberated, and his theories of psychoanalysis emphasised the development of an essential masculinity through boys' Oedipal complexes and girls' penis envy (Freud 1905). Sexuality was seen as an a-historical phenomenon, although social attitudes towards sex were believed to have caused varying degrees of repression. During the last twenty years, a more historical appreciation of sexuality has emerged, one influenced particularly by the works of Michel Foucault (1981, 1985, 1986), by historians of medicine and the body, and by feminist and queer theorists.

Foucault proposed that sexuality was the pivotal transfer point for relations of power (1981: 103). Its history was bound up with discourses of power that resulted from the control of knowledge. Especially in the eighteenth and nineteenth centuries, this was achieved through the professionalisation of the study of sex, procreation and desire, through pedagogy, medicine and psychiatry. Foucault's history of sexuality has been criticised on a number of counts, particularly for its concentration on the male perspective, and for its characterisation of relations of sexuality as solely bound up with control, articulated through domination and repression. Nevertheless, his contribution provoked enormous interest in the development of attitudes to sex and the body, and the place of medicine in shaping our contemporary understanding of categories. Our modern preoccupation with gendered dichotomies such as nature/culture has been traced to the period of the Enlightenment, when gender polarities ossified to form accounts of gender that appeared naturalistic (Jordanova 1989). The new language of physiology created biological, social and pyschological portraits of two opposites in every respect: male and female.

Thomas Laqueur has tracked perceptions of the body from antiquity to Freud, revealing the significance of eighteenth-century thought in shaping modern categories of sex and gender (1990). He argues that sexual difference between men and women was not voiced clearly until the end of the eighteenth century, when such distinctions became critical to feminist and anti-feminist debates over women in education and public life. In the classical and medieval worlds, a one-sex model had prevailed, in which men and women were perceived as more or less the same sex. This view stemmed from Aristotle (d. 322 BC) and Galen (d. 199 AD), the latter of whom formulated a physiological theory of heat and the humours that would hold sway until the Renaissance (see pp. 114–15). The correct balance of heat was considered to be of crucial importance in physical and intellectual performance. Galen believed that the female was cooler than the male, and therefore a less perfect version of him. Moreover, from Galen to the Enlightenment it was believed that men and women shared identical sex organs, with the female containing hers inside, and the male carrying his outside. According to Galen, the female did not have sufficient heat to extrude the organs of reproduction, and the resulting situation provided a safe place for conception and gestation. Laqueur concludes that the classical and medieval metaphysics of hierarchy in the representation of women in relation to men, was replaced during the Enlightenment by an anatomy and physiology of incommensurability. Right into the seventeenth century it was argued that sex, which was determined by bodily fluids, was mutable; women in particular could change their sex by thrusting their testes outward (Laqueur 1987, 1990). An understanding of changeable, relatively more or less perfect bodies, was replaced by one of fixed, different and opposing bodies. It seems that categories of biological sex, therefore, must also be seen as historically created and contextually perceived. Classifications of sex, as much as gender, are socially constructed.

And what of sexuality? It is commonly held that gender is expressed through sexuality, and that each sex has its own sexuality (Caplan 1987: 2). Yet if sex and gender are socially specific, is sexuality also socially constructed in relation to prescribed gender categories? It has been argued that this emphasis on sexuality as defining personal expression or identity is very much a modern preoccupation (Turner 1996; Shilling 1993). Studies of ancient sexuality, therefore, run the risk of anachronism, and the projection onto the past of presentist concerns of the sensual body. Care must be taken to problematise sexuality, not as a timeless, natural category, but as an historical construction. Certainly modern perceptions of sexuality emerged only in the nineteenth century, with homosexuality and heterosexuality discussed as distinct sexual natures only from c. 1870 onwards (Herdt 1994: 28). That is not to say that single-sex sexual acts have not been prevalent amongst all societies, but rather that this preference was not used as a basis for the social classification of individuals until relatively recently. In this way the modern, western, 'four gender classification' emerged, based on male and female heterosexual and homosexual dispositions (*ibid.*: 22). Politically loaded debate still rages as to whether sexual orientation is essential or socially constructed, in other words, biologically or socially defined (Stein 1990).

Further, some contend that sexuality may be either voluntary or determined. That is to say that one either *chooses* to be hetero- or homosexual, or the psyche and/or biology *determine* sexual orientation (hormonally, or through the 'gay gene', pp. 12–13) (*ibid.*: 327–31). These sexual categories were viewed as fixed, at least until Alfred Kinsey's report on *Sexual Behavior in the Human Male* (1948) proposed that only 50 per cent of the American (white, male) population is exclusively heterosexual thoughout their adult life. Although Kinsey's ethics and methods have since been questioned, he opened the debate by arguing that the categories of hetero-, homo- and bisexuality were obsolete, since individuals could be all or none of these (Stein 1990: 3).

Historical and sociological accounts have problematised our categories of sex, gender and sexuality. These insights resonate with those of queer theorists and feminist theorists of difference, who break down distinctions of sex and gender, refuting the notion that sex is a stable point of reference (Butler 1990). But to what extent is this sexual theorising relevant only to the modern West, the inheritors of the classical, medieval and Enlightenment traditions? Anthropologists have come to realise that in non-western societies bodily categories are also contextual and permeable. In some cases gender is ascribed; among the Hua of Papua New Guinea, individuals are classified as male or female, but their bodily fluids are believed to change over the course of the lifetime, shifting the balance between masculinity and femininity (Moore 1994: 24). A similar belief has been studied closely among the Sambia of Papua New Guinea, where male and female are believed to possess the same sex organs at birth, but to develop gendered essences at different rates. For a boy to achieve manhood, or warrior status, *jerungdu*, he must shed the female essence (blood) and gain the male essence (semen). This balance is acquired ritually through two acts: nose-bleeding, and fellatio with tribal elders (Herdt 1987). Henrietta Moore has observed that gender may be grounded in culturally specific theories of the physiology of the body, with categories of sexual difference varying between societies to produce ontological statuses for hermaphrodism, androgeny and a third sex, amongst others (Moore 1994: 13).

In the midst of such shifting sands, surely biological categories of sex remain stable? In an archaeological cautionary, Jarl Nordbladh and Tim Yates observed that male and female are simply two extremes on the same physical scale, with sex a relative rather than fixed status. Hormones can vary to create the secondary sexual characteristics of the opposite sex, while genetic sex varies greatly from the ideals of female (XX) to male (XY), with a further nine categories in between (Nordbladh and Yates 1990: 225). Indeed, chromosomes are no guarantee to the phenotype, the physical characteristics of an individual. The outward appearance of 'sex-reversed' individuals (male XX; female XY) might not be visibly affected, while other 'intersex' chromosomal variants might impede the development of secondary sexual characteristics (e.g. male XXY; female XO, XXX) (Brown 1998). Indeed, the intersex XXY is known traditionally as the hermaphrodite: an individual with a congenital condition of ambiguity of the genitalia, a phenomenon historically recognised and deified in the bisexual Greek god Hermaphroditos (fourth century BC), combining Hermes and Aphrodite. It has been proposed that today, perhaps one or two people in every thousand are born as intersex individuals, possessing the internal and external reproductive organs of both sexes (Taylor 1996: 64).

Hermaphrodites are sometimes perceived culturally as a distinctive sex, or as individuals who may transform their gender in puberty. Gilbert Herdt has studied a rare form of hermaphrodism that occurs in New Guinea (5-alpha reductase deficiency) and in the Dominican Republic (steroid 5-alpha reductase deficiency) which causes the delayed onset of anatomical maleness. In New Guinea the *kwolu-aatmwol* is perceived as anatomically distinctive, and occupies an assigned ritual role and place in mythology; while the Dominican *guevedoche* is permitted to change gender at puberty if desired, allowing flexibility in gendered dress and tasks (Herdt 1994: 16, 68). The cultural status of hermaphrodites varies, with the condition highly valued amongst the Native American Navajo, for example, and stigmatised amongst the Pokot of Kenya (Bolin 1996: 24). These societies do have one thing in common, however; they have assigned an ontological status to individuals who are neither male nor female. In our society, the absence of such an institutionalised ontological role results in surgical intervention being sought by transsexuals (Herdt 1994: 71), individuals who have the physical characteristics of one sex and the emotional and pyschological identity of the other.

Multiple genders: life on the edge

In many social and historical situations, examples can be cited of gender reversals or cross-gender roles, consisting of a change which brings a person closer to another gender (Ramet 1996: 3). Such transitions are sometimes inspired by individual pragmatism: for instance, women who have cross-dressed in order to take up exclusively male vocations, as varied as early Christian hermit saints and nineteenth-century soldiers. Cross-gender roles may also arise from social adaptation, such as the Balkan practice of raising biological females as male, in cases where there is no male heir. Among the Serbs, Montenegrins and Ghegs, these *muškobanje* are sworn to a life of celibacy (Grémaux 1994). In some societies the cross-gender role occupies a permanent ontological space between male and female, through an institutionalised third gender. Such roles are frequently linked with sexuality, but are defined more often by social or economic gender roles. They may be articulated through material culture, for instance signalled by cross-dressing or distinctive costume, separate dwellings or communities, and specific burial rites.

Here, three examples of institutionalised third-gender role are considered, the Indian *hijra*, the Byzantine eunuch, and the Native American two-spirit, all blurring the boundaries of sex, gender and sexuality. All three may be considered distinct genders that break down binary categories of male and female. These cross-gender roles alert us to the myriad possibilities to be considered in an archaeological context. Single-sex communities may be more common, and represent a broader range of social possibilities, than simply military barracks or medieval nunneries; take, for example, convents of Byzantine eunuchs or communities of *hijra*. Cross-gender roles or individuals have physical and archaeological manifestations. It is not unusual to encounter skeletons that, according to the criteria of physical anthropology, have the traits of one sex, yet are associated with grave goods linked culturally with the opposite gender. Celebrated cases include females buried with weapons, and males buried with the paraphernalia of weaving, ranging from Iron Age Italy to Anglo-Saxon England (Vida Navarro 1992; Lucy 1997).

Within Hinduism, all individuals possess both male and female essences. For the sexually ambiguous, a particular vocation exists which provides an alternative sex and gender role. These *hijra* are followers of the mother goddess, *Bahuchara Mata*. According to the research of Serena Nanda, the *hijra* are perceived as 'sacred and erotic men' (Nanda 1994: 373). Yet the composition of this group is mixed, including those who are born as hermaphrodites, men who are sexually impotent with women and therefore undergo surgical castration, and more rarely, non-menstruating women. The *hijra* adopt female dress and are endowed with the divine power of the goddess and the ascetic. There are considerable numbers of *hijra*: they live together in communities or households, with pooled resources and a hierarchy based on seniority.

Impotent men are said to attribute their condition to a defective sex organ, and to interpret their impotence as a call to serve the goddess. They choose a new sex and gender identity through emasculation by removal of the genitals. The operation is undertaken by a *hijra* midwife, who removes the penis and genitals and buries them under a tree. Afterwards the new *hijra* is treated like a woman following childbirth, and is integrated into her new community as a bride, wearing the erotic female colour of red. They take on female roles, gestures and tasks, such as caring for children. The *hijra* occupy certain culturally sanctioned ritual roles: they perform at marriages and at the birth of male children. But they also engage actively in prostitution, and when performing in public they flout the conventions of Indian femininity, acting aggressively, swearing and behaving in a burlesque fashion.

The *hijra* is a permanent cross-gender role in which an adult chooses to transform their gender identity, sexuality and, in many cases, their biological sex. They elect to renounce their family life, kinship and any possibility of marriage, and for these reasons it is not surprising to find that they are not drawn from the upper castes. They are liminal, sometimes intimidating, individuals, who are regarded ambivalently. Their allegiance with the goddess, who can be a malevolent force, endows them with a certain reverence, and they are known for both blessing children and cursing adults; yet their subsistence is gained largely through prostitution with men. Physically they are perceived as eunuchs, who are seen as cool, ascetic and residually male, but their behaviour displays an exaggerated female sexuality that is associated with heat (Nanda 1994).

The marginal situation of the *hijra* can be contrasted with that of the historically known Byzantine eunuch, a category of individual who performed courtly, ceremonial, religious and political functions through 1,000 years of the Byzantine empire (fifth–fifteenth century AD) (James 1997). The eunuch is now widely regarded by Byzantine scholars as a third gender, neither male nor female, although the precise physical definition of this category is insecure. Up to the ninth century, the term eunuch might refer to anyone who could not procreate, including castrates, celibates, sterile or impotent men. Castrated men were considered to lose the essential heat that Aristotle and Galen considered defining of masculinity. They were described as lacking masculine musculature, body hair and beards; they had an elevated voice range and seldom went bald. Like women, eunuchs were considered to lack self-control. With this mixture of male and female, it has been suggested that they were perceived as similar to adolescent boys. Eunuchs were changeable, both male and female, and it was reported that they enjoyed sexual activities with both sexes (Ringrose 1994: 90–1).

The Byzantine eunuch was a position of considerable political status, and parents would volunteer their sons for castration if they might achieve social elevation. Castrates acquired a distinctive bearing and set of mannerisms to set them apart from men and women, and at court wore a distinctive costume. Especially under the rule of empresses, eunuchs at the Byzantine court were trusted political advisers and administrators. Ringrose proposes that they 'supervised the boundaries', acting as go-betweens, and serving corporeal functions: preparing the dead for burial, and acting as barbers, bloodletters and doctors. But like many liminals, they were regarded with both awe and suspicion (Ringrose 1994). In contrast with the *hijra*, the Byzantine eunuch seems to have been adopted primarily as a social role, and was not motivated by a personal sense of cross-gender identity or sexuality. Physically, both groups arrived at the same phenotype of biological sex, but their mental journeys and genders were markedly distinct.

The Native American 'two-spirit' is simultaneously the most celebrated and diffuse of third-gender roles. In this case an individual would assume the sex, sexuality, roles, gestures and dress of their biological opposite. The two-spirit formed his or her own identity through the very choice of transition. This cross-gender role was widespread among indigenous peoples of the Americas, but seems to have been regarded among them variously as a revered or stigmatised status. Oral history, ethnohistorical sources and anthropological accounts are sometimes confused or contradictory, and even the terminology for this status is inconsistent. The two-spirit is the name used to refer to this role by contemporary native peoples, but it has been discussed as the 'man-woman' or the *berdache*, a term now considered to have been used perjoratively by the Spanish who first encountered cross-dressing homosexuals in Central and South America (Fulton and Anderson 1992: 604). In North America, 150 tribes are documented as having recognised the two-spirit, until its disappearance from the mid-to-late nineteenth century. It was a more common role for men, particularly among Plains tribes, but nearly half of the tribes recognised a cross-gender role for women (Roscoe 1994: 330), generally among the more egalitarian, western tribes such as the Mohave (Blackwood 1984: 28).

Two-spirits assumed the tasks of their opposite gender. The male two-spirit undertook domestic and craft work, such as weaving baskets and making pottery, often becoming celebrated for their skills, and was frequently prohibited from warfare or handling male weapons. The female two-spirit took up male tasks including hunting, warfare, social leadership and cultivation of crops. In some cases the two-spirit was an esteemed role, linked with the status of a shaman or healer. The dress and gestures of the opposite gender were usually adopted, and the two-spirit could marry a member of the opposite gender and engage in same-sex relations. There was no stigma attached to this, and the partner of the two-spirit could have heterosexual marriages before or after this particular union, sometimes bringing children into the marriage. Indeed, homosexuality does not seem to have been the defining characteristic of this cross-gender role, as not every two-spirit was devoted exclusively to same-sex relations (some were bisexual or heterosexual), nor were all homosexuals two-spirits (Fulton and Anderson 1992: 608).

What motivated the transition into the two-spirit? This seems to have depended on the attitudes prevalent within a particular tribe, but it was frequently linked with a vision, dream, or some other supernatural validation of the choice. It was not necessarily linked with physicality, such as stature, under-developed secondary sexual characteristics, or, in the case of women, absence of menstruation (Blackwood 1984: 32). Where high prestige was accorded, there may even have been recruitment of children to the role, for example where female children displayed an interest in the male role, they would be taught the same skills as boys (*ibid*.: 30). The transition was publicly sanctioned through an initation rite, after which the two-spirit became a new gender in all respects. Anthropologists have interpreted this role variously as institutionalised homosexuality, an economic strategy (Whitehead 1981), a mixed gender, cross-gender, third gender and unique gender. Clearly the precise status was specific to a tribe, but the transition was voluntary and personally desired. Its deeper meaning can be glimpsed through additional social roles performed by the two-spirit: participating in burial and mourning rituals, giving secret names to newborn infants, acting as go-betweens, assisting the wounded in battle, collecting scalps and dancing at the return of successful warriors (Callender and Kochems 1983: 447–9). As Fulton and Anderson propose, the two-spirit was a sacerdotal role, an intermediary between two sexes, between the living and the dead, and between the gods and humanity.

In contrast to the *hijra* and the Byzantine eunuch, the two-spirit was defined principally by mentality, over physical or sexual factors. Moreover, the two-spirit could occasionally be a *temporary* cross-gender role, more akin to the Polynesian *mahu*, for example, who adopted the dress and tasks of the opposite gender, along with homosexuality, but could take up this status temporarily or intermittently (Bolin 1996: 28). Again, this stresses the fluid, changeable nature of sex and gender, frequently perceived as voluntary. Amongst the Inuit, for instance, it is believed that a foetus can change its sex while being born (Saladin D'Anglure 1988: 25). Evidence for belief in such gender ambiguity may sometimes be detected in symbolic material culture.

Miranda Green has argued that the figural iconography of prehistoric Europe adopted a deliberate duality of gender representation, including hermaphrodism. From figurines and images on Iron Age coins, she proposes that double meanings of sexual representation were conveyed through deliberate visual punning. She concludes that such iconography signalled a sense of otherness of the spirit world, a crossing of boundaries to the liminal place of cross-gender (Green 1997).

It is realistic to anticipate third or fourth genders in the Native American context, and two case studies have dealt with the archaeology of the two-spirit. Sandra Holliman has considered the role among the Californian Chumash, Yokuts, Mono and Tubatulabal, among whom it was linked with occupational specialists who were responsible for funerary rites, including preparation of the corpse, burial, graveside and mourning rituals. She has tentatively identified two-spirits' burials through the study of grave goods in association with pathology; in particular, degenerative joint disease linked with occupation. Females from this region generally show much greater degeneration in the spine than males (regardless of age). Two young males with severe spinal arthritis, aged about eighteen years, are proposed to have engaged in repeated activities that could place their spines under mechanical stress. In addition, both individuals were buried with the tool kit known to have been associated with the two-spirit undertakers: digging-stick weights and baskets (Hollimon 1997: 186).

Mary Whelan identified a possible two-spirit grave in a cemetery in Minnesota, as the result of factor analysis that revealed artefact clusters, which she proposes designate gender categories that were not ascribed on the basis of biological sex (Whelan 1991). The Eastern or Santee Sioux cemetery was in use c. 1830–1860 AD, and artefacts included beads, medals, buttons, a coin and Euro-American ceramics. Thirty-nine individuals were recovered, with roughly equal numbers of male and female, and approximately equal representation of adult and juvenile. Whelan stressed that sex and gender were distinguished analytically: skeletal remains were analysed independently of artefacts associated with each burial, using multivariate sexing and ageing methods where possible. No absolute age or sex artefact correlates were found, and no artefacts related to subsistence activities were present in the grave goods, perhaps indicating that burial was reserved to signal symbolic statuses. When gender was examined without reference to sex, certain artefacts appeared to suggest gendered social categories. Artefacts with documented ritual associations (pipestone pipes, mirrors, pouches) were associated with seven people; when compared with evidence for biological sex, six of this group were male. According to Whelan, the predominance of male sex in this group suggests a gender category because sex played an important, although not exclusive, role in defining membership. The woman in this group was young (20–25 years) and associated with more artefacts of more types that any other in the cemetery. This woman's burial may be indicative of a two-spirit who changed her gender and achieved a respected, shamanistic role in her community.

Masculinity: the making of a warrior

In our own culture, gender identity is conveyed outwardly by the dress, mannerisms and gestures of masculinity or femininity, or more realistically, some combination of the two across a wide spectrum. Assumptions are made regarding the essential qualities of masculinity: for example, men are active, ardent, dominant, aggressive or violent; in contrast to an essential female who is passive, maternal, gentle and tender. Masculinist scholars have challenged such universal notions with studies of conflicting and diverging masculine values, such as those displayed by machismo *versus* 'the new man' (Segal 1990; Cornwall and Lindisfarne 1994; Connell 1995).

Hegemonic and counter-hegemonic masculinities can be seen to co-exist within the same culture, while characteristics and values of masculinity and femininity are selectively adopted by both men and women. Hegemonic masculinity may be seen as those aspects of maleness that are viewed as particularly empowering within a society; counter-hegemonic masculinities may evolve in different sexual identities, social classes, ethnic groups, institutions, regions, or stages in the lifecycle. Masculinity often conflates physicality, learned behaviour and sexuality, and is culturally mystified to create a naturalised equation of maleness with power. Cornwall and Lindisfarne have commented on the role of material culture in this process, as images and instruments of power (such as weapons) construct masculinity through a metonymy that can be acquired or lost (Cornwall and Lindisfarne 1994: 21). Such aspects of masculinity can be taken up by women, or be perceived in them by their communities: witness female police officers in the United States, who adopt elements of masculine behaviour as a strategy for professionalism (McElhinny 1994); or the North Piegan 'manly hearts', and 'shark women' of the Marquesan Islanders, both of whom are named in reference to their aggressive behaviour and vigorous sexuality (Bolin 1996: 30).

Archaeological studies have frequently portrayed masculinity as an essential quality that is exclusive to men, and achieved metonymically through weapons or phallic imagery. In a study of gendered symbols from Neolithic through to Iron Age Italy, for example, John Robb argues from an explicitly structuralist perspective that binary, and mutually exclusive, categories of male and female emerged. In Neolithic figurines and Copper and Bronze Age stelae, he proposes that female representations are distinguished anatomically, primarily by the inclusion of breasts, while in Neolithic rock art distinctions might be drawn between phallic figures, and those shown with dots between their legs; these tentative 'female' figures are more consistently shown with the addition of a necklace. The proposed 'male' figures, in contrast, are regularly depicted hunting (Robb 1997: 45–6). From the later Bronze Age, anatomically specific representations of males disappear, but weapon symbolism becomes common, with carvings of daggers and halberds, which are traditionally interpreted as male images. Robb tests this assumption against his reading of the Bronze Age stelae of Lunigiana, and concludes that breasts and weapons were mutually exclusive markers for female and male.

Robb argues that this theme is developed in Iron Age Italian cemeteries, by which time spears, and less commonly swords, are associated with male burials: 'weapons were the primary material symbol of masculinity' (*ibid.*: 50). Female graves became associated with ornaments, such as earrings, pendants and fibulae, which are found less frequently with males. This is interpreted as the symbolic clothing of women, through which 'ornamentation probably served to mark an abstract conception of beauty as a valued part of female identity' (*ibid.*: 52–3). Finally, violence is attributed with defining 'categories such as active and passive which would have been easily mapped on to social divisions and prestige hierarchies' (*ibid.*: 55). The expression of violence and its symbolism through weaponry are seen as crucial to constructing concepts of male honour that would have controlled access to women, a situation prefiguring the patriarchal Mediterranean family (*ibid.*: 56). Robb acknowledges the possible counter-hegemonies that would have been signalled by differences in class and age, but adheres to an evolutionary account that assumes the presence of binary gender structures and hierarchical prestige systems. No gendered alternatives are explored for the contrasting imagery (such as men of different ages, initiants, or masculine women) nor is the possibility of a more complementary gender structure considered. Moreover, the ornamented female is considered a metonym for the historically constructed, aesthetic notion of female 'beauty'.

The same period of European prehistory has been considered by Paul Treherne, who interprets the emergence of the male weapon burial as the reflection of a lifestyle in which 'central to both life and death was a specific form of masculine beauty unique to the warrior' (Treherne 1995: 106). The 'warrior grave' developed in the mid-second millenium BC, when it is proposed that the communal mortuary rituals of the Neolithic were replaced by aspects of personal display that accompanied the development of Bronze Age chiefdoms. Treherne argues that imported and prestige goods were used to signal a male symbolism and ethos which, through repeated associations, became increasingly natural. In particular, this 'naturalised' image of masculinity was represented by four themes: warfare (weapons), alcohol (drinking vessels), riding/driving (horse fittings and vehicles) and bodily ornamentation (metal ornaments and toilet articles such as combs, tweezers, razors, mirrors and awls). He acknowledges that many ornaments are also associated with women, although some are exclusive to men, including the toilet articles. Alternative interpretations for these items are not countenanced, such as razors, which could have been used for depilation by men or women, or could have been tools used for preparation of hides. The social bonding of drinking rituals is assumed to have been an entirely male preserve. He postulates a concern with grooming that inscribed masculinity onto the warrior, including a particular emphasis on long hair that supposedly signalled sexual potency (*ibid.*: 126).

Treherne explores the ways in which elements of material culture and their repeated associations may come to represent a 'naturalised' masculinity; his approach also underlines the extent to which beauty, and the aesthetics of the body, are culturally constructed. However, the bodily experience of these would-be warriors is left unresolved; for instance, the changes in gendered status that might accompany the onset of facial hair at puberty, and the fading and thinning hair of later years. To what extent was the warrior status linked with a specific age or ethnicity, and was it exclusive to biological males? Treherne's approach to the warrior ethos assumes unacceptable long-term continuities stretching from the Homeric warriors of the Iliad to those of Hrothgar's hall in Beowulf. Certainly in the latter example, dating to the eighth century AD, the most ferocious being was personified as female, the monster Grendel's mother, and the bonds of the drinking rituals were cemented by a woman's offering of the mead-cup, a common Anglo-Saxon motif: 'Hrothgar's queen, mindful of customs, gold-adorned, greeted the men in the hall; and ... went about each of the retainers, young and old, offered them the costly cup ... the ring-adorned queen, mature of mind' (trans. Donaldson 1966: 11).

In the context of Anglo-Saxon warrior graves, Heinrich Härke has proposed the contingent nature of warrior status. In a study of forty-seven Anglo-Saxon cemeteries in England, fifth–eighth century AD, he has shown that the weapon burial rite was almost exclusive to males (Härke 1990). The weapons have been interpreted previously as part of the *hergewede*, part of a man's property that could not be inherited, and was therefore buried with him (Figure 4.1). As such, most previous scholars have taken the weapons to be directly reflective of wealth. Härke has proposed that there is also a clear correlation between physical stature and the presence of weapons. In addition, the incidence of the weapon burial rite in fact peaked during periods when there appears to have been an *absence* or *decline* of actual military activity (according to historical sources). Those commemorated by a weapon burial, therefore, were not necessarily seasoned soldiers or military heroes. These graves represent individuals of 'warrior status': perhaps an ethnic identity based on Anglo-Saxon descent, and characterised by men of the tallest stature and strongest physique.

Through burial evidence, Treherne and Härke have presented different profiles of hegemonic masculinities. But there are contexts in which the 'warrior status' of masculinity might be attributed equally to females, such as the Scythian and Sauromatian 'Amazon' burials. Throughout the regions of the Steppes and Caucasus are found warrior burials containing the sexed skeletons of females. These graves include weapons and armour in addition to more 'feminine' artefacts such as jewellery, mirrors and spindles; further, the female skeletons exhibit physical evidence of violence, including severe head injuries resulting from blows and stabs to the head, in addition to arrowheads still embedded in the skeleton. Forty of these graves have been discovered in Scythia, while in Sauromatia, to the north of the Black Sea, they account for 20 per cent of known warrior graves (Rolle 1989: 88–9). Such burials are accepted as female warriors largely due to historical provenance: writing in the fifth century BC, the Greek Herodotus introduced the 'Amazons', a race of warrior women of the Steppes. Saxo Grammaticus wrote emotively of Viking warrior women in his *History of the Danes* (*c.* 1200 AD):

There were once women in Denmark who dressed themselves to look like men and spent almost every minute cultivating soldiers' skills. ... Those especially who had forceful personalities or were

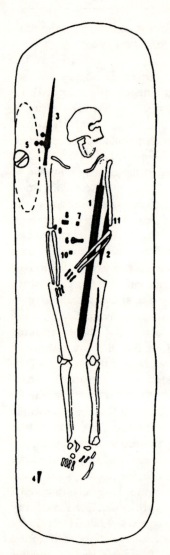
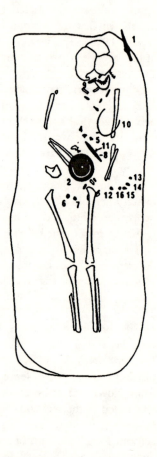

Figure 4.1 Anglo-Saxon weapon burials (*c.* 400–600 AD). Left: grave 56 from Dover-Buckland, Kent, showing sword (1), seax (2), spear (3–4) and shield (5). Right: grave 33 from Andover, Hampshire, showing spear (1) and shield (2–7)

Source: From Evison 1987: fig. 72; and Cook and Dacre 1985: fig. 35.

tall and elegant embarked on this way of life. As if they were forgetful of their true selves they put toughness before allure, aimed at conflicts instead of kisses, tasted blood, not lips, sought the clash of arms rather than the arm's embrace, fitted to weapons hands which should have been weaving, desired not the couch but the kill, and those they could have appeased with looks they attacked with lances.

(Saxo Grammaticus, quoted in Jesch 1991: 176)

One such woman has been identified tentatively in the burial of a proposed Viking raider from London's Saxon foreshore, one of two sexed burials from Queenhithe Harbour, radiocarbon dated to 670–880 AD. This woman died as the result of a blow to the head caused by a wedge-shaped implement, possibly an axe or sword. She was carefully wrapped in bark and laid on a bed of reeds before interment, with moss placed over her face, pelvis and knees, and her grave marked by stakes (Ayre and Wroe-Brown forthcoming). Where no equivalent literary accounts exist, archaeologists are reluctant to postulate such a female warrior status.

This has certainly been the case in relation to Anglo-Saxon burials, although the reasoning has developed from circular arguments, with favour given to the sexing of the burials by artefacts over anthropological sex (Lucy 1997). Where biological sex is separately determined, considerable ambiguity appears, such as the occurrence of weapons with female skeletons, or jewellery with males (12 per cent at Buckland, Kent and 15 per cent at Sewerby, Yorkshire). Certain cases might be excluded on the basis of the context of the artefacts; for instance, many of the weapon parts associated with female burials are examples of secondary use, such as detached spearheads being used as knives or weaving swords. This cannot explain away all instances, however, and the lack of reliability of anthropological sexing is sometimes raised as a defence. These methods can be used with up to 95 per cent confidence where the pelvis is present, and 85–95 per cent confidence where the skull is complete (Brown 1998). However, it must be emphasised that robusticity varies between individuals, so that prehistoric women may very well be identified as male by the methods of physical anthropology. Further, even where DNA determinations are carried out, it must be recalled that chromosomal sex and physical phenotype do not necessarily coincide. Through DNA we might identify as female or male, individuals who possessed the secondary sexual characteristics and outward appearance of their opposite sex.

Archaeologists display a remarkable reticence to address women's adoption of 'masculine' symbols to convey authority. An infamous example from the Central European Iron Age is that of Vix, a cemetery of 500–480 BC, which included the burial of an anthropologically sexed female (aged 30–35 years), contained in a wooden burial chamber and laid out on a four-wheeled, highly decorated wagon box (Arnold 1991: 366). The grave included imported bronze and ceramic drinking equipment, a large bronze cauldron, two bronze basins, a gold torc, pins, earrings, bracelets and anklets, the last of which are generally seen as exclusively female items. Although no weapons were present, three other aspects of masculinity (after Treherne 1995) are represented: alcohol, driving/riding and bodily ornamentation. Bettina Arnold has observed that previous commentators have identified this and similar burials as transvestite priests or cross-dressing warriors, fantastic interpretations that have been preferred over that of a woman wielding masculine symbols of power.

Similar ambiguity arises where symbols of male sex are associated with females. Explicit representations of phalluses, for instance, are generally interpreted as unassailable references to the biological male (Robb 1997; Yates 1993). Yet, in the context of Iron Age burials from Hasanlu Tepe in northwestern Iran, females were interred with pins showing an erect penis (Figure 4.2) (Marcus 1996). These flat bronze or iron pins were worn on the chests of five females (aged 21–45 years), who were members of an elite class of women buried with elaborate bronze headdresses, beads of amber, carnelian, shell and gold, finger rings, bronze pins, imported goods and rich metal (*ibid.*: 46). Chronologically these burials are thought to correspond with a period marked by the increasing militarisation of Mesopotamia, at a time when the Assyrian and Urartian empires were expanding into the region (*c.* 1000–800 BC). Michelle Marcus has compared the phallic bronze pins to larger iron plaques, of similar shape and design, that were found associated with military equipment in a burnt building at Hasanlu, which are thought to have been horse trappings or helmet flaps.

Marcus argues that together the pins and plaques are part of a response to external threat, in which the Hasanlu elite attempted to create an image of 'an armed and well-defended society', with the female body decorated with phallic pins in order to signal 'the illusion of a potent and secure society'. She offers various possibilities for the status represented by the phallic pins and those wearing them, including signs for women's fertility, sexual unions, ancestral authority,

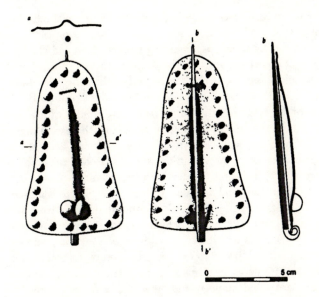

Figure 4.2 Reconstruction drawing of an Iron Age pin from Hasanlu Tepe, Iran, length 83mm (HAS 64-193)

Source: Drawing by D. L. Hoffman. Reproduced from Marcus 1996: fig. 17b.

or as identifiers of the wives or daughters of high-ranking military men (*ibid.*: 51). Judging from their size (80–130mm × 50–70mm), the phallic pins signalled a reasonably subtle message, and can hardly have been intended to intimidate enemies beyond Mesopotamia's borders. The remainder of accompanying artefacts reinforces the femininity of those buried wearing the pins, yet these women must have possessed some extra quality or status more usually linked with masculinity. Rather than reflecting their status relational to male prestige (as wives or daughters), did the pins perhaps reflect the sexuality of the women, or were these particular individuals somehow linked with the proposed campaigns for enhanced militarisation, as patrons, strategists, spies? In some sense, were these women from Hasanlu regarded as masculine by their contemporaries, conveying the aspects of maleness that were viewed as particularly empowering by their community?

Written on the body

Archaeological approaches have sometimes reified the body, rendering it a mannequin, to be dressed, inscribed, invested with social meaning. Representations of the body in ancient art are taken to be commentaries on particular social groups, including women, men and children, in the belief that power relations will be decoded through formal analyses of anatomical sex, bodily gestures and archaeological context (e.g. Rogers 1995; Hitchcock 1997; Kokkinidou and Nikolaidou 1997). Such studies of the body run the risk of conflating gender with anatomical sex, although they hold potential for discerning the naturalisation of gender through the sexualised body. Within classical archaeology there is a greater legacy of interest in the sexualised body through the study of 'erotic art', although here categories are often collapsed to confuse gender with sex, and sexuality with sex acts. There is a broad concern with the notion of 'the gaze': a concept deriving from film theory, which examines the way in which a particular visual medium stereotypes or objectifies its subject through the voyeuristic eyes of its creator and audience (Mulvey 1975). In this context, representations of the body are considered in terms of how different viewers or audiences see the sexualised subject, and how desire for the subject is staged (Kampen 1996: 5–6; Lyons and Koloski-Ostrow 1997: 4).

Analysis of the body has been characterised by an interest in dress, body ornament and body modification. In the study of ancient art, Natalie Kampen has proposed concentration on the uses and meanings of the nude, clothed or decorated body; and the relationship of the body to contextual values of morality, religion, medicine and politics (Kampen 1996: 5–6). Marie Louise Stig Sørensen has approached gender through the archaeology of bodily appearance. In particular, she is concerned with the meaning of dress as a form of social knowledge through which specific 'messages become naturalised in appearance codes' (Sørensen 1991: 122). Dress is seen as a means of communication between individuals and groups, subject to temporal change and superimposition, and distinguished through constituent parts of cloth, clothing and costume. In a study of costumes of the Danish Bronze Age she detected clear distinctions between male and female dress; there were two costumes for women and only one for men, with female differences signalled additionally through head-dresses and elaborate coiffure. She argues that the contrasting female costumes were not representative of age, region or seasonality, but rather the women's position relative to men, with a specific costume having designated the social or marital status of a woman (Sørensen 1991: 127).

Lynn Meskell has criticised such archaeological approaches to the body for their tendency to focus on exteriority, on the body as artefact or exhibit: 'Archaeology has been seduced by Foucauldian notions of control, where power relations are mapped on the body as a surface which can be analysed as a forum for display' (Meskell 1998b: 141). She has called for studies which examine bodily experience and seek 'individual contextualised bodies' (Meskell 1996: 5), over those which view bodies as signs for social categories. Here, two case studies are introduced which take distinctive approaches to the gendered body: the first considers masculinity as a quality that is acquired socially (Yates 1993), while the second probes representations of the self and individual, effectively deconstructing gender as an ontological category (Knapp and Meskell 1997).

Tim Yates has studied the Bronze Age rock carvings of the west coast of Sweden to explore the way in which the body and sexual identity are represented (Figure 4.3). There are some 2,500 individual panels at 2,000 sites, consisting of images incised or pecked onto the surface of exposed bedrock (Yates 1993). Six categories of image have been observed, including cup marks, ships, human and animal figures, foot marks and circular designs. Yates is particularly concerned with the human figures, and classifies these according to the presence or absence of weapons, with four categories cross-referenced to the presence of physical characteristics, including an erect phallus, exaggerated calf muscles, exaggerated hands and/or fingers, horned helmets and long hair (*ibid.*: 35–6). Because no firm chronological framework exists for the rock carvings, Yates treats these images as one group. He proposes certain shared characteristics, with armed phallic figures being twice as common as non-phallic, and non-phallic figures four times as likely to be shown unarmed. These phallic 'warriors' are less common than other types of figure, but are consistently depicted on a larger scale than other figures. Yates reports a general consensus that 'the society which produced the carvings was dominated by ideals centered upon aggressive masculinity' (*ibid.*: 41). The intriguing figures are the non-phallic ones, which have sometimes been interpreted as representing women (Mandt 1987). Yates argues that the absence of a parallel symbolism of female sexual characteristics (such as breasts or vaginal symbolism) mitigates against a binary male/female vocabulary in rock art. Rather, he proposes that the opposition demonstrated is between male sexual identity and sexual ambivalence.

Yates explores the manner in which sexual identity can be acquired, citing Gilbert Herdt's study of the Sambia (see pp. 57), among whom the young male must shed female essences (blood) and gain that of the male (semen) (Herdt 1987). Yates proposes that ontological identity is

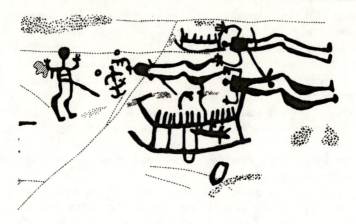

Figure 4.3 An example of Swedish rock art from Torsbo, Kville, showing human figures with phalluses, exaggerated calf muscles and
exaggerated hands

Source: Drawing by Steve Allen, after Fredsjo 1981: 241.

not natural but a 'cultural-linguistic construct' making use of general
codes of symbols. In the context of Bronze Age Sweden, he argues
that male sexual identity was not perceived as an inherent part of the
body, but required supplementation of some kind. Within rock art the
male was shown with weapons, erect phalluses, exaggerated calf
muscles or in association with antlers: 'Masculine identity must be
guaranteed by signs applied to the surface of the body, and these signs
are detachable – they do not inhere in the body, but can be separated
from it' (*ibid.*: 66). While Yates perceives masculinity as synonymous
with an aggressive, male sexual identity, he views this as a principle that
is applied to bodies from the outside. Thus masculinity is an acquired
identity, and binary categories in rock art are interpreted not as
male/female, but instead, as male/lacking male. This approach
assumes a single, hegemonic masculinity as a quality that is exclusive to
the male. However, Yates has offered a reading of sexualised imagery
that stresses the acquired, changeable status of masculinity.

In their study of prehistoric figurines from Cyprus, Bernard Knapp
and Lynn Meskell reject commentaries on social groups, in favour of
concentration on the individual. Approaching the individual in this way
requires three layers of appreciation: the cognitive tendency to experience oneself as a distinct entity; the culturally specific experience of
being a man or woman in a particular time or place; and the sense of

self that is experienced through age, status, sex, ethnicity and other contributors to social identity (Knapp and Meskell 1997: 198). The figurines in question are anthropomorphic figures in clay or stone, which are frequently classified in a binary framework of male or female (*ibid.*: 190). Further distinctions are drawn between Chalcolithic stone pendants and Bronze Age plank figures, mainly in clay. Although many figurines lack clear signs of biological sex, and others exhibit both vulvic and phallic components, there has been a tendency to assign a female identification, and in addition to treat the figurines as manifestations of mother goddesses (*ibid.*: 191). Knapp and Meskell propose that the discernment of dichotomous gender categories in the figurines is by nature an essentialist enquiry. Instead of generic representations, many of these should be seen as expressions of the self. Rather than expressing binary dichotomies, they assert that some forms (such as the Chalcolithic cruciform with elongated neck) 'may represent an attempt at harmonizing, or at least incorporating, the sexual characteristics of males and females' (*ibid.*: 194).

Knapp and Meskell argue that Bronze Age Cyprus is distinguished by an increased use of figurines, and by increased differentiation amongst the figurines, including plank figures with individual markings of personal adornment and jewellery, and facemarks that might be interpreted as masks, tattoos or face-paintings (Figure 4.4). These changes follow an emerging concern for individual status in the Chalcolithic, evidenced in urn burials, the use of seals and the development of household storage of resources. The Bronze Age witnessed an increase in settlement numbers and size, refinement of craft technologies, agriculture, and the emergence of elites who participated in a prestige-goods economy. Knapp and Meskell attribute the rise in incidence and diversity of the figurines to the enhanced sense of self-identity that would have accompanied this magnification of social complexity. They discount any attempt to discern gender in the figures through male or female anatomical sex. Rather than normative categories, they propose that gender should be contemplated as a spectrum, a principle that is selected, experienced and expressed integrally to individual identity. Meskell stresses that this notion of the individual as a cognizant, singular person should not be conflated with individualism, a modern, humanist concept that attributes the capacity for autonomous, rational thought to each human subject (Meskell 1999). As Marilyn Strathern has demonstrated in relation to contemporary Melanesia, concepts of the individual are culturally specific (Strathern 1988). Gender identity, sexuality and the constructed body, are drawn

Figure 4.4 Red polished ware double-headed plank figurine from Dhenia, Cyprus (height 300mm) showing individual facemarks and jewellery

Source: Reproduced by kind permission of Lynn Meskell

upon variously to create each society's ontologies of gender, and each actor's sense of personhood.

Beauty and the beast

Sex, gender, and sexuality are permeable categories that are created through culturally constructed models of physiology. Gender identities are classified and drawn upon through relative understandings such as the functioning of the human body and the degree of difference between males and females. Gender is mystified, or naturalised, through a conflation of physiognomy, ethnicity, religious or social beliefs, learned behaviour, and in some cases sexuality, creating apparently natural gender categories of masculine, feminine, and specified others. Perhaps the most common gender construction will be binary, based on male and female biological differences; the evidence of human biology, history, anthropology and archaeology, however, demands that consideration be given to multiple or mutable gender categories. Gender is a cumulative ontology, acquired by individuals through processes of socialisation and through their own performances of repeated activities that naturalise their gender. The lived experience of gender shifts, changes and develops with stages in the lifecycle, and physical transformations can be wrought in the body through the addition of costume, adornment, coiffure and cosmetics, or permanent adaptations, including scarification, male or female circumcision, tattooing, piercing, foot-binding, head-flattening, ear-elongation, and so on.

Gender identity is not always synonymous with physicality and sexuality. In some cases third or cross-genders may be physiologically distinct, such as the Byzantine eunuch, the Indian *hijra*, or in some societies the hermaphrodite; or alternatively, in the case of the Native American two-spirit, defined by mentality or supernatural belief. In premodern, non-western contexts, there is frequently a lack of fit between gender categories and sexuality, and these statuses are sometimes adopted only temporarally, so that the application of labels such as hetero- or homosexual may be inappropriate. Further, the practice of same-sex sexual acts does not presuppose the recognition socially or personally of a distinct sexuality. Even institutionalised third genders, such as the two-spirit and the Byzantine eunuch, cannot be defined by exclusive sexual mores. Certain cross-gender roles may be accorded their own gender category, yet frequently this status requires the renunciation of all sexual activity, such as the modern Balkan *muškobanje*, or the cross-dressing female saints of the late Antique deserts of Egypt, Syria and Palestine.

Gender identity is a contingent quality: a phantom constructed, selected and applied through cultural notions such as beauty, chastity, virility, and warriorhood. An understanding of masculinity or femininity must be sought that is comparative and contextual, in contrast to essential binary assertions such as feminine beauty and masculine violence. Clearly, in certain contexts women ascribe to masculinity, while men borrow feminine traits for their counter-hegemonic masculinities. Masculinist archaeologies must resist the perpetuation of such stereotypes. They will need to search beyond the hunter, warrior, pillager or rapist, to consider man the farmer, craftworker, priest or politician; the father, son, husband or lover who is not accounted for by commentaries on universal male aggression.

Gender is in the body, but it cannot be reduced to mere differences of biological sex, hormones or brain chemistry between males and females. Gender is experienced as an identity that is personal and mutable, rather than externally inscribed and fixed. Our binary perceptions of gender are blurred by evidence for multiple gender categories, and indeed their recognition may confirm that all such types may be no more than our western desire to classify and rationalise the individual. It has been suggested that gender should be regarded physically and mentally as a spectrum, rather than conceptualised as concrete categories (Nordbladh and Yates 1991; Knapp and Meskell 1997). But is gender merely the sum or total part of selfhood, which individuals choose, experience and perform? We must recall that the individual may not be the primary social actor in all societies (Moore 1994; Strathern 1988). Fundamental to any identity, or experience of personhood, are connections between families, communities and generations: the intimate gender relations that result from cycles of time, space and the body.

Chapter 5

Performing the past

Gendered time, space, and the lifecycle

Gender is consolidated through the course of a lifetime, as ideas about gender difference and the physical changes of the lifecycle are brought together in the cultural definition of the lifecourse. Through the metaphors of gender, time and space, the lifecycle is given specific meaning. This chapter examines how gender is performed at different scales and in distinctive settings to create personal identity, cohesion of age groups and vital connections between generations. Here 'performance' conflates the repetition of everyday tasks and time; gendered learning through children's play; the theatrical performance of rites of gender conferment; and the performance of life itself, as the gendered body is transformed by age.

Time: the gender clock

Physicists generally concur that 'time' is no more than an illusion, a concept invented by people to make sense of the world around them (Hawking 1988). Archaeologists, in contrast, are professional time-keepers, measuring human experience according to sequences of events dated by chronologies, whether relative or absolute, resulting from artefact typologies or methods of scientific dating. It has been argued that the resulting periodisations may be androcentric. Joan Kelly-Gadol observed that historians have perceived male experience and male status as the traditional markers for conventional periodisation, such as wars, political events and transitions of rulers (Kelly-Gadol 1976). With reference to archaeology, Marina Picazo has proposed that previous periodisations have been based on the occurrence of male artefacts, resulting in linear chronologies that may neglect more female measures of cyclical time (Picazo 1997: 64–5). She cites research by Paloma González Marcén on chronologies of the Argaric Bronze Age of southeast Spain, where female grave goods, in particular the pairing of the domestic knife and chisel, show longer durations of use than the weapons associated with male burials (González Marcén 1992).

Recently this gulf between measured, sequential time and the experienced time of daily life has been addressed by archaeological theorists. A particular concern has emerged for the way in which daily and long-term time scales construct the identities of both individuals and social groups (Gosden 1994; Thomas 1996). Christopher Gosden has argued that time and social cohesion are created over the long term, in contradistinction to the anthropologist Emile Durkheim, who viewed time scales as having derived from the rhythms of social life, through the repetition of rites, feasts and ceremonies (Durkheim 1965). Following Paul Ricoeur, Gosden stresses the importance of two temporal scales, the personal time of daily habits *versus* the more public time of social rites, with meaning created through the intersection of big, cosmological time *versus* small, personal time (Ricoeur 1988: 245; Gosden 1994: 136). Identity is enhanced by a collective drawing on the past, a social memory, which provides a structure for creating cosmologies, through origin stories, links with ancestors and future afterlives. Archaeologists have tended to stress the linear, long-term character of socially created time (Thomas 1996: 31). Anthropologists like John Davis, on the other hand, have stressed that time has contextual meaning. He has contrasted perceptions of cyclical *versus* generative time, in other words time structures that emphasise either the circular or the sequential nature of experience, and their significance in constructing personal, political and ethnic identities (Davis 1991: 13, 15).

> Times are a setting, a metaphor, analogy, model, which we use to generalize our experience of duration. People have construed the past variously as an alternate state or condition; as one phase in a cycle; as a series of precedents; as part of an unfolding story which culminates now or at some time in the future.
>
> (*ibid.*: 18)

The importance of personal, daily time was stressed in the works of the philosopher Martin Heidegger ([1927] 1962). Julian Thomas has developed Heidegger's concept of *Dasein* for application to archaeology (Thomas 1996). The term *Dasein* summarises the way that humans engage with the world, a sense of being or subjectivity that is lived in an embodied form (*ibid.*: 47). Heidegger proposed that time derives from the body, with 'being' – involving practical action – elevated over knowing. Heidegger developed hermeneutic phenomenology as a means of understanding everyday life and the way in which the senses perceive the world (Gosden 1994: 108). His notion of 'being' relies on perceptions of time, in that the cultivation of three time-scales or *ecstases*, a past, present and future, are said to model personal identity (Heidegger 1962: 377). Thomas has argued that Heidegger's notion of 'being' links together identity, materiality and temporality, with potential for examining 'experiential space': the way in which place is experienced through the human body (Thomas 1996: 83, 85, 90). Thomas adds the dimension of the human lifecourse to Heidegger's model, noting that everyday time is gendered, in that 'women are forcibly and repeatedly reminded of the cyclical character of their own biology', with the result that their own understanding of personal time may differ from men's (*ibid.*: 52). In his own work on the later Neolithic, Thomas proposes that there was a heterogeneous quality to life with 'multiple overlapping communities' created by lifecourse events that may have involved practices such as initiation or the transmission of secret knowledge.

> Individual persons might have been present at quite different sets of events, and these would have contributed to quite different narratives of personal identity. Each person would have moved through a range of different contexts in the course of their life.
>
> (Thomas 1996: 180)

Space, identity and everyday time are connected through the concept of *habitus*, developed by anthropologist Pierre Bourdieu (Bourdieu 1977). *Habitus* is a practical logic and sense of order that is learned unconsciously through the enactment of everyday life. In his study of the Kabyle house, for example, Bourdieu proposed that the organisation of space was structured according to the same sets of contrasts that informed the everyday knowledge of its inhabitants (Bourdieu 1970). Bourdieu developed an embodied notion of *habitus* in the concept *hexis*, whereby the different social experiences created by gender, class and age are inscribed on the body (Bourdieu 1990). *Hexis* might be seen as the cumulative experience of gender, in that knowledge acquired during childhood is built upon throughout the lifecourse, reinforced by physical movement through cultural spaces, and public endorsement through rites and ceremonies: a combination of private and public temporality.

Bourdieu's *hexis* and Heidegger's *Dasein* provide some insight to social identity and the importance of both everyday practice and long-term social memory. Yet both concepts assume a remarkable degree of continuity and homogeneity in social practice; further, they remain abstract in that the actual processes by which identity is created remain elusive. In comparison, Judith Butler's model of performance provides a more concrete bridge between the body and everyday experience, proposing the mechanisms through which the body is gendered and identity is attained. Butler contends that gender does not express an existing psychic reality, but instead that gender and sexual identity are created by 'performance': repetitions that constitute and contest the coherence of personal identity. In her reading, gender is not a category or classification but rather 'being' in the Heideggerian sense, 'an ontology of gender whereby the meaning of *being* a woman or man is elucidated within the terms of phenomenology ... the "being" of gender is *an effect*' (Butler 1990: 32). Here gendered identity is created through the repetition of postures, gestures, dress, language and so on, performed as the repeated citation of a gendered norm, in a manner not dissimilar to the *habitus* proposed by Bourdieu (Butler 1993: 12–16). In this way the everyday time of gender is made visible and material, tangible qualities amenable to archaeological study.

Through a sense of 'being' and repeated 'performance' the details of everyday life provide the experience of gender difference. The contextual meanings of such differences are conveyed through gender ideologies that draw on longer-term perceptions of time, the cosmologies of belief and social memory. Yet the personal experience of gender difference is also inwardly corporeal: the physical and mental processes of time and age are gendered. None of these conceptual models of time and the body interweave the everyday and the long term with the corporeal and the natural: the temporal scales of the physical lifecycle and those of the natural world, the daily and cyclical scales of the sun rising and setting, and the changing of the seasons. These temporal experiences – the attainment of adulthood, growing old, the passage of the day, autumn waning into winter – balance cyclical and linear time, continuity and discontinuity. Gender is created through this merging of being, performance and the corporeality of the lifecourse; conversely, time may take on meaning through the embodiment of gender.

Gendered cosmologies: marking time and space

For me, the most vivid example of this convergence of time, space and the lifecourse, one which is still very perceptible in the modern English landscape, may be found in the medieval parish church (Gilchrist 1999). By the thirteenth century, the fully developed ground plan of the church represented the body of the crucified Christ; but the siting of particular rites, features and images also connected physical movement through the spaces of the church with the passage of a Christian life (Figure 5.1). Churches are invariably oriented east/west, with the most sacred space, the high altar, located in the eastern portion, the chancel. Burials also followed this east/west orientation, ostensibly to allow the resurrected souls to rise from their graves on Judgement Day and walk towards the holy city of Jerusalem. Such an orientation also followed earlier practices in facilitating a focus on the rising sun in the east, perhaps symbolising the dawning of a new life. Bell-towers were constructed at the western end of the church (or over the crossing of cruciform churches). Right up to the nineteenth century, the only common measure of daily time was the pealing bells that called people to services at their local parish church.

Parishioners entered the church through the west (or southwest) door in the nave, the main (western) body of the church where the congregation gathered. The priest(s) entered through a separate door in the chancel, the eastern part of the church that was reserved solely for liturgical use. The junction between the chancel and the nave, or the sacred and secular space, was bounded by a decorated screen that supported the rood, the image of the crucified Christ, flanked by the Virgin Mary at the north, and St John the Evangelist at the south. This screen not only marked the division between the space of the priest and that of the parishioners, it served to obscure the people's vision of the high altar, thus emphasising the sacred/secular divide, and further mystifying the mass (Figure 5.2).

Fonts for infant baptism were placed at the western end of the nave, to denote both entry to the Church and initiation to the lifecourse. By the twelfth century it was common to have a substantial, sculpted stone font placed permanently by the main door in the west of the nave. Popular iconography for the font included representations of the

Figure 5.1 The parish church of Gedney, Lincolnshire, looking from west to east. This fully developed church dates predominantly to the thirteenth and fourteenth centuries. It consists of a structurally distinct chancel and nave, and aisles (with their own altars) to the north and south of the nave, divided from the nave by large arcades that would have been screened. The screen below the chancel arch is a nineteenth-century reconstruction of the medieval arrangement.

seasons and the labours of the months, combining images of the agricultural cycle with overtones of the human lifecycle. The west door was frequently decorated with the iconography of the zodiac and/or the seasons, linking the natural year, the human lifecourse and cosmological symbols. The most arresting imagery was reserved for the space over the chancel arch, the tympanum, above the Crucifixion on the rood screen. Here, visions of Doom and Judgement Day depicted the weighing of good and bad souls, the torments of Purgatory and the passage to Heaven or Hell. This didactic imagery punctuated the division between the secular and sacred space of the nave and chancel, and symbolised the distinction between earth and heaven. Its placement underlined the passage of the Christian life: entry through baptism at the western extreme of the nave; moving eastward through life towards judgement at the rood screen; and the promise of heavenly afterlife in the mystified, eastern area of the chancel, often embellished

Figure 5.2 Reconstruction of a screen typical of those that would have marked the division between the nave and chancel of a medieval parish church. The screen was topped by a loft, which supported a three-dimensional 'rood' or Crucifixion, flanked by the figures of the Virgin Mary to the left (north) and St John the Evangelist to the right (south). It distinguished the spaces of the priest and parishioners, together with the dichotomies of sacred and secular, heaven and earth, future and present. It also served as a boundary which impeded direct vision to the high altar.

Source: Drawing by Steve Allen

with an image of Christ in Majesty (Figure 5.3). It was believed that at Judgement Day the inequities of age would be resolved: all would be resurrected at the prime of life, thirty-three years old, taking on the age of the crucified Christ (Shahar 1997: 53 n71).

These broad canvasses of space and time were experienced differently according to social status, sex and age. Proximity to the chancel during services, and thus visibility of the high altar through the rood screen, was determined largely by class, with parishioners further segregated by sex (Aston 1990). It was more common for women to be

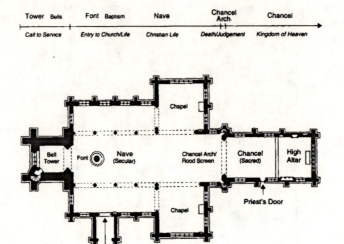

Figure 5.3 Plan of a later medieval parish church, illustrating the conjunction of the passage of a Christian life with physical movement from west to east through the spaces of the church

Source: Drawing by Steve Allen

allocated areas to the west or north of the nave, and men to the south of the nave, perhaps corresponding with placement of figures that peered down from the rood screen: the Virgin Mary at the north and John the Evangelist at the south. It was usual practice to stand during services up until the fifteenth or sixteenth century, with special benches provided for the elderly and infirm, flanking the north and south side walls. The axes of the church were sometimes gendered further through images painted on panels of the rood screen, in wall-paintings, stained glass, and carved on the fixed benches that filled the interior of the nave in the later middle ages. In particular, the rood screen that faced the congregation was often decorated with images of male and female saints, occupying respective halves of the screen (Duffy 1990); while examples survive of elaborate schemes of benches, dividing male and female iconography into cardinal points of the church, as at St Mary the Virgin, Wigginhall, Norfolk. Of course, the status of priest was reserved for men, so that space to the east of the rood screen was their preserve, both during their lives and to a great extent afterwards, with burial in the chancel limited to that of priests and founders of the church. The priest faced the altar during mass, towards the cosmological future, presenting his back to the congregation, away from the earthly present and ancestral past. Only he could touch the venerated host or holy water, drink from the chalice, or wear the sacred vestments.

From the twelfth century onwards, burial of wealthy families in the interior of the church became more common, focusing on the nave and aisles (see Daniell 1997). These ancestors underfoot became a tactile presence from the thirteenth and fourteenth centuries, when effigies – individual likenesses or representations of the dead – became part of the tombs of prominent families. These mausolea were erected in private chapels that had grown up in the aisles, particularly as chantry masses for the dead became more popular: prayers that were believed to hasten the passage of the soul through Purgatory. These chantry masses connected the living and the dead, a lifeline that was performed repeatedly through obits – anniversary masses for the dead that might be continued for decades after an individual's funeral. In some cases a wooden effigy of the deceased would be brought out for subsequent re-enactments of the funeral.

Male and female parishioners experienced daily, seasonal and anniversary rites equally, a reflection of the Christian belief in the equality of souls, despite earthly inequality of sexes. The exception to this rule was the rite of the 'rechurching' of women after childbirth, an act of purification that was practised in porches or outside doors at the western end of the nave, symbolising the woman's re-entry to the Church after giving birth. The spaces of the medieval parish church united the sacred with the profane; the living with the dead; and personal, daily time and public, cosmological time with corporeal and natural time scales: those of the sun, the seasons and the lifecourse. Personal, family and community identities were emphasised through space, imagery and hierarchy, experienced through attendence of daily and/or weekly services, seasonal festivals, baptisms, marriages and funerals (Graves 1989). Through the medieval parish church, gendered identity was reinforced through performances that were both repetitious and theatrical in character.

Syncopated lives

Men and women experience time differently through the vehicle of the human body: most women experience menarche, monthly menstruation and menopause. Their lives are characterised alternately by cyclical continuity and discontinuity, in contrast to the greater physical continuum of men's lifecycles. The cultural inscription of stages in the lifecycle can encourage gendered scales of time, with men and women drawing upon distinctive pasts, presents and futures, the gendering of Heidegger's *ecstases* of personal identity. In relation to Classical Greece, Lin Foxhall has argued that men and women accessed conflicting discourses of time and monumentality (Foxhall 1994). She describes how girls were believed to reach adulthood sooner than boys, with boys slipping more gradually into full adult status around thirty years of age. A woman's influence increased as she grew older, with her power over kin and the household accelerating until she held sway over three generations of the family. In this position she took a special role in rites of passage for her children and grandchildren, including childbirth, weddings and funerals. Foxhill argues that men 'were dependent on women for access to the three-generation time scale which framed most of everyday life' (*ibid*.: 136) through children and the household; at the same time, men controlled the formal network of kinship through the *ankhisteia*, the group of people who shared an ancestor three genera-tions retrospectively. Men, in contrast to women, achieved greater public power and a larger-scale past, but retained this authority for a shorter period, with influence decreasing with age and cessation of military activity. Men adopted larger-scale notions of past and future, and cultivated a concern for monumentality, for instance through rhetoric about fame, glory, reputation and memory, and material culture ranging from grave stelae to monumental architecture. These artefacts of a 'hegemonic masculinity' marked 'their relatively short period of full, powerful adulthood' (*ibid*.: 137).

The female and male lifecycles were out of step in Classical Greece, with women marrying earlier (aged 12–14) and living longer, with the result that they bridged generations and spanned over two formal genera-tions of men. Women had more control over the present and short-term past, perhaps conveying an oral history through the teaching of children in the household, in contrast to the male realm of longer-term past and future, through monumentality and the *ankhisteia*. Foxhall's vision of Classical Greece reveals the gendering of the two time scales postulated by time theorists: here, personal, everyday habitual time was female, while public, long-term social memory was male.

Gender's metronome: archaeology and the lifecourse

In its narratives of life in the past, archaeology seldom represents the full diversity of age ranges; on the whole, gender archaeology has been no exception in this, with its telescoped view of binary gender structures, focused on adult male and female. From the evidence of palaeodemography we can propose that most prehistoric populations endured a childhood mortality rate of at least 50 per cent, with the implication that half the living population of any community were children (Chamberlain 1997: 249). Extremes of age are especially overlooked: methods of ageing skeletal evidence under-represent individuals over fifty years of age, while the difficulties of recovering, ageing and sexing infant skeletons are considerable (Rega 1997). In common with the disciplines of sociology, anthropology and history (Featherstone and Wernick 1995; Ginn and Arber 1995; Keith 1985; Laslett 1995; Shahar 1997), there has been a notable absence in archaeology of the study of ageing, and theorisation of the relationship between age and gender.

The first studies to tackle such issues paralleled early discussions in gender archaeology, with a focus on matters of visibility and the disentanglement of biological sex from cultural gender. Similarly, discussions of age and gender have emphasised visibility (particularly of infants and children), and the distinction between physical age *versus* the cultural construction of gendered age (Derevenski 1997b: 486). Sociologists propose three meanings of age: chronological age, which is measured by accepted calendaric means; social age, which reflects the normative behaviour that is culturally imposed on particular age groups; and physiological age, a medical construct that estimates levels of functional ability or impairment (Ginn and Arber 1995: 5). Anthropologists stress that age, like time, is calculated differently in specific cultures, with varying significance placed on chronology as opposed to function, and divergent numbers of recognised stages in the lifecourse (Keith 1985: 240). Jennie Keith has proposed that function is the most common measure of age (*ibid.*), one which draws attention to social and economic productivity, and emphasises the difference in rates of ageing between individuals.

Societies vary in the number of life stages that they recognise in the lifecourse, indicating that physiological factors, such as changes in fertility, are not always of paramount importance. Certain Inuit groups of the St Lawrence area of Quebec, for instance, use age only to distinguish between immature and mature males and females. In marked contrast, the Arusha of Kenya observe formal age statuses, or grades, for males: youths, junior warriors, senior warriors, junior elders and retired elders. Male age-sets have been recognised more commonly than female, and can be linked to formal age systems that connect age with social hierarchy. The African Masai are a classic example of this, who share egalitarian status amongst junior grades with overall control exercised by those in senior male grades (Keith 1985: 249). The lack of recognition of comparable, female age-sets may reflect the bias of ethnographic field-work, or, alternatively, may be a measure of the gendered differences between age and time. As the example of Classical Greece has shown (above), it may be more common for women to form social or productive groups that span and influence a number of generations simultaneously.

To date, the archaeological study of ageing has concentrated on infancy or childhood (Moore and Scott 1997; *Archaeological Review from Cambridge*, 13.2, 1994). The first discussions were raised by Scandinavian archaeologists, who sought to identify children in the archaeological record (Lillehammer 1989), just as they had pioneered the recognition of women archaeologically (Bertelsen *et al.* 1987). Following trends set in the social history of childhood (Ariès 1965), archaeologists have argued that the modern idea of the passive, depen-dent, adored child may be inappropriate to the past, and have set about examining the cultural specificity of infancy (Scott 1992), childhood (Lillehammer 1989), child labour (Derevenski 1997c) and ideas about parenting (Bolen 1992). Children have been considered as more inde-pendent, productive agents, capable, for example, of producing small, roughly worked flint tools (Finlay 1997).

More important than recognising individual children or their work, however, is an understanding of the process of gendering through enculturation, so that 'childhood can be regarded as a time of appren-ticeship to a culturally defined gender norm' (Derevenski 1997c: 199). This process can be envisaged through Bourdieu's concepts of *habitus* and *hexis* (see above), through which children learn about gender via the material world: the coding of buildings and space, artefacts such as toys and tools, dress and food. Through *habitus* they learn what is appropriate behaviour for a boy or girl. This unconsciously constructed, and apparently common-sense knowledge of the world is further devel-oped through the bodily experience of *hexis*. In the modern West, children are said to develop an awareness of their own gender identity from the approximate age of two, when gender is perceived as constant, linked with physical characteristics and dress. By the age of three or four they comprehend gender as stable and consistent across time and situations within their social experience (Derevenski 1997c: 195, after Golombok and Fivush 1994).

The way in which material culture interacts with this gendered apprenticeship can be glimpsed from artefacts recovered from children's burials, such as those at Birka in Sweden. Grete Lillehammer classifies these as objects linked with music, work, games and sport (Lillehammer 1989: 98). Further, it has been postulated that miniature items were associated with children for recreational or educational purposes (Figure 5.4), such as the tiny weapons and domestic crockery that are known from the later medieval period (Egan 1997), or the extensive, miniature material culture that Inuit children used in 'playing at house' or 'playing at hunting' (Park 1998). In many cultures, miniatures have also been used as amulets or votives in healing and pilgrimage cults. Where they can be firmly associated with children, however, they provide a firm insight into the use of material culture for establishing normative gender behaviour. Through miniature items of utilitarian character children could mimic the gendered, adult world through their play. In this sense, children's play can be seen as performance, in which children begin to create their gender identity through the emulation and repetition of gendered work, tasks, postures, gestures, and language.

The notion of childhood as a period of gender apprenticeship assumes a continuity between child and adult gender statuses; moreover, it dissolves the distinction between ascribed and achieved gender. This may be inappropriate in some contexts, however, where gender and the lifecourse may be viewed as discontinuous, or gendered status

Figure 5.4 Toys from medieval England in the form of miniature lead and tin jugs, scale 1:1.

Source: Drawings by Nick Griffiths and Tracy Smith in Egan 1997. Reproduced by kind permission of Geoff Egan.

is regarded as earned. Where gendered status is linked with full reproductive capacity, for example (both economic and physical reproduction), children might be perceived as gender-less. In her analysis of the Dakota burials from the Black Dog burial site (see also above, pp. 63–4), Mary Whelan observed that there were no artefact categories found exclusively with juveniles of any age, but a surprising number (twenty-six) associated only with adult burials (Whelan 1991: 28–9). She proposed that prepubescent individuals may have been perceived as a separate, gender-less category.

Before puberty, and the greater awareness of gender difference, males and females may sometimes have enjoyed similar access to activities, resources and cultural status. In this situation boys and girls were not gender-less, but rather shared a greater fluidity in elements of social identification and recognition. This may have pertained even to aspects of masculinity, such as the Anglo-Saxon 'warrior status' that was conveyed through the weapon burial rite (see above, p. 67). Heinrich Härke has examined the practice of burial with a simple iron knife, which occurred in 45–50 per cent of fifth to seventh-century burials in England (Härke 1989). From a sample of 925 knives he concluded that adult men were buried consistently with longer blade lengths, with knives becoming a symbol of masculinity during the decline of the full weapon burial rite. In juvenile burials, however, while males were more likely to have knives, females could have longer blades. It appears that until puberty, it was possible for some females to earn the equivalent of the masculine 'warrior status'.

Joanna Sofaer Derevenski has proposed that gender and age should be regarded as linked processes, rather than as separate categories of analysis (1997b). She argues that a satisfactory study of gender must examine change over each individual's lifecourse, since 'Gender is not static through the life course but must be constantly renegotiated in the light of increased gendered knowledge and changes in social situations' (ibid.: 487). She believes that through attention to age-related gendered statuses we can study the economic and social activities of specific age grades. Membership of such age grades provides a sense of similarity, of belonging, which may balance the perception of difference built up through sexual or social inequalities. She suggests that through burial evidence it should be possible to examine the age distribution of artefacts within a binary categorisation, in order to identify age cohorts and possible changes in gendered perceptions of the male and female individual (ibid.: 489).

Derevenski has used this approach in her analysis of the cemetery of

Tiszapolgár-Basatanya, an early-to-middle Copper Age site in eastern Hungary (4500–3600 BC) (Derevenski 1997a). Amongst this community gender difference was articulated potently and pervasively: in all periods binary sidedness in burial resulted in the interment of males on their right side and females on their left side. Anthropological sexing confirmed the near consistent bi-modal pattern, and from this evidence Derevenski extended her discussion to burials of unsexed, younger individuals who were also represented through sidedness. She examined the artefacts associated with 156 single burials in two major phases of the cemetery, not to identify sex-correlates, but rather to consider 'a continuous variable showing differences in age-related distribution between men and women' (*ibid.*). Contrasts were also observed between the two chronological periods, with difference expressed particularly through costume and the incidence of objects, including ceramic vessels, blades and stone artefacts. These differences were not absolute, but represented significant trends. In period 1 the medium of costume seems to have been sensitive to gendered age differences: women wore limestone beads as a girdle around the pelvis and a finger ring on the left hand; men wore armrings on the right arm and beads were found scattered around the torso. The armrings were associated with males between 5–25 years, while older males (35+) displayed copper beads. The association of the girdle with females does not appear to have been age-linked, although copper beads were found only in the graves of women below the age of about thirty-seven years. In period 2, in contrast, there seems to have been no distinctive male costume, with gender instead represented through the presence or absence of items. In period 1 the ocurrence of ceramic vessels increased with males over *c.* 25–30, while in female burials the incidence of vessels increased gradually up to forty years of age, and then steadily declines. In period 2 the distribution of ceramic vessels was less marked according to age, but there were greater contrasts between male and female graves. Stone artefacts were also used to express difference: worked stone artefacts were found almost exclusively in male graves, with pebbles occurring only in female graves. In period 1 the stone objects were associated with men over about twenty-five years of age, while pebbles were found in graves of females between *c.* 12–43 years. In period 2 the age distribution of stone items evened out, with objects occurring in male and female graves over *c.* 19–20 years of age. Blades and scrapers were associated predominantly with male burials, and distinctions according to blade length and morphological type may have been age-related.

Derevenski does not attribute specific meanings to these age-related gender differences, but proposes that in period 1 gender was linked more to prestige, reflecting gendered achievement, while in period 2 gender may have been ascribed according to sexual difference. Her approach to gender assumes a consistent binary structure, and concentrates on the recognition of homogeneous age cohorts, leaving little room for the expression of social status or personal gender identity. The broader social and economic context is not considered, factors that might shed light on the apparent changes between periods 1 and 2. However, the patterns yielded by her analysis suggest that the community at Tiszapolgár-Basatanya was concerned with symbolic signification of both cultural and physiological gendered age. For example, it is possible to detect a greater number of age grades for males in period 1, with important thresholds at ages c. 5 (when armbands were gained), c. 25 (when armbands were discarded) and c. 35 (when copper beads were displayed), perhaps reflecting junior, adult and senior male grades. Females, in contrast, were consistently represented by the wearing of the girdle; yet fertile women, between the ages of menarche and menopause, appear to have been distinguished by copper beads, ceramic vessels and pebbles. In period 2, however, there seems to have been a more equal emphasis on gendered age, with the occurrence of stone objects and pebbles in the graves of both males and females c. 19–20 years of age, perhaps denoting adult status. Derevenski's analysis reveals the potential of examining gendered age statuses, and emphasises the tendency for complexity and change in gendered signification, even within a single cemetery. Where age and gender have been carefully considered in mortuary analysis, as for example in the study of Anglo-Saxon cemeteries (e.g. Pader 1982), a great deal of variation has been detected in the emphasis placed on gender and/or age, within and between regions, in specific cemeteries and across relatively short periods of time.

Lifecycle rites: footprints in the sands of time

Where it can be detected that age grades or statuses were emphasised, as at Tiszapolgár-Basatanya, the transition between stages may have been marked by cultural rites. These 'rites of passage' (van Gennep [1908] 1960) have been recognised by anthropologists to be present in a broad range of societies, generally marking important moments in the lifecourse that are linked with either physiological or social changes.

Selected events often include birth, puberty, initiation, marriage, widow-hood and death. Such rites are a public means of consummating the passage, and it has been proposed that they involve three classic stages: separation, marginality and reincorporation (Turner 1969). Rites involving adoles-cents, including initiation and puberty, have attracted greater ethno-graphic attention, and it is to these public rites of passage, especially those of young males, that the three classic stages particularly pertain. Archaeologists have limited their discussions predominantly to rites of passage that are thought to have involved initiation, including the trans-mission of secret or 'esoteric' knowledge, and the practice of hunting magic or shamanistic rituals. A particularly evocative example is that of the postulated cave rituals of Upper Palaeolithic Europe, natural places that provided the total darkness and seclusion to separate initiates. The participation of adolescents in some kind of social rite is implied by the small foot and handprints that survive in the paintings that embellish these caves (Owens and Hayden 1997).

There has been a tendency to distinguish physiological from social transitions, for example the distinction between puberty ceremonies (such as the marking of menarche) from social ceremonies (such as initiation to exclusive societies or training for warriorhood). Paul Roscoe has argued that this is a false distinction, and that rites associ-ated with adolescence should be viewed as just one of several 'life-cycle rites' (Roscoe 1995: 233). Further, the apparently greater incidence and emphasis placed on male rites of passage (La Fontaine 1985) reflects an ethnographic bias. Although group initiation of males is more common than female, recorded in 30 per cent *versus* 10 per cent of known societies; individual initiation is actually more common for women. Individual female initiation is practised in 50–60 per cent of known societies, in contrast to 30–40 per cent practising initiation of individual males. In general, female rites are now recognised as being of a smaller scale, focusing on the individual and occurring more frequently than those of males (Lutkehaus and Roscoe 1995: xiv). Importantly, the physical impact of puberty, or the formal ceremonies of initiation, do not always confer adult status. Among the Melanesian Manam, Murik, Babae and Yangoru Boiken, women achieve adult status only by giving birth or adopting a child (*ibid.*: 23); whilst the complex process of achieving full manhood amongst the Sambia is reached only after the formal marriage rite and the birth of the first child (Herdt 1987: 167). In such cases, motherhood or fatherhood denotes the full status of adult.

Female initiation is linked more intimately with changes in the physical lifecycle, reflecting the more abrupt and dramatic first menstruation; which contrasts to the more tentative and gradual male indicators of puberty, such as the development of facial hair, the deepening of the voice or the first nocturnal emission. Commonly, the onset of menstruation prompts training for young girls in female sexuality and/or maternal nurturance. It is well known cross-culturally for menstruation to carry overtones of pollution and taboo: menstrual blood is perceived as a powerful substance (Lutkehaus 1995: 19; Moore 1988: 16–17). Protection for the initiate is afforded by ritual washing of the body to achieve purity; while frequently her community is protected by the practice of seclusion during menstruation. Material culture may sometimes be used to convey knowledge to the initiate about the female body, or to assist with the process of achieving womanhood. Joan Reilly has explored this possibility in relation to so-called 'dolls' occurring on the grave reliefs of young girls from Ancient Athens (5th–4th century BC) (Reilly 1997). The girls are depicted holding figures of naked females, which display mature proportions and developed breasts. Reilly compares these images to terracotta figures which are generally interpreted as children's toys. She proposes that rather than dolls, these figurines and their representations on grave monuments were anatomical votives linked with female health, and the particular diagnosis of ancient Greek medicine that a girl may require assistance to achieve menarche.

Lifecycle rites do not cease with puberty or parenthood. Retirement rituals for men include those of the Kenyan Boran: when they enter the most senior grade, men publicly recite their life exploits and achievements (Keith 1985: 246). In contrast, public recognition of menopause seems nonexistent; yet women certainly progress to new statuses in later life (see below, pp. 106–8). Amongst Saniyo-Hiyowe women of Papua New Guinea, rituals of widowhood unravel the purity rites of puberty: the widowed woman undergoes a period of symbolic menopause during which she is prohibited from washing. After several years, she is again free to wash and eventually to remarry (Townsend 1995).

Archaeologists have viewed prehistoric rites of passage as one means of creating and maintaining social inequalities. Owens and Hayden reviewed ethnographic evidence for 'life maturation events', including: growth payments, such as feasts to mark a child's development; puberty ceremonies, encompassing spirit quests and seclusion rites; initiations to secret societies; and training, for instance for male occupational specialisms or the conferment of administrative or esoteric knowledge (Owens and Hayden 1997: 128). They propose that certain rites of passage are indicative of greater social complexity, particularly growth payments and initiations, that require substantial material investment and may be limited to higher status children. They argue that because such rites of passage are accompanied by gift exchange and the creation of marriage alliances between families, they serve as a means of investment of surplus that stimulates the evolution of more complex cultural forms. In this scenario, 'aggrandizers use their children as pretexts for generating and investing surpluses and creating ongoing exchanges in surplus wealth' (*ibid.*: 150). Such an approach divorces maturation events from the lifecycle rites that are more deeply rooted in the human and social body. Further, the place of such rites in establishing personal identity, and clinching age cohorts, is lost in the image of initiates as passive pawns in a plot towards greater socio-economic complexity.

Increasingly, anthropologists view initiation rites as creating personhood and individual gender identity, but at the same time integrating this personal perspective with a wider political economy and cosmology (Lutkehaus 1995: 13). Particularly in relation to Melanesia, it has been observed that no meaningful distinction can be drawn between the individual and their society. Marilyn Strathern has argued that such rituals 'witness the formation of the cultural or social person, and the passage from childhood to adulthood becomes a metonym for all the processes by which persons are moulded' (Strathern 1992: 67). Melanesian initiations make an individual complete, so that they may become reproductive members of the community. A child is seen first of all as cross-sex; the process of the initiation embues them with a single sex essence of masculinity or femininity (*ibid.*: 66). The child is considered to be a product of multiple relationships: this 'multiple person' gains his or her identity and kinship from a combination of bodily substances (semen, blood, breast milk, bones), food, and objects or gifts, which also symbolise these multiple relations (Strathern 1988). Considerable resources are required to sponsor initiations and endow gifts to the initiate. In female initiation such gifts act as adornments to beautify the girl, but they may also influence later bridewealth negotiations.

Ethnographers traditionally viewed rites of initiation that involve strict sexual separation as characteristic of antagonistic gender relations. Complex, public rituals of male initiation were interpreted as separating boys from their mothers and developing male solidarity and aggression (Lutkehaus 1995: 10). Strathern argues that gender is a metaphor, and that sexual symbolism does not necessarily reflect the actual relations between men and women (Strathern 1988). Generally this ritualised antagonism is balanced by a concept of gender complementarity, in which both male and female are recognised as necessary for the reproduction of both the individual and the cosmos (e.g. Barlow 1995). As Nancy Lutkehaus concludes, initiation rites create gender difference, but 'the message conveyed in these societies is of the social necessity of both "male" and "female" powers and potentialities' (Lutkehaus 1995: 15).

Group lifecycle rites are public performances in the theatrical sense, with actors and audience participating in the creation of gender difference and identity. Exceptionally, archaeologists may encounter the stages for such performances, such as the caves of the Upper Palaeolithic, or possibly the sweat lodges, hunting stands, menstrual and birth huts of Native North America (Bolen 1992: 55; Galloway 1997). We may regularly retrieve fragmentary evidence of gifts and costumes indicative of initation to a new age grade, and perhaps ritual items integral to the transition. It has been argued, for instance, that the so-called 'venus figurines' of the Upper Palaeolithic represent the full lifecycle of the reproductive woman (Figure 5.5), including premenstrual and postmenopausal states, and could have been used to teach girls about the female body (Rice 1981); further, it has been proposed that such figures were modelled and fashioned by women as representations of their own bodies (McDermott 1996). Following this line of argument, it might be postulated that such figurines formed part of more private, female rites of initiation and transition. There is considerable ethnographic evidence, however, to suggest that male initiation rites regularly involve figurines. Amongst the Murik, for instance, boys sleep with carved figurines of cult spirits who convey magical knowledge about seduction (Barlow 1995: 97). Moreover, many male initiation rites invoke metaphors of pregnancy or female fertility. The female body is viewed as a metaphor for social reproduction: amongst the Manam and Murik, men secretly 'give birth' to canoes during their initiations (Roscoe 1995: 222). The Maconde of Tanzania, in contrast, bury figurines of pregnant women during the seclusion of boys, and re-excavate them for the boys' reincorporation into the community. Gunnar and Randi Haaland use this analogue to propose one alternative interpretation for the supposed 'goddess figurines' of prehistoric Europe. They argue that such female images may have been used in connection with the formation of male identity, for example through rites of initiation (Haaland and Haaland 1995: 118).

Figure 5.5 A so-called 'venus' or 'goddess' figurine of the Upper Palaeolithic: the Venus of Willendorf (Austria)

Source: Drawing by Steve Allen

Rather than seeking to identify the location or details of the rites themselves, there is potential in focusing on the ways in which the life-cycle is culturally segmented into age statuses that are marked materially. It is seldom possible to reconstruct the physical transformations that initiation rites wrought on the body, such as circumcision, scarification or tattooing. However, through the evidence of burial we can glimpse the association of particular artefacts or sets of objects that denote an age grade, or specific costumes that were connected with gendered age. At the early Bronze Age cemetery of Mokrin in Hungary, Beth Rega has noted the presence of bone needles in the graves of female children aged 6–13 years (Rega 1997: 233). She proposes that the association of such objects with individuals who had not yet acquired the strength or dexterity to sew, indicates that these needles were 'girl-symbols carried to adulthood'; in other words, objects given to mark the first female age grade.

Conversely, the special status of adulthood was chosen for symbolic representation at the Mesolithic sites of Téviec and Hoëdic in Brittany (Schulting 1996). Rick Schulting has observed that pierced marine shells were used to distinguish the burials of young and middle-aged adults, whose graves contained a greater quantity of ornamentation and artefacts than younger or older individuals. In addition, there was a subtle distinction in the use of local marine shells to represent male and female adults. The species *Trivia Europea* was used primarily in association with male graves; while the species *Littorina obtusata* primarily marked females. It cannot be certain whether these differences corresponded with gendered clothing during their lives, but the men and women of these Mesolithic communities were marked in death according to their status of adulthood. Such recognition is not indicative simply of having attained puberty, but perhaps the acquisition of social or economic skills, the achievement of marriage or parenthood. This careful use of two locally abundant species of shellfish seems to suggest both gender difference and complementarity in adult statuses.

Gendered metaphors: space and the household

Space serves as a stage for gendered performance: the daily and seasonal repetition of tasks, routines, conversations and personal exchanges. Particularly in the arena of domestic space, we see the everyday experience of gender difference and the nexus of relations between generations. Space is given meaning through various avenues, including the mental interpretation of spatial arrangements and the physical sensation of movement through spaces (Moore 1986). Space takes on gendered meaning as a metaphor for social relations and cosmologies, through the disposition of buildings and their interiors, differential access and mobility, materials and notions of permanence (Gilchrist 1994: 150–69; Meskell 1998a). The meanings of space are perceived contextually, and through processes such as *habitus*, space assists in establishing and reproducing social order. While the precise social configuration of the household is seldom evinced archaeologically, the physical forms and activities carried out within domestic structures have been linked with gender relations. In particular, issues of land inheritance have been studied through the household, together with ideas about continuity of landholding that connect living generations with the ancestors (Hodder 1990; Tringham 1991; Lyons 1998). Further, the lifecycle of the house has been viewed as a metaphor for social relations and the passage of the lifecourse.

In her study of 'households with faces', Ruth Tringham emphasises the importance of architectural and spatial studies at the micro-scale, proposing that more generalised approaches fail to discern significant differences of use and meaning, and evidence for social transformations at the local level (Tringham 1991). She examined the houses of Opovo-Ugar Bajbuk, associated with the Late Neolithic Vinça culture of the former Yugoslavia (4400–4200 BC), focusing on evidence for the lifecycle of the house: construction, duration, use, maintenance, abandonment, destruction and replacement of buildings. She observed important differences between the Opovo houses and those typical of the Vinča culture. In particular, they were built less substantially and were shorter-lived, and only one house possessed an oven and internal partitioning. From this evidence Tringham postulates that Opovo may have been a seasonal or short-term village. Because the full complement of activities associated with the Vinča are not represented, she proposes that Opovo was a settlement predominantly composed of a single gender or age group (*ibid.*: 114).

Single-gender settlements may result from seasonal occupations practised in tandem with an exclusive sexual division of labour, for example transhumance, or seasonal trading. The proto-urban trading places of early medieval Europe are a case in point; cemeteries excavated at 'wics' such as Southampton (*Hamwic*) are dominanted by male burials (Gilchrist 1997: 45). There are ethnographic examples, however, of more permanent 'age villages', such as those of the Nyakyusa of Tanzania. In this case, age cohorts of boys (of about ten years of age) set up their own small village to which they eventually bring their wives. The village expands when a new generation of younger boys moves to its centre, while the older men retire to the outskirts. This arrangement is thought to mitigate conflict over resources between generations of males (Wilson 1951).

Tringham stresses that issues of inheritance may have been resolved through the physical household, and that insight may be provided through cycles of destruction, abandonment and replacement (Tringham 1991). Spatial partitioning of the household, either vertically or horizontally, can also be connected with the cohabitation of generations. In the case of medieval English peasant households, such subdivision occurred with intense pressure on agricultural land in the twelfth and thirteenth centuries. There are examples of two dwellings contained within the same toft (farm enclosure), and the addition of independent extensions to residential buildings (Astill 1988: 58); the development of solars (upper storeys) in East Anglian houses may have served the same purpose. This extra accommodation was used to house younger or older generations of the same family, perhaps a young married son or widowed mother or grandmother. Alternatively, it could denote the terms of a tenancy agreement, in which a young farmer took over the holding of an elderly stranger, and provided shelter for them for the remainder of their lives.

The house itself may take on the symbolic connotations of daily or seasonal time, and the transitions and transcience of the gendered lifecourse. Diane Lyons has pulled together these threads in an ethnoarchaeological study of Mura compounds in Déla, northern Cameroon (Lyons 1998). Mura men control the land through ancestral connections that are represented through the spatial treatment of the house and compound (Figure 5.6). The Mura practice patrilocality and polygamy; men control the resources of land and rights over women's fertility (*ibid.*: 348). Divorce is common among the Mura, so that a woman may relocate to a new village or compound several times during her life. As part of the ritual cycle she returns regularly to her father's ancestral village and compound for festivals and rites. In contrast, men remain permanently located: compounds are passed from fathers to the youngest son, and sons construct their own compounds behind that of their father's, resulting in spatial clusters of closely related men. Men and women of the Mura have access to different supernatural powers: men enjoy the protection of the ancestors, to whom offerings are made by the lineage head; women invoke witchcraft, which is seen as highly dangerous to those with whom they share close contact, including husbands and co-wives. Through their witchcraft, mobility, and disinheritance from the land, Lyons proposes that Mura women are constructed as anti-social.

The Mura house is designed and built by men, and serves as a medium for representing gender through permanence or impermanence in space and architecture (Figure 5.6). The compound is aligned on an east/west axis, with the husband's entry/bedroom at the front, west and uphill; the first wife's kitchen is to the back, east and downhill. On either side are houses for male children and animals, and the kitchens and bedrooms of additional wives. The husband controls access to the compound through the single entrance to the inner courtyard. Satellite buildings are erected to house elderly relatives or divorced or widowed sons. Lyons notes that a hierarchy of superior spaces is constructed, with notions of above/front *versus* behind/below. Men's spaces are placed to the west with the door facing east into the courtyard, in order to be awakened by the morning sun for work in the sorghum fields; the women's spaces are in the east with the kitchen door facing west, so that the setting sun will prompt her to prepare the evening meal for the men returning from the fields. Thus 'cardinal orientation is a metaphor for men's and women's relationship to resources', in which men are providers and women are processors (*ibid.*: 352). During the lifecourse men and women move through the space of the compound differently, to produce an association of male/front and female/back. Children are born at the back of the compound, where they reside with their mother and siblings until the

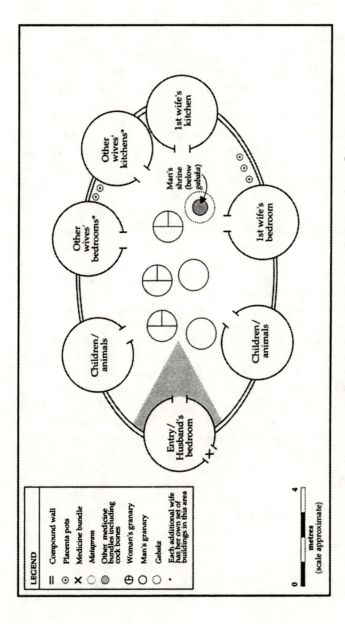

LEGEND

= Compound wall
⊙ Placenta pots
✕ Medicine bundle
◯ *Malaprum*
⬤ Other medicine bundles including cock bones
⊕ Woman's granary
◯ Man's granary
· *Gabaka*
Each additional wife has her own set of buildings in this area

Other wives' kitchens*

1st wife's kitchen

Other wives' bedrooms*

Man's shrine (below *gabaka*)

1st wife's bedroom

Children / animals

Children / animals

Entry / Husband's bedroom

0   4

metres
(scale approximate)

Figure 5.6 Representation of a space within Mura compounds in Déla, northern Cameroon

Source: Drawing by Shannon Wood in Lyons 1998: fig. 2, 353. Reproduced with kind permission of Diane Lyons.

age of eight, when boys move to the front of the compound. Girls remain at the back of their father's compound until they move to the back of their husband's.

Space reflects the distinction between men's permanence and women's impermanence, corresponding with the greater physical continuum of the male lifecycle. The transitory, anti-social character of Mura women is further emphasised by men in their choice of building materials in the compound. Men's houses are built in a more substantial form, with skilled construction in daub. Women's houses are made from a mixture of daub, termite-mound soil, stone and vegetable materials. Despite their more fragile construction, the placement of the women's houses to the west of the compound ensures that they absorb the major impact of seasonal rains. The men are wary of female witchcraft, and if a man's wives leave him for fear of witchcraft, he will abandon his compound, leaving it to collapse. Ultimately, however, the men's ancestral magic is considered more powerful. Among the Mura, gender difference and relations of production are ordered through a cosmology of competing supernatural powers that is represented through space and time: a system of beliefs that allows the appropriation of both land and women's labour.

Gendered concepts of space and time are not fixed, but instead change alongside social and economic transformations. Perhaps the most marked transition is the separation of public and private that was spurred by capitalism. Diane DiZerega Wall has proposed that this bifurcation of male and female spheres was particularly stringent in the urban United States, where men indulged in the new arena of commerce, and women elaborated their domain through the creation of a cult of domesticity (Wall 1994). She contends that this change took place between 1790 and 1840, a period which she examines through the microscope of developing, middle-class New York. This period saw the separation of home and workplace, with the gendering of architecture and space emerging along with class difference. The commercial centre was based by the East River port, with more residential neighbourhoods segregated by class. By 1840, only the poor lived in the central parts of the city, while the profusion of new churches was concentrated in the residential, outer areas. Architectural style was used to define 'boundaries between the commercial center and the residential neighborhoods (or man's and woman's spheres)' (*ibid.*: 39). Commercial and government buildings employed the Greek Revival style, while churches 'as part of the women's sphere' were constructed in the Gothic Revival style.

Wall argues that women used material culture in the ritualisation of family and the domestic, with increasing consumer choice feeding the desire for more complex rules of etiquette. The middle-class household grew with the addition of servants, and the physical and social distancing of children. The timing of daily routines altered with the separation of home and workplace, including the shift of the main meal from the afternoon to the evening, when men returned from work (*ibid.*: 114). Dinner was a new social occasion, which was cultivated through increasing specialisation of course structure, presentation and table settings. Gender roles were reinforced by associations with certain foods and the daily cycle and etiquette of mealtimes: despite the presence of domestic servants, 'the mistress served the soup at the beginning of the meal and master served the roast, or main meat dish' (*ibid.*: 139). Afternoon tea, in contrast, was 'feminized as a social ritual for women' (*ibid.*: 139). Through analysis of ceramic assemblages from eleven excavated households, Wall chronicles the increasing range of dishes that heralded the gendered, formalisation of meals, including an apparent tendency for 'Gothic' style dinner wares that may have been consistent with the choice of Gothic architectural style for domestic and ecclesiastical buildings. Wall is adamant that American women were active agents in the separation of public and private spheres, and that they carved an elevated niche for themselves through the cultural elaboration of a distinct, feminine space. Further, her case study takes us some way towards a phenomenology of gender, through which men and women of nineteenth-century New York experienced gendered perceptions of time, space and architecture, food, etiquette and domestic material culture.

Growing old: gender at the close of day

The most neglected age groups in archaeological study remain those of the middle-aged and elderly. One reason for this may be the difficulty of accurately ageing skeletons over fifty years of age, but a more likely cause is the gerontophobia which until very recently has characterised sociological and historical research. In our own society we approach old age with heightened anxiety and even embarrassment, a dread of our own mortality which we seem to have projected onto the past.

Four major approaches have represented social research on the aged: gerontology, which studies the impact of age on the body (Binstock and Shanas 1985); modern social policy (Ginn and Arber 1995); historical demography, consisting of the reconstruction of age composition through time (Laslett 1995); and, most recently, the embodiment of ageing through the lived body (Featherstone and Wernick 1995). Sociological research on the modern elderly reveals that men and women experience ageing differently, with contrasts in both physiological and social measures of age (Ginn and Arber 1995). From archaeological evidence we can begin to consider the gendering of old age, including cultural definitions of productivity, social recognition and physiology. First, the special case of human longevity must be acknowledged.

The extended lifespan of the modern human, stretching well beyond the years of fertility, is not characteristic of any other primate. It has been argued that the postmenopausal stage of life evolved as a form of reproductive fitness (Hawkes *et al.* 1997). In particular, the older woman ensured the survival of her daughter's offspring by assisting with provisioning. This hypothesis has been compared with ethnographic data on time allocation among the Hadza of Tanzania. Male contribution to the feeding of children was seasonal, and much less important than that of the mother and grandmother, the latter of whom spent most of her time foraging for her infant grandchildren when the mother's time was absorbed by a new sibling (*ibid.*: 559–60). Female foraging strategies, and the continuing productive role of older women, may provide the evolutionary link in social organisation that has been attributed previously to male hunting strategies (*ibid.*: 562). In other words, the tremendous longevity enjoyed by modern humans may have evolved on *grandmother's* coat-tails (*contra* Darwin 1871).

The social status attributed to middle and old age varies culturally, depending on factors such as inheritance, land ownership and family structure. Male status can be seen in some cases to diminish in later life, as we have seen, for example, in Classical Greece, where masculinity was drawn from public and military roles (above; Foxhall 1994). Although in our own society a double standard of ageing disadvantages women, there is cross-cultural evidence that 'women's lives appear to improve with the onset of middle age' (Brown 1982: 143). In this context 'middle age' may refer to women who have either reached menopause or have already raised their children. Thus the measure of calendar years will vary according to biological and social factors, such as age at marriage. The precise timing of menopause also fluctuates; estimates based on modern populations are age 51 for women in industrial societies, and age 42–3 for women in non-industrial societies (Sperling and Beyene 1997: 144–5).

In comparison with younger women, these middle-aged women frequently enjoy greater social recognition and personal freedoms. Judith

Brown has argued from ethnographic evidence that female mobility increases once women are freed from the strictures of menstrual taboos, and from notions of chastity that limit female sexuality during the fertile years (Brown 1982: 144). Institutionalised roles for women, such as matron, mother-in-law and grandmother, increase their influence in later years. Particularly in patrilocal contexts, the mother-in-law has control over her daughter-in-law's labour and household resources. Where strict sexual segregation is practised, for example in Moroccan Muslim society, the mother-in-law is the go-between who has physical access to the young wife, and holds the keys to her purdah. In matrilocal societies authority may be contingent on age; among the Mundurucú, for example, the oldest woman is in charge of the household (*ibid.*: 145). The older woman may also be considered to possess valuable knowledge and experience that should be passed on to the next generation. In Pacific West Britain she becomes a 'big woman', *tamparonga*, when her children marry and leave home. She progresses to the senior generation, membership of which is determined by age and character rather than sex (Counts 1982: 149). The older women of the community frequently hold responsibility for passing on oral traditions and maintaining social networks. Among the !Kung, for instance, they are considered experts in kin terms and are entrusted with the classifications of people that form the basis for marriage (Brown 1982). After their own childbearing years have ceased, some women take on designated social and ritual roles, such as midwife, matchmaker, healer or presider over initiation rites. Among the Maya, for example, older women became ritual assistants, supervising feasts and burning censers in purification ceremonies (Joyce 1996: 186), a task that presumably would have been made impure by a younger, menstruating woman.

Archaeologically, the ageing and elderly may rarely be glimpsed through visual sources, such as the funerary sculpture and portraiture of Ancient Egypt or Rome. In prehistoric contexts, burial evidence may hold the greatest potential for discerning the special treatment of older men or women. One such example is that of the Hohokam of Arizona, whose mortuary practices altered substantially in the Classic period (1150–1400 AD). Patricia Crown and Suzanne Fish have discussed changes in Hohokam burial from the cremations of the pre-Classic period to the inhumations of the Classic. Men were buried more often with ornamental and ritual items, while women were accompanied by more utilitarian objects (Crown and Fish 1996: 808). Crown and Fish measured the relative prestige of individual burials by assigning values to artefact types. While this reductive approach fails to consider the contextual meanings and values of grave goods, and the initial sample was small, certain age-related patterns were observed. Classic period burials appear to indicate that status was higher for younger male adults than older men. For women the opposite was observed, with highest values demonstrated for adult female burials over forty years of age. The burials of older women were more costly and in more prestigious locations, including a woman of 40–50 years of age from Las Colinas, interred on top of a platform mound, and buried with a leather pouch under her head which contained a large quartz crystal, asbestos and hematite covering her pelvis. Crown and Fish postulate that among the Hohokam, postmenopausal women, such as the one commemorated at Las Colinas, took on roles of shaman, midwife or herbalist (*ibid.*: 810).

An archaeology of the lifecourse should not consist merely of the recognition of isolated age groups, such as children or the elderly. Nor should the aim of gendered archaeology be limited to making certain social categories of persons visible, whether defined by sex, sexuality or specific age cohorts. In each cultural context we must consider the interaction between gendered embodiment, social definitions of ageing and the physiological effects of age on the body. Here the emphasis must be placed on temporality: gender through the day, season, year, lifecourse or epoch. The corporeal properties of gender may be perceived to be transformed by ageing, according to culturally constructed understandings of physiology. In the ancient and medieval worlds, for example, the theory of the humours (below, pp. 114–15) proposed that the physical and temperamental differences between men and women reduced with age, following the loss of essential heat. Elderly men and women were defined as cold and dry, although older women were believed to retain poisons that they could no longer expel through menstruation (Shahar 1997: 44). Chapter 6 will pursue medieval ideas about the gendered body and lifecourse, where attitudes towards spatial segregation and the female body are explored in a study of the medieval English castle.

Chapter 6

The contested garden

Gender, space and metaphor in the medieval English castle

This chapter explores metaphors for gendered discourses in later medieval England. The relationship between space and the body is examined through the complex imagery of the castle, an institution most often characterised as a bastion of male warrior ethos. The castle provides a case study of the seclusion of high-ranking women, and the meanings of gender segregation in a specific cultural milieu. Too often archaeology reduces the connection between gender and space to the identification of exclusive, and static, gendered domains: bodies become sexed artefacts suspended in time. Here, a more phenomeno-logical approach is attempted, one which emphasises the link between space and the embodiment of gender. Such embodiment is perceived materially through the concrete, everyday world, and the physical processes of the lifecycle. The centrality of the body to experience is highlighted, with the aim of recapturing the perceptions of gendered bodies in a particular point in time and space (Merleau-Ponty [1945] 1962). In short, we consider what it was like for a man or woman to *be* in a medieval castle, and how this bodily experience differed according to gender, social status and age.

The function of the castle in western Europe has long been acknow-ledged as twofold, serving both domestic and military roles. Yet its study has been dominated by military concerns, and an emphasis on warfare has led to the personification of the castle as a purely masculine domain. During the period under consideration, English castles were constructed also in Wales, and the English nobility shared both language and chivalric values with France. Within the feudal order, castles were symbols of lordship; they were the family residences of knights, barons and kings. They were, and still are, evocative of medieval chivalric values. As such, they were a locus in which gender was critically negotiated, and, perhaps ironically, where discourses surrounding the female body were realised materially. Gendered constructs and relations can be studied through the corporeal spaces of the castle: the contrasting locales, concerns and textures surrounding its men and women.

Issues raised in the preceding chapters are pursued through multiple lines of evidence, allowing a sensitive reading of gender as it was mediated by medieval models of physiology. Within historical archaeology, the variety and abundance of archaeological and documentary evidence provides tremendous potential for gender archaeology. This greater diversity of sources can also be inhibiting, however. Much greater care is needed to achieve a fully contextual approach, combining the archaeology of standing buildings with that of artefacts, iconography and buried deposits (often deriving from multi-period, deeply stratified sites); further, each literary, visual or historical genre has its own well established form of source criticism. In common with prehistory, there are problems with the use of these sources as analogy to inform interpretation. In particular, documentary sources should not be used to *explain* material evidence, but rather to complement and amplify. The use of multiple sources of analogy is crucial, in addition to the examination of contradiction and ambiguity between analogues and source (Wylie 1985). Historical archaeologists seek to employ documents critically, drawing texts from different contexts for comparison and contrast (Beaudry *et al.* 1991). The method adopted here is one of contextual analogy, in which contemporary historical and literary evidence is used together with archaeological data, not to provide illustration or explanation, but to link themes between media (Gilchrist 1994: 12). Material culture is used together with contemporary literature, medical and theological treatises, house-holding books, manuscript illuminations and documents, in particular the building accounts that detailed annual expenditure on royal castles and palaces. These complementary sources are interwoven to address difference, ambiguity, and to reduce dependence on single analogues or sources of evidence (Andrén 1998: 171). While these diverse medieval sources are used 'also by other disciplines, they are harnessed here to address a distinctively archaeological problem: a descriptive account of the role of the body and perceptual experience in the medieval castle.

This chapter first sets out cross-cultural assumptions regarding female seclusion and gender domains, before introducing spatial and bodily concerns in medieval England. Turning to the medieval castle, the nature of its social and physical forms are outlined, and archaeological evidence is presented for gendered spaces in castles of the thirteenth and fourteenth centuries. In addition to approaching the embodiment of gender, the case study focuses on cultural metaphors for gendered discourses. A metaphor may be defined as the use of an object or idea to expound a concept to which it is not literally applicable. Hence gender metaphors do not literally represent the relations between men and women (Strathern 1988), but are rather an expression of gender as it is embedded in social practice and beliefs about sexual difference. Metaphors of the castle and the female body were used in medieval England to represent the gendered and bounded spaces that both defined and perpetuated the social order of feudalism.

Sexual spaces: female seclusion and the domestic domain

A recurring motif in spatial studies of gender is the physical distancing of men and women. Spatial oppositions of public/private, culture/nature and male/female have been invoked to portray the emergence of an inferior, female domestic domain, strictly delineated from the more prestigious, male public domain. Such studies have drawn on cultural stereotypes, and on early works of feminist anthropology that attempted to identify underlying tendencies for the supposed cross-cultural subordination of women (Rosaldo 1974; Ortner 1974; see Moore 1988: 21–4; and above, pp. 32–5). In particular, there has been an interest in the origins of gender domains, and the practice of segregating women spatially, the latter frequently read as the control of female sexuality by men exercising patriarchal power (Turner 1996: 126). The incidence and meaning of spatial segregation have been attributed variously to increasing scales of socio-complexity (Ortner 1978), an exclusive sexual division of labour (Kent 1990), the control of land or property as a critical resource (Hodder 1984), together with an intense cultural investment in the concept of male honour (Small 1991).

The physical enclosure of women, as practised in parts of contemporary Latin America, the Mediterranean, Africa, India, China and so on, has been linked by Sherry Ortner with the notions of female purity that are common in state-level societies (Ortner [1978] 1996: 43–57). Female purity, or chastity, is taken as a measure of the status and honour of the woman's family: the female body becomes a contested resource through which property-holding kin groups protect their patrimony. Ortner argues that in non-state societies women are viewed as polluting or threatening, while in state societies they are seen as vulnerable, and requiring male protection (*ibid.*: 50). This view underestimates the ambiguity with which the female body is frequently perceived. In the complex nation-states of medieval Europe, for example, it was commonly held that woman's nature was a danger to herself, requiring protection from the consequences of her own voracious sexual appetite. The belief that spatial segregation increases with social complexity has been put forward by Susan Kent, among others, in a cross-cultural study of the ethnography of space (Kent 1990). In fact, Kent observed gender-specific spatial areas in *less* complex societies, concluding that sexual segregation is not a measure of social complexity, but results instead from gendered divisions of labour based on biological sex (Kent 1990: 149). Her conclusion is in itself essentialist, and, contrary to contemporary archaeological and geographical theory (McDowell 1996: 29), assumes that spatial regularities correspond with cross-cultural norms and social values.

Ian Hodder has argued that a fundamental duality emerged during the Neolithic between perceptions of nature and culture, with the house (*domus*) used to express oppositions between men and women, and a shift in critical resources from labour to land (Hodder 1990). He has proposed that the complexity of house plans can be taken as an index of investment in the domestic realm, and the status of women as reproducers and links to lineage claims (Hodder 1984). It seems that the spaces of the house have been used to control female mobility and sexual opportunity where wealth is bound up with property, and lineage claims depend on demonstration of the paternity of legitimate heirs. Under the medieval feudal system, for instance, the accumulation of property in land required monogamy and inheritance by primogeniture (inheritance through the eldest male). Female fidelity, and its display through the physical confinement of women, became essential to the perpetuation of successful lineages.

The functioning of female seclusion in patriarchal societies has been studied with reference to Ancient Greece by Lisa Nevett (1994) and for contemporary Islamic purdah by David Small (1991). Both conclude that the significant aspect of female seclusion is not the absolute segregation of women from men, but rather the separation of women from strangers – men outside the family and household. They argue respectively that in both contemporary Tunis and Ancient Greece, the courtyard house was used to limit physical access and visibility of women from outsiders. The emphasis of spatial control is on thresholds, entrances and boundaries, allowing relative freedom of movement for women in the house interior and courtyard. While this distinction breaks down more simplistic gendered oppositions of public/private, it continues to treat all men and women as a homogeneous group, regardless of social status or stage within the cultural lifecourse.

Further, it has been proposed widely in archaeological literature that segregation of the sexes is coincident with lower female prestige, whether evidenced through segregated social rites, architecture or burial. Examples include those as far afield as early medieval Europe, where the provision of segregated burial or separate cemeteries for men and women has been interpreted as indicating lower female status (Hinton 1990: 131; Gebühr 1997), and Native American Arizona, where the development of walled courtyards among the Hohokam is seen as reflecting the 'declining autonomy' of women and their lower status relative to men (Crown and Fish 1996: 804, 806). In the latter case, the greater separation of women's domestic work in house clusters contained in walled enclosures is said to have decreased women's 'access to community activities, interaction and gossip', in addition to providing the increased privacy that allows domestic violence against women (*ibid.*: 806). Domestic tasks and spaces have been attributed universally to women, with values applied that assume exclusive spatial domains and the lower prestige of women. In his discussion of Iron Age and Roman households in Britain, for instance, Richard Hingley offered a typical series of binary oppositions: male/female, public/private, cooked/raw, light/dark and clean/dirty (Hingley 1990: 133).

While historical and ethnographic evidence confirms that sexual segregation is practised widely, its meanings and resulting spatial patterns may differ enormously. Does segregation imply antagonism between men and women, or lower female prestige? Does female seclusion indicate male control over female sexuality, and the limiting of women's influence beyond the home? Or, alternatively, is spatial segregation one means of conveying gender difference, or even complementarity? With reference to medieval England, it is proposed here that segregation is used to convey a sense of social order, while the actual physical practices of female seclusion varied according to social status and age.

The medieval body politic

Medieval people understood their own place within a highly-structured universe. The social order was feudal, with a pyramidic hierarchy established through bonds of military or labour service. At the pinnacle, the king provided lands for the aristocracy in return for their loyalty and the obligation of military service. The aristocratic lords were therefore landlords, who allowed peasants to work some of their land in return for labour service (or cash rent). From *c.* 1000 AD onwards, the feudal system was represented as comprising three estates: those who prayed (the clergy and religious), those who fought (the aristocracy), and those who worked (the peasants). This model of the three estates was considered to offer the recipe for a harmonious, cohesive society. The clergy prayed for the peasants and the aristocracy; the aristocracy protected the clergy and the peasants; and the peasants worked to support the others. From the fourteenth century, sumptuary laws dictated appropriate dress by social class, and even the cosmos was understood to be hierarchically structured, with the kingdom of heaven staffed by ranked orders of angels. An emphasis on sexual segregation resulted from this mania for strict representation of social place, together with anxiety about the body and sexual congress.

Medieval power was invested in the land, and the future of aristocratic dynasties lay in the protection of patrimony. Only the eldest son was encouraged to marry, and it was essential that his progeny were legitimate, so that the inheritance, the 'honour', could be passed through his line unfragmented. To facilitate this primogeniture, the twelfth century witnessed a heightened emphasis on monogamy, but at the same time marriage was actually denied to the majority of aristocratic males (the younger sons). The church stressed that sex was appropriate only between married couples, yet this status was withheld from many in the aristocracy (Duby 1997: 67–8). This dichotomy was potentially disruptive to an ordered society, so that new codes of behaviour were developed to structure relations between aristocratic men and women, expressed by the values of chivalry. Increasingly, the female body was regarded ambivalently: the fertile wife was essential to the promulgation of patrimony, but the seductive woman was the greatest threat to a meticulously spun social order. Women were personified according to extremes. The good woman and the evil woman were represented by the opposing figures of the Virgin Mary and Eve, the virginal mother and the ruinous temptress (Grössinger 1997). Ecclesiastical writings became increasingly misogynistic, and medical and philosophical discourses stressed the contrasting moral and physical properties of men and women.

Medieval society perceived men's and women's bodies as having dichotomous qualities. Patristic theology characterised women's bodies as more naturally given to sinfulness, requiring taming and containment. Medieval medicine drew upon the classical tradition of humoral theory, rooted in the works of Aristotle and Galen, which proposed that the human body was made up of four basic elements, which also made up the universe: fire, water, earth and air. Fire, which was hot and dry, produced yellow bile in the body, and led to a choleric complexion. Water, which was cold and wet, produced phlegm, and the phlegmatic disposition. Earth, thought of as cold and dry, was also black bile in the body, and associated with the melancholy complexion. Air, hot and wet, made blood, and the sanguine temperament. A balance of these temperaments, or humours, was required for good health in each individual, but it was believed that age and sex influenced the overall humoral balance. Women were regarded as watery and changeable, with a cold, wet humoral balance which contrasted with the hot, dry male (Rawcliffe 1995: 172). Masculine and feminine shapes, complexions and dispositions were typologised according to reproductive roles, with relative degrees of heat considered to be a crucial sex difference. Women's bodies were perceived as too cool to be able to produce semen. It was believed that this resulted in their softer, smoother, more hairless appearance, and made them more suited to a sedentary life (Cadden 1993: 167–72). Both sexes grew colder, drier, more brittle, with age. Classification of male and female physiology was essentially binary, although explanations for hermaphrodism were proposed, and through the theory of humoral disposition, the physical body was linked to gender constructs, such as personality and deportment.

Even in death, or perhaps especially so, embodiment was crucial to medieval people. To be resurrected as a complete person after the Last Judgement required material continuity (Bynum 1995: 186). Caroline Bynum has argued that in the thirteenth and fourteenth centuries the body became essential to the resurrection of the soul, and that visions of the afterlife began to particularise souls by gender and religious status, depicting individuals with characteristics of sex, age and rank (*ibid.*: 297, 308, 319). Following Augustine's teachings, it was believed that the souls of men and women would rise with their respective sexes intact (*ibid.*: 100). Further, the perceived physical qualities of the female body lent women a distinctive religiosity. Because humoral theory accorded women a colder, wetter, more changeable character, the female body was thought to be closer to decay. Resurrection of the body and soul required special feats of self-mortification for women to triumph over organic process: consequently, stories of women 'living without eating, and dying without decay', are prominent in medieval miracles (*ibid.*: 221).

Through medieval literary, theological and medical discourses, gender difference was contrasted starkly. Male and female bodies were regarded as essentially dissonant: offering a pun on Ortner's classic work (1974), Bynum proposed that the medieval 'woman is to man as matter is to spirit' (Bynum 1987: 262). The female symbolised the material, physical, lustful side of human nature, while the male represented the spiritual, rational and intellectual half. These corporeal preoccupations resulted in a profound concern for sexual segregation in public places, including medieval hospitals, religious houses and parish churches (Gilchrist 1995: 21, 110, 122). At formal events, such as entertainments, banquets and jousts, men and women were often separated, with the women watching the proceedings from galleries or seated separately in the hall. Difference was further underlined by the foods consumed by noble men and women at such occasions. Men were associated with 'heavy' foods, such as meat, while 'lighter' foods were thought more appropriate for women, especially fruit, dairy products and sweets. They were to avoid meat, wine, and strong liquors: anything believed to aggravate lust (Bynum 1987: 191). At aristocratic funerals men and women were segregated in the funeral feast and procession, and women were excluded from carrying the funerary bier (Binski 1996: 56). Travel outside the home was restricted for women: even pilgrimage was gendered, and masculine cults drew men from considerable distances, in contrast with cults appealing to women, which attracted more local audiences (Finucane 1977: 127-9). In the noble household, which was frequently peripatetic, travelling between the castles and estates owned by a baronial lord, the mobile, 'riding household' was essentially male (Girouard 1978: 19).

The extent to which segregation was experienced personally depended on social status and age. Among the medieval peasantry women were more closely associated with work in the house and toft, as evidenced by accidental-death patterns provided by coroners' inquests and manorial court rolls. Women died in the home, around the village, at neighbours', gathering water from wells and doing laundry in ditches, while men died in the fields, forests, mills, construction sites and marl pits (Hanawalt 1986). Adherence to spatial domains was seasonal, however, with women assisting in the fields at harvest time and men spending more time close to the home during winter months. In the later middle ages (after c. 1350), younger peasant women actually enjoyed greater personal mobility than men; it was common for them to enter servanthood or apprenticeship in a nearby town before returning to their local manor to marry (Goldberg 1992). It has been argued that young men and women in northwestern

Europe married in their early to mid-twenties, much later than their southern counterparts. The nobility did not engage in this practice, however: it was common for girls to be married at twelve years of age, and boys at fourteen (Ward 1992: 13); whilst the royal female age at marriage appears to have been fifteen, at least among the Plantagenets (Parsons 1994: 66). Without doubt, widowhood offered the most independent time of life for a woman of the urban or landed classes. As a *femme sole* she could act freely and legally, as a merchant or artisan, or head of household and estate.

The children of the nobility began rehearsals for their gendered roles at age seven, when boys were separated from their mother's realm to be trained as knights. Three stages of childhood were recognised in medieval medical and didactic literature: *infantia* (to age seven), *pueritia* (to twelve for girls or fourteen for boys) and *adolescentia* (from twelve or fourteen to adulthood). Two very different experiences were cultivated for young men and women. After separation from his mother, the oldest son would be raised at home by his father, while his brothers would be sent to a noble sponsor for training in the skills of horsemanship, hunting and warriorhood, in addition to courtly skills such as music, chess, conversation, dancing and table etiquette. Girls were tutored at home (or sent to local convents) to learn literacy, numeracy, music, etiquette and pastimes, including embroidery, chess, falconry and storytelling (Shahar 1990: 209–22).

The social and sexual tensions of medieval noble society were addressed to some extent by the codes of chivalry and courtly love that demanded respect for all noble women, and fidelity and service to a lady. The main protagonists in such literature were two lovers unsuited for marriage, frequently a landless knight who falls passionately in love with the unattainable (usually married) queen or lady of the castle; notable examples include Lancelot and Guinevere or Tristan and Iseult. The relationship is adulterous, and therefore in strict opposition to the elevated virtues of chastity and virginity; yet fidelity, courtesy and humility are shown by the hero. In this context the woman is dominant, dictating military missions to test the honour of her knight. Indeed, it has been argued that the genre of the courtly romance played with concepts of gender reversal between the lady and the knight (Burns 1997). Such tales were commissioned by, and written for, predominantly male audiences, but were owned and read by both men and women. They were regarded by contemporaries as misleading for young girls to read, encouraging a false sense of superiority and security over their suitors (Pratt 1997: 243–4). Tensions between generations were also teased out through courtly love. The two lovers are young adults (*juventus*) at the peak of their physical beauty and prowess, while the cuckolded husband is frequently elderly, and the enemies of true love (in the *Roman de la Rose*) are personified as old women (Shahar 1997: 49).

The medieval lifecourse was gendered according to cultural models of physiology, status and gender role. For males and females of the aristocracy the first phase of life was shared (to age seven), after which members of different sexes cultivated distinctive perceptions in contrasting environments (to age 12–14). Early years of marriage saw men and women emerged in different concerns, physical cultures and degrees of mobility (aged 12–14 to adulthood). Such dichotomies were broken down in later life, when physiologies grew less dissonant, and women achieved greater legal and spatial liberties.

The medieval English castle and its household

The English castle may be defined as the fortified and defensible home of a member of the feudal nobility (Pounds 1990: 6). Its more specific forms and functions changed dramatically from the eleventh to the fifteenth centuries, until eventually the military and domestic functions were disjoined. Perhaps the earliest timber and earthwork castles, the ringworks and motte and baileys that were built immediately after the Norman Conquest, were fully masculine in outlook, functioning as Norman forts in hostile territories from which a mounted garrison could dominate a large area. Excavations at the motte and bailey castle of Hen Domen (Montgomeryshire), for instance, revealed an extensive complex of timber buildings dating from *c.* 1071, but no artefacts indicated the presence of women or children at the castle. Indeed, there was no evidence of an aristocratic presence of any sort, with an absence of indicators of literacy, imports or religious devotions (Barker 1987: 53–4). Permanent accommodation for more heterogeneous households was provided certainly in the first masonry castles of the late eleventh and twelfth centuries: the tower keeps which provided at least two storeys of accommodation in the highly fortified core of a free-standing tower. By *c.* 1200, the emphasis of defence was shifting from the heart of the castle to its outer walls, so that it was possible to provide more varied accommodation in halls ranged within a large, defended enclosure (Figure 6.1). From the later fourteenth century, courtyard castles were built to include ranges of stacking accommodation around a central courtyard, with the emphasis on decorative facades and symmetry betraying their more domestic purpose.

Castle studies have concentrated almost entirely on the military half of the castle's dual functions, with only recent consideration of its everyday life (Kenyon 1990), the symbolism of its architecture (Heslop 1991, 1994) and its place in the medieval landscape (Austen 1984). This more holistic scrutiny has revealed the castle as a medium for the display of lordship. For example, certain royal tower keeps extended an iconography of kingship, through the deliberate use of archaic style and significant elevational proportions at Orford Castle (Suffolk, 1165–73) (Heslop 1991). Elsewhere heroic, masculine emblems were displayed, such as those carved on the capitals and voussoirs on the main door into Norwich Castle keep (Norfolk, 1090s), of a kneeling warrior, Pegasus and hunting scenes (Heslop 1994: 55–6). At the baronial castle of Bodiam (Sussex, 1385) a designed landscape was

Figure 6.1 Carisbrooke Castle, Isle of Wight. The enclosure castle consisted of a large space contained by curtain walls, within and against which halls and ancillary buildings could be constructed. To the left of the picture are ruined buildings against the curtain wall; in the background is the earlier shell keep (*c.* 1136) perched on a motte; in the middle ground is the residential block built by Isabella de Fortibus (*c.* 1262–93), with later additions at both ends of the block.

contrived as backdrop, complete with gardens, water features, modelled vistas and viewing terraces (Taylor *et al.* 1990).

The household itself might travel between dispersed castles and manors, with a mobile baronial household numbering up to *c.* 100 people, and a royal household up to *c.* 500, comprising perhaps one third of the total household (Girouard 1978: 14, 20). The household was the power base of lordship, providing administration, defence and hospitality (including education of young knights), and it was predominantly male. In the fifteenth-century household of the Earl of Northumberland, for instance, there were nine women and 166 men. This included the mainly male servants of the house, with only a small number of female launderers, chamberers and nursery servants (Mertes 1988: 57–8). It seems that the noble women were concentrated spatially in a separate female household. Practical instruction books for women, such as Christine de Pisan's *The Treasure of the City of Ladies* (1405) portrayed women at court as occupying female households, entertaining and living separately from men. The Princess's household was accounted separately, and her companions resided in the 'apartments of the ladies and maidens' (II.3). Despite occupying self-contained spaces, ladies were left frequently to manage the household and estates, while the lord was away at leisure with his 'riding household', or at war. Indeed, it was not uncommon for a woman to successfully defend the castle from siege, including Norwich Castle in the twelfth century by Queen Emma, and Lincoln Castle by Nichola de la Haie in 1216. In more peaceful times the noble woman forged alliances between aristocratic families, sometimes arranging marriages, and occupied herself with charity and hospitality. In his praise of the Countess of Hereford, Etienne de Fougères (chaplain of Henry II) wrote of the close connection between gentlewomen and piety, suggesting that they should occupy their time building chapels, decorating altars, caring for the poor and honouring and serving high personages and churchmen (Labarge 1965: 41). This role was amplified for medieval queens to include an official intercessory function, from the thirteenth century linked overtly with the traits and cult of the Virgin Mary (Parsons 1997).

A man's world: spatial models of the medieval castle

Modern writers characterise the medieval castle as fundamentally masculine (and peculiarly equine). It is proposed that the presence of a garrison or private army, in addition to the masculine pursuits of the knights of the lord's household, resulted in the extreme physical distancing of the domains of its men and women.

> Two species dominated castle life, men and horses ... the society was overwhelmingly male. ... Given the crowded nature of the accommodation, it was probably best for everyone, especially the women themselves, if they kept away.
>
> (McNeill 1992: 29)

> Women were never far from dozens of violent men, practising their horsemanship, furbishing their breastplates, smelling of sweat, leather and the piss of the horses they looked after more carefully than they did them; one must imagine them in great danger, shut up in the fortress, anxious, obliged to handle some defeat alone, to go out in search of money for a ransom.
>
> (Duby 1998: 105)

> They [young knights] were raised in the male world of sweat, weapons, stables, horses and hounds, with its ethos and courtly culture, as well as its lusts and unrestrained urges.
>
> (Shahar 1990: 211)

> The contrast between this island of womanhood and the masculine world that surrounded and served it must have been a violent one, and one likely to lead to tension.
>
> (Girouard 1978: 28)

Thus, archaeologists and social historians have eulogised the male domain of the castle, reeking of sweat, testosterone and horses. Just like commentators on prehistoric masculinity (e.g. Treherne 1995), they have adopted weapons, armour, horses and violence as metonyms for masculinity. But we know that aristocratic women were also skilled in riding and hunting, sometimes participated in siege warfare, and certainly lived in castles. What can be said, therefore, of gendered experience in the castle's interior, presumably with horses *in absentia*?

Consideration has been given previously to the rules which governed the social use of space inside the English castle. Discussion of precise room functions has remained problematic, however, since it is difficult to identify with certainty any rooms other than the hall, chapel, kitchen and latrines. The heart of the castle was its hall, a public meeting and eating space, which was also used for administration. From the thirteenth century, a castle might contain several halls, each the focus of a household, in addition to the great hall, which was the ceremonial and administrative nexus. By 1400, however, a 'retreat from the hall to the great chamber' had occurred, with the lord and lady eating and entertaining in a chamber, which served also for sleeping, playing games and receiving visitors (Girouard 1978: 46).

Spatial analysis of the castle has touched indirectly on the theme of the body: in particular to the placement of the body of the king, and the hierarchy of male bodies which ranked below him in the feudal order of the body politic. Medieval kingship was imbued with divine sanctity, and the body of the king himself became sacred. Royal and saintly power were closely synonymous, so that the corporeal presence of the king, and, following death, any part of his body, was considered to emit sanctity (Bynum 1995: 204–5). Within castle studies there has been an interest in the origins of *enfilade*, a male etiquette known to have been widespread in baroque palaces, and evident in embryonic form at the royal castles of medieval Windsor and Warwick. A filtering system of rooms was used to regulate access according to male status in relation to the body of the king (Girouard 1978: 144–6). The earliest written evidence for this 'axis of honour' is found in an Elizabethan copy of the Harleian regulations, dated to the late fifteenth century (*ibid.*: 64). From this it has been argued that a social hierarchy was reflected in the spatial arrangement of the castle and its separate households, including those of the lord and lady, other generations of their family, the constable or keeper, the deputy or lieutenant, and other retainers of the lord.

In a highly influential study, the architect Patrick Faulkner proposed that such households could be identified as sets of rooms sharing common facilities such as kitchens, service areas and a great hall. A hierarchy of households was articulated through regulation of public access, room size, situation and degree of luxury; for example the presence of a fireplace and garderobe (latrine) *en suite*. He suggested that 'it would seem axiomatic in medieval domestic planning of the scale under consideration that the most remote apartment shall be reserved for the most select occupant and that difficulty of personal access shall be a mark of rank' (Faulkner 1963: 228). In other words, the chamber of the highest ranking male (the king, followed by the lord of the castle) would be situated in the deepest space. It has been argued further that accommodation for higher-ranking individuals will correspond with upper floors and the control of roof-tops, and that distinctions

should be made between private chambers which were linked directly
to the hall *versus* secondary chambers which were isolated and free-
standing, the latter becoming more common in the fourteenth century
(Fairclough 1992: 362).

The female household: a room of their own

Castle studies have remained largely silent as to the gendering of the
physical spaces of the castle, and have ventured little on the location of
the female household. We know from contemporary chronicles and
poems that spatial segregation was practised at formal occasions. In the
Romance of Guy of Warwick (*c.* 1300), during the Earl's feast at
Whitsuntide, the 'Knights sat in the hall, Ladies in the chamber all'
(quoted in Girouard 1978: 46). Geoffrey of Monmouth's *Historia
Regnum Britanniae* describes how

> The King went off with the men to feast in his own palace and the
> Queen retired with the married women to feast in hers; for the
> Britons still observed the ancient custom of Troy, the men cele-
> brating festive occasions with their fellow-men and the women
> eating separately with the other women.
>
> (quoted in Pratt 1997: 245)

On a daily basis the women also occupied separate spaces. Even in the
manor house privacy could be found at the upper end of the hall, as
illustrated in Chaucer's fourteenth-century tale of *Troilus and Criseyde*,
in which Criseyde has a 'paved parlour' at the upper end of the hall, in
which she sits with her ladies, and a maiden reading to them (Smyser
1956) (II, 599). The anonymous English poem *Sir Gawain and the
Green Knight* (*c.* 1400), describes the *chambre* of the ladies, located in
the upper reaches of the castle, and their *cumly closet*, a private, female
pew in the chapel (Barron 1974: lines 975, 1373, 933, 938). Many
castles had a principal chapel for general use and a number of smaller
private ones. Where only one chapel existed, or had to be shared, it
seems that a private pew or gallery was provided for the women. It is
likely that the private pew referred to in *Sir Gawain* was the upper
storey of a two-storey chapel, an arrangement common in castles and
manor houses, which seems first to have been made fashionable in
England by Henry III, as an act of refurbishment after his marriage in
1236 to Eleanor of Provence. From royal building accounts it is
possible to examine the type of accommodation commissioned for

royal women by the king, in addition to building work specifically detailed as 'the queen's work' in royal castles or properties owned personally by the queen. Chapels at the palaces of Winchester and Windsor and the manor house at Havering (Essex) had upper storeys inserted especially for the queen's use (Allen Brown *et al.* 1963 II: 862, 867, 1013). In the Chapel of St George at Windsor the queen's 'closet' still remains in the north aisle of the chancel, a fully screened gallery with private access, with an oriel overlooking the high altar at the east end.

Special provision was required in the physical placement of the lady's household, her chamber and nursery. Details are provided by Lambert of Ardres in his history of the Counts of Guînes (1194). He describes the *domus* of Arnold, lord of Ardres, built in the castle *c.* 1117. The three-storey keep contained the chapel at the highest level and the cellars and granaries on the ground floor. On the second floor were the residential apartments, including:

> the great chamber of the lord and his lady, where they slept, on to which adjoined a small room which provided the sleeping quarters of the maidservants and children. Here in the inner part of the great chamber there was a small private room where at early dawn or in the evening, or in sickness, or for warming the maids and weaned children, they used to light a fire.
>
> (Mortet 1911: 183–5)

This account indicates that the lady's chamber was in the innermost space of the castle, and was provided with some form of warming apparatus. Accommodation for the maidservants and nursery continued to be provided adjacent to her chamber. For instance at Woodstock (Oxfordshire) in 1240 the queen's chambers included a small room immediately outside the entrance for her attendants (Allen Brown *et al.* 1963 II: 1012). In 1298 at the palace of Westminster a fire destroyed an area which included the queen's hall, the royal nursery, and the 'Maydenhall' (Allen Brown *et al.* 1963 I: 505). The women's household would have been more socially mixed than other high-ranking households in the castle, including as it did the lady's chamber, the nursery and accommodation for her maids and attendants. At times these rooms would have been open to a wider female public, including midwives and wet nurses. Certainly queens, and possibly noble women, received guests and petitioners of both sexes in their chambers (Parsons 1994: 10), thus dissipating its private connotations.

Positioned in the upper ends of halls or the upper reaches of castles, the female household may have been characterised by a greater degree of luxury, embellished by warmth, rich colours and soft textures. It would have been provided with better facilities, such as fireplaces and private garderobes, and made more hospitable by furnishings such as tapestries, room hangings and cushions. Themes portrayed on such tapestries included hunting scenes, exotic animals and gardens, and tales of courtly romance. Indeed, the creation and transmission of luxury seems to have been a particular concern of high-ranking women. In her chamber, the lady of the castle and her ladies-in-waiting would have embroidered soft furnishings and church vestments; such articles of the *opus Anglicanum* were highly valued by contemporaries. Where they survive, medieval textiles are difficult to provenance, but patterns in their commissioning and transmission can be detected from written sources. Inventories of noble women's goods include items such as tapestries, rugs and linens, in addition to clothes, jewels and books (Ward 1992: 73–82). Wills indicate that these luxury items were passed through the female line, connected perhaps with the female role of providing hospitality and upholding family prestige (Sekules 1987: 44). Joan Beauchamp, for example, a fifteenth-century Lady of Abergavenny, bequeathed beds and tapestries in gold cloth, blue brocaded silk, black and white velvet, and green, red and blue fabrics embroidered variously with swans, leopards and foliage (*ibid.*: 82). Throughout the middle ages queens also took a special interest in certain aspects of luxury. It is clear that they held responsibility for the planting of gardens (James 1990: 83), while innovations in waterworks and sanitation were implemented by Eleanor of Castile, and icono-graphic ceramic tiles may have been first introduced to England by Eleanor of Provence (*ibid.*: 98).

Nature meets culture: 'a garden enclosed is my sister'

An external, private space was provided for the perambulation of the female household, through the provision of pleasure gardens of herbs or flowers (Figure 6.2). 'Ladies who lived on their manors', as Christine de Pisan recounted, should reserve separate work for their women and chambermaids, namely attending livestock and weeding the courtyard and working in the herb garden 'even getting covered in mud' (*The Treasure of the City of Ladies*, II.10). The expectation that women should be closely associated with gardens is repeated in the instruction book of *Le Menagier de Paris* (*c*. 1393), written by an elderly husband for his young wife. The second article of this treatise on household management gives practical and detailed instruction for young wives on 'the art of gardening' (Power 1928). Many royal and aristocratic women commissioned gardens, where they could take their leisure in feminine places that were colourful and sweetly scented, a world away from the acrid smells and drab greys of the stable and garrison. Turf lawns hosted violets, daisies, periwinkle and primroses; aromatic herb beds or lawns contained lavender, camomile, marjoram, sweet basil, thyme, feverfew, mint, balm and sage (Harvey 1981), many used by women in traditional herbal remedies (Rawcliffe 1995); and flower gardens, reserved for the wealthiest, boasted scented lillies and roses (McLean 1981: 94, 164, 183–4). The sounds of the garden also contrasted with the male voices and clattering hooves of the barracks and training ground: caged animals such as squirrels and songbirds were housed in women's gardens, for example in the aviary built by Master Richard at Westminster for Eleanor of Castile (Allen Brown *et al.* 1963 I: 505).

Our knowledge of medieval gardens comes largely from documentary evidence, including early gardening treatises and accounts of building works (Harvey 1981; McLean 1981; Landsberg 1998). Increasingly attention is paid to their material remains, including evidence for hard-landscaping that survives as earthworks or buried foundations (Moorhouse 1991; Taylor 1991), and, more problematically, rare palaeobotanical evidence for possible plantings (Taylor 1991: 4). Royal building accounts reveal the importance of gardens to medieval queens.

In the building of Rhuddlan Castle, work in 1282–3 detailed as the 'queen's work' included a courtyard garden laid with 6,000 turves and fenced with staves of discarded casks (Allen Brown *et al.* 1963 I: 324). At Guildford Castle in 1260 improvements included a pentice (covered walkway) to the queen's lawn and a garden for the queen (Allen Brown *et al.* 1963 II: 952). At King's Langley (Hertfordshire) between 1278–84, Queen Eleanor of Castile had her own cloister, great and middle chambers rebuilt and gardens repositioned nearby, introducing the Moorish tradition of paved courtyard and fountain gardening, together with imported apple trees and vines (James 1990: 93; McLean 1981: 102), and at Banstead (Surrey) between 1276–9 Eleanor built a new timber-framed chamber with a new cloister and well-house and a park enclosed with ditches and hedges (Allen Brown *et al.* 1963 II: 896). She continued her innovative landscaping at Leeds

Figure 6.2 Medieval illumination showing a female servant being instructed by a lady in the planting of a herb garden

Source: *Die Lof der Vrouwen*, translation of Christine de Pisan's *Cité des Dames*, Dutch, 1475. British Library Additional MS 20698 (f. 17 recto).

Castle, Kent, between 1278–90, where she had a large lake formed with an inner island that was approached by a bridge (Harvey 1981: 106).

In bishop's palaces, a private court or garden was sometimes provided for the queen's visits, as at Knole (Kent) from the fifteenth century (Faulkner 1970: 141). At the bishop's palace of Wolvesey (Winchester) in 1306, Queen Margaret fitted up the northern chamber of the high range of the west hall for her own use, and laid out a garden which consisted of a turfed enclosure with water running through the middle (Allen Brown *et al.* 1963 II: 863). Literary sources are consistent in these associations. Chaucer's Criseyde had her private chamber overlooking a garden, with stairs giving her direct, exclusive access to it, where she could walk with a 'gret route' of her women (*Troilus and Criseyde*, II: 813):

> Adown the steyre anonright thro she wente,
> Into the garden, with hire neces there
> > (*Troilus and Criseyde*, II: 599)

A strong association emerges between women and gardens, which was central to gendered metaphors (see below).

Case studies: 'a history of the queen's works'

Closer understanding of the female household can be provided by archaeological study of the specific physical spaces that can be identified as having been used or built by women. Here, six cases are described briefly before turning to the gendered meanings of their spatial patterns. These examples provide contrasting situations of female accommodation in a royal palace, and in royal and baronial castles, thus illustrating arrangements in both undefended and defended royal residences, and castles of the aristocracy. They date from the thirteenth and fourteenth centuries, a period when the castle's dual residential and military functions were achieved through the provision of freestanding households within defended enclosures. These particular examples have been chosen to explore the evidence of both extant buildings and excavated archaeological deposits, with attribution of female spaces made with reference to historical documentation. In this context, identification of male and female spaces according to artefacts is not possible.

Evidence for supposedly male artefacts is in abundance, consisting largely of militaria and horse equipment, yet exclusively female artefacts

Figure 6.3 Portchester Castle, Hampshire (see discussion on pp. 130–1).
A Norman keep (centre) was built on the site of the former
Roman town in the early twelfth century. Subsequently a
series of buildings was constructed in the inner bailey to
the south and east of the keep. The ruined palace to the
south (left) of the keep, dated 1396–9, was preceded by a
similar arrangement of three ranges of accommodation
facing onto a private garden (mid-fourteenth century).

are seldom discerned. Objects associated with needlework, such as the
thimbles excavated from Sandal Castle (West Yorkshire) (Mayes and
Butler 1983: 236), may equally have been associated with male servants;
while gaming boards, such as those recovered from Castle Acre
(Norfolk) and Gloucester Castle, would have been used by both noble
men and women. Both sexes wore jewellery, as did children, in addition to precious stones and amulets. Occasionally the symbolic
connotations of an artefact indicate possible use by a woman, such as
the Middleham Jewel, found near Middleham Castle (North Yorkshire).
This combines the symbolism of the Nativity with an *Agnus Dei* (lamb
of God) inscription; the latter was believed to have held therapeutic
properties for pregnant women (Cherry 1994: 32–4). In general,
however, very few finds of this nature have been yielded by castle excavations. Indeed, the majority of artefact types represent a fluidity in

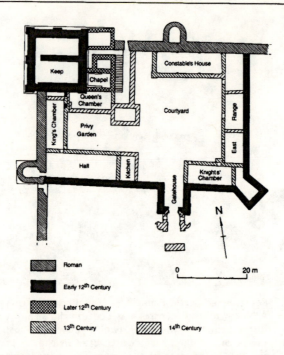

Figure 6.4 Plan of the excavations in the inner bailey at Portchester
       Castle, Hampshire, Period 4 (1320–50)

Source: Drawing by Steve Allen, after Cunliffe and Munby 1985: figs 7, 57.

gendered activities and adornment. The approach of 'gender attribution', therefore, has little to offer. More can be deduced from the
surviving architecture and excavated structures of medieval castles.

Portchester Castle (Hampshire)

The site of this royal castle has been excavated extensively, and it retains
very substantial standing remains; further, an attempt has been made to
link excavated and surviving structures with documented buildings
(Cunliffe and Munby 1985). By the middle of the fourteenth century a
series of domestic ranges was constructed in the inner bailey, to the
south of the Norman keep, providing residential accommodation
around a small private garden, separated from the rest of the courtyard
by a fence (*ibid.*: 124). Today this area is occupied by the ruined buildings of a palace built by Richard II in 1396–9 (see Figure 6.3 on p. 129).

Excavations have shown that this palace was preceded by royal accommodation in three ranges that faced onto a garden (see Figure 6.4 opposite): the south range contained the hall and kitchen, the west range housed the king's chamber, and the north range is thought to have accommodated the chamber of the queen (Cunliffe and Munby 1985: 124–6, 142–3). The north range appears to have had direct access to the chapel (in the keep forebuilding), via a communicating door at the upper level; this door still remains in the south wall of the former chapel. On the basis of an account of building repairs made in 1337–8, the excavators have identified the north range tentatively as the 'queen's chamber', and proposed that it would have enjoyed a 'pleasant, south-facing room overlooking the privy garden' (*ibid*.: 142–3).

Clarendon Palace, Wiltshire

At this undefended royal residence, the arrangements of the queen's household can be reconstructed through the evidence of documents, and the survey and excavation of former structures (James and Robinson 1988). The queen's household formed the four most easterly structures of the north range, which was substantially improved for Eleanor of Provence, who married Henry III in 1236. Her household was positioned to the east of the king's apartments and was housed, like his, in two storeys, consisting of a hall, wardrobe and at least three chambers (see Figure 6.5 on p. 132). The buildings were plastered internally and provided with innovative, high quality ceramic tile floors. The main structure comprised a ground-floor hall and an upper storey with wall fireplace. This is likely to have been the queen's 'high chamber', which was later screened and provided with a gallery. From here a doorway provided direct access to a building to the south, which housed the queen's chapel in its upper storey, with a hall below. A building attached at right angles to the other, but without direct access between, is thought to have provided accommodation for the queen's chaplains, who were Franciscan friars. This structure was aligned east-west, and comprised two rooms at ground-floor level with hall above. The eastern, lower room housed an altar, while the western had a raised dais (platform) at its eastern end, and benches along the walls. The queen's privy tower was near her chamber, and her private garden extended to the north, forming a private ward of the palace. It was ordered in 1250 that a window should be made for her 'toward the garden, well barred with iron' (James and Robinson 1988: 21).

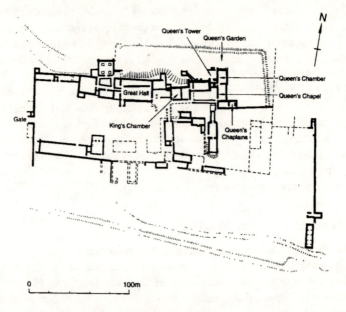

Figure 6.5 Composite plan of Clarendon Palace, Wiltshire, based on excavated and surveyed structures

Source: Drawing by Steve Allen, after James and Robinson 1988: figs 5, 12.

Castle Rising (Norfolk)

In 1329 this baronial castle was sold to the Crown. In 1331 it became the residence of Queen Isabella, the notorious 'She-Wolf of France', who had been accomplice in the murder of her husband Edward II. Isabella was resident primarily at Rising until her death in 1358, although she was never a prisoner there; she could travel freely, entertain guests, and was given a generous pension (Morley and Gurney 1997: 3). The foundations of a series of ruined buildings survive to the south of the extant Norman keep (Figure 6.6). These formed a separate household of the castle, and have been linked with the period of Isabella's occupancy of the castle. Excavations have dated the structures closely to *c.* 1330, from three jettons (tokens) of this date deposited during the construction of the west range (*ibid.*: 56). The excavated structures indicate two residential ranges and a chapel, with a courtyard contained within the space between the three buildings (see Figure 6.7 on p. 134). Direct access to an upper gallery in the chapel was provided from a chamber on the first floor of the western

Figure 6.6 Castle Rising, Norfolk. Structures attributed to Queen Isabella (*c.* 1330) have been excavated to the south of the Norman keep (*c.* 1138).

range; stairs down from this chamber led to a covered passage leading to the south range. The upper floor of the west range is therefore the best candidate for Isabella's own chambers, with easy communication with her chapel, courtyard to the south and keep to the north. The south range contained a fireplace in its gable wall and was subdivided internally, possibly to provide guest accommodation, and/or an audience chamber and antechamber for receiving guests (*ibid.*: 60). The complex was provided with its own well and nearby kitchen, ensuring that Isabella's enemies had no opportunity to poison her. It is likely that the great hall and kitchen of the Norman keep would have continued in use for the purposes of ceremony and hospitality.

Chepstow Castle (Gwent)

Earl William fitz Osbern built this baronial castle by *c.* 1070, as a hall keep perched on a steep natural rock slope above the River Wye (J. K. Knight 1991). Substantial remains of the castle survive, comprising three baileys and a barbican, defended by a sheer cliff to the north and a plunging valley to the south. Like many castles, the plan of Chepstow developed organically over several generations. During the thirteenth

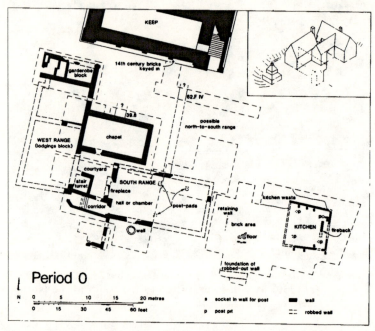

Figure 6.7 Plan of excavated structures south of the keep at Castle Rising, associated with the occupancy of Queen Isabella

Source: Drawing by Stephen Ashley, from Morley and Gurney 1997: fig. 46. Reproduced by kind permission of East Anglian Archaeology.

century, accommodation was added by the Marshals to include a hall and kitchen block in the lower bailey, adjacent to the outer gatehouse, and a chamber block in the upper bailey (Figure 6.8). This extant chamber block, located in the southwestern corner of the upper bailey, adjacent to the barbican, has been identified as the *camera comitisse* (chamber of the countess) that was recorded in the thirteenth century (*ibid.*: 8). It consists of a single chamber at upper storey level, overlooking a substantial private enclosure that separated it from the keep to the east. From the keep the countess's chamber could not have been visible; its western elevation having been provided with only circular splayed windows that precluded observation.

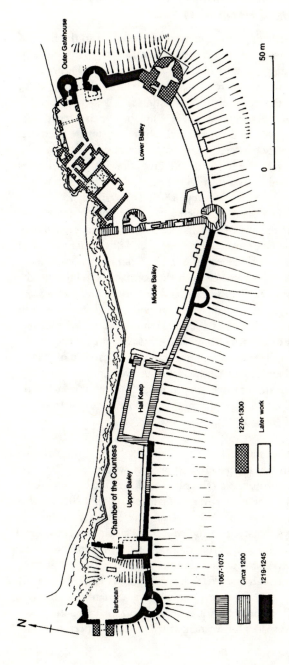

Outer Gatehouse

Lower Bailey

Middle Bailey

Hall Keep

Chamber of the Countess

Upper Bailey

Barbican

N

50 m

0

1067-1075
Circa 1200
1219-1245
1270-1300
Later work

Figure 6.8 Plan of earthworks and ruined buildings at Chepstow, Gwent

Source: Drawing by Steve Allen, after J. Knight 1991.

Pickering Castle (North Yorkshire) and Carisbrooke Castle (Isle of Wight, Hampshire)

The royal castle at Pickering was conferred by Henry III to the Earls of Lancaster. Today, remains of the castle include the original shell keep and the ruined buildings of subsequent freestanding halls (Figure 6.9). In the fourteenth century new residences were built in the inner ward, including in 1314 the 'new hall' for Countess Alice, wife of Earl Thomas of Lancaster (Thompson 1985: 8). Documents record that this was an expensive, two-storey hall with an upper chamber, including an elaborately plastered room with a fireplace, that may have covered only the northern end of the building. Surviving foundations show that the hall had a door in its north side which gave access to a covered walkway (see Figure 6.10 on p. 138). This walkway led in turn to the west wall of the chapel, in which a blocked doorway can still be detected. The arrangement of the hall and walkway enabled direct, private access for the Countess to the western end of the chapel, where a private pew is likely to have been sited. The Countess's accommodation was screened to allow privacy from the constable's lodging to the north, the tower and keep to the east, and the prison and barbican to the south. This sequence of hall, chamber and chapel is repeated at Carisbrooke Castle on the Isle of Wight (Hampshire), which was held by Countess Isabella de Fortibus from 1262–93 (see Figure 6.1 on p. 119). Isabella owned not only the castle, but the whole of the Isle of Wight. She built a new residential block, which still survives, comprising a hall, great chamber, private chambers and chapel, including a squint through which she could view the high altar in the chapel from her adjoining chamber (Jones 1984).

Very clear spatial patterns emerge from these six cases. Private chapels (or direct access to private galleries or closets within chapels) were provided in all but one example (Chepstow), illustrating the significant religious role of the noble or royal woman (above p. 120). Further documented examples include Nottingham and Windsor, where the queen's chamber was adjacent to the chapel (Allen Brown *et al.* 1963 II: 758, 879), and those where porches, oriels or vestibules were constructed between the queen's chamber and the chapel, such as Woodstock, Marlborough and Westminster (*ibid.*: 1012, 736; I: 502). Private enclosures, courtyards or gardens are evident in all cases, reflecting the female association with gardens, and the emphasis placed on private, enclosed spaces for women. It seems to have been especially

Figure 6.9 Pickering Castle, North Yorkshire. The ruined hall associated
with Countess Alice (1314) (left) was built adjacent to the
chapel (which has been restored) and shared direct access
with it.

important that these gardens or courtyards were not overlooked by any
buildings other than those of the women themselves (or the
king's/lord's household), so that they were squeezed discretely
between ranges at Portchester and Castle Rising, or tucked into an
angle of the defences at Chepstow, Carisbrooke and Clarendon. In
common with the private chambers of all high-ranking people, those of
the women were located at an upper level. Occasionally the tower was
incorporated explicitly into female quarters in castles, such as the privy
chamber of Eleanor of Provence at Winchester, which in 1269 was
rebuilt in the form of a tower with double vaulting (*ad modum turelle
cum duplici vousura*) (Allen Brown *et al.* 1963 II: 861). From this
elevated position women would have enjoyed substantial views of the
castle interior, while remaining out of view themselves. This control of
sightlines was even more important in public spaces, such as the
chapel, where through a squint or screened closet, the woman could
observe everything around her without being seen. Such towers and
galleries did not imprison feckless, fairytale princesses: these female
spaces were carefully sited for dioramic views, a 'female gaze' that did
not display the viewer.

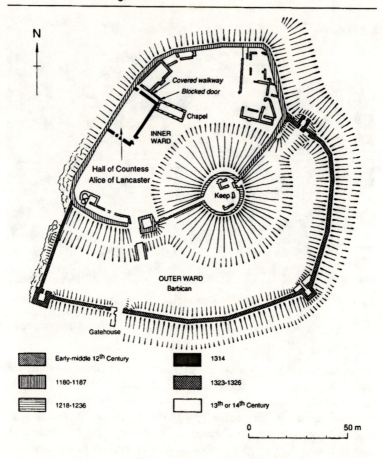

Figure 6.10 Plan of earthworks and ruined buildings at Pickering Castle, showing the central motte and shell keep (early twelfth century) and halls built subsequently in the inner ward

Source: Drawing by Steve Allen, after Thompson 1985.

Body metaphors: 'the secret places of women'

Female quarters were positioned in the innermost spaces of the medieval castle, at the greatest distance from the main ceremonial entrance. Where formal spatial (access) analysis has tested this hypothesis, it has been confirmed that the female household was located in the deepest space on the ceremonial route through the castle, although its actual spatial relationship to secondary entrances, such as posterns and barbicans, rendered it physically vulnerable (Kitson 1997; Richardson 1998). Symbolically and ritually, at least, women were positioned in the most secluded spaces of the castle, cocooned even more deeply than the sacred body of the king. Further, the female body served as a metaphor for the interior, protected spaces of the castle.

Later medieval thought was dominated by a concern with the physicality and substance of the body: through the mass the body of Christ transformed substance, and through the cult of saints, body parts had the power to heal (Bynum 1987: 251). The body is frequently used as a metaphor for bounded systems, such as castles, and Mary Douglas has observed that such imagery is pertinent particularly where the boundaries are threatened or precarious (Douglas 1966: 115). The metaphor of the female body, more specifically, provides the connotations of safe, contained spaces (Best 1995: 187; Irigaray 1985). Conversely, medieval medicine explained the physiology of the body through architectural metaphors, with the body's interior perceived as contained, domestic and feminine. In his *Chirurgie* (1306–1320), for example, Henri de Mondeville explained that 'interior space, be it of the house or of the body, is a feminine place; for the first dwelling-place of man is buried deep in the secret places of women' (quoted in Pouchelle 1990: 130). Medieval understanding of the womb was based on the assumption that the female carried her sex organs internally, which were a mirror image of the external genitalia of the man, in order to provide a safe place for conception and gestation (Laqueur 1990). These 'secret places of women' were inner, watery, changeable places, in keeping with the proposed phlegmatic humour of women.

The honour and patrimony of lordship rested on the impermeability of both the castle and the female body. It is not surprising, then, to find the castle used as metaphor for the female body, a tabernacle protecting the precious virginity contained within. The bride on her wedding night is described as a 'fortress', her virginity 'the keep' in the fifteenth-century collection of tales, *Cent Nouvelles Nouvelles*: 'before reaching the central keep of the castle, he had to take ... bulwarks, palisades, and several other strong places by which the castle was surrounded, like one which never before had been captured' (quoted in Pouchelle 1990: 130). In the genre of medieval romances, the female body was equated with land, and that of the queen came to symbolise the integrity of the kingdom. As Karen Pratt has noted, the lady of courtly romances used the 'terminology of land tenure as she handed over her body to her lover in return for his service' (Pratt 1997: 255–6).

Female virginity was demanded in secular and religious contexts, and the spatial segregation of women in castles may be compared with the absolute enclosure experienced by religious women. Indeed, works written for anchoresses, who were permanently enclosed in their cells, likened the virgin to the fortress. In *The Letter on Virginity*, written in the West Midlands in the late twelfth or early thirteenth century, the chief metaphor for the religious virgin is her enclosure in a tower (Millet 1982: II.27). In the *Ancrene Wisse*, a guide for anchoresses contemporary to the letter, the image used for the soul of the recluse is that of a courtly lady under siege in an earthen castle (Millett and Wogan-Browne 1990: 112/33–114/21). It is no coincidence that iconographic representations of chastity included the tower, and that the image of the tower was central in the popular martyrdom stories of virgin-saints, in particular Barbara.

A second metaphor was used for the virginal, female body: that of the garden, a feature so consistently paired with the accommodation of the female household. The link between women's chastity and the enclosed garden was made in the Old Testament *Song of Songs*:

> a garden enclosed is my sister, my spouse
> a spring shut up, a fountain sealed
>
> (4: 12)

This passage served as one image in constructing the iconography of the Virgin Mary, who was symbolised by the *hortus conclusus*, the enclosed garden and fountain of water which referred to the Virgin's purity, her enclosed womb. It also influenced spiritual writings, introducing a language of 'florescence and germination' which equated the soul with the bride, and the body with organic analogies such as the garden or the flowering plant (Bynum 1995: 224–5, 319). These overtones may have informed the close connection that was drawn between women and gardening (above pp. 125–8), and the Marian frame of reference for the queen's sacerdotal roles. Enclosed gardens built for queens included that built by Edward I at Conwy: the *herbarium Regine* was next to the queen's chamber, a lawn of turf fenced in with staves (Allen Brown *et al.* 1963 I: 338). In the park at Odiham (Hampshire), the queen's garden consisted of an outer hedge and an inner enclosure of a boarded fence, with five doors and seats protected by a turfed roof and screened by a hedge (*ibid.*: 767–8). At Woodstock

(Oxfordshire), the queen had a 'walled garden to walk in', placed adjacent to her chambers (*ibid.*: 1012), one of a series of walled or hedged gardens entered through locked doors. In addition there was a cloistered water pleasance nearby, and an elaborate maze, Rosamund's Bower (sketched by John Aubrey in the seventeenth century), where Henry II is conjectured to have made love secretly to his mistress, Rosamund Clifford (McLean 1981: 100–1; Landsberg 1998: 21).

The enclosed garden represented chastity iconographically, but its meaning could be ambiguous to a medieval audience. In medieval literature the garden was a venue for lovers' trysts, such as Henry and Rosamund's. The rose-garden was a symbol of Paradise, with the rose another icon for the Virgin Mary, while the enclosed garden could represent the Garden of Eden (Genesis 2: 8–20), with its overt connotations of sexual temptation and the treachery of woman. Even the enclosed garden of the biblical *Song of Songs* was seductively scented:

> Breathe over my garden, prays the bride to the north and south winds
> To spread its sweet smell around.
> Let my beloved come into his garden,
> Let him taste its rarest fruits
>
> (4: 16)

In medieval art, depictions of the Garden of Love satirised women, emphasising man's foolishness and woman's deceit, with lust at the root of sexual obsession and sinfulness (Grössinger 1997: 103).

This tension is most clearly expressed in the first section of the *Roman de la Rose*, the apogee of courtly literature, written by Guillaume de Lorris (1225–30) and continued by Jean de Meun (1269–78). The young male narrator is admitted by Lady Idleness to the walled garden of Pleasure, which is visited by Lord Pleasure and his comely male and female companions. In the tradition of the courtly love-lyric, the garden serves as an allegory for a love affair. The focal point is the rose-garden, enclosed by a hedge, where the narrator is pierced by Love's arrows. His lover's quest is encouraged by Fair Welcome, and discouraged by Reason, who comes down from her tower. The roses are guarded by Shame, Reason's daughter, but still the young man enters the enclosure. Jealousy is aroused, who warns of Lechery and Lust, and chastises Shame, 'Chastity is no longer safe in the abbey or in the cloister. Therefore I will have the rose-bushes and the roses enclosed within a wall ... I shall not delay in building a fortress to enclose the roses' (line 3587 onwards) (Horgan 1994).

The enclosed garden was a contested space: chastity encountered lust, social order was breached by love, and youth triumphed over old age. In Chaucer's fourteenth-century *Canterbury Tales*, the lovers Emelye and Palamon of the 'Knight's Tale' meet when Emelye walks in the garden below the keep where Palamon was prisoner (line 1065). January, the elderly lover of the 'Merchant's Tale', jealously guarded his young wife, May, by building a beautiful garden enclosed with stone, in which only he could visit her (line 784) (Blake 1980). Like the female body, the garden was evidently regarded ambivalently. It was a female preserve, a metaphor for purity and the soul, a means of creative expression and tranquility within the apparent rough and tumble of male life in the castle. But the seclusion of its hedges and walls offered the potential for secrecy and the breaking of social conventions which segregated the sexes. The body of the chaste woman, like the enclosed garden, was a chrysalis ripe for sexual encounter.

The chaste female body was the key to patrimony, and the young noble woman or queen was protected by an ideology of enclosure. Even when she travelled between castles and palaces, the men rode on horseback, while her household was enclosed in a carriage, as depicted in the early fourteenth-century Luttrell psalter (Figure 6.11). At home or with the mobile household, the female body was veiled. Yet the oppositions of public and private were permeable; for instance, by the custom for her to receive visitors in her bedchamber. The ideology of female seclusion marched in tandem with the lifecourse, diminishing once she had fulfilled her obligation to produce the heir apparent, and, according to humoral theory, as her moist female body dried with age, and became closer to the male. The matron or widow held court openly, presiding publicly in the great hall as lord of her own household. In the late thirteenth century Bishop Grosseteste advised the Countess of Lincoln to 'Make your own household ... to sit in the hall, as much as you may ... and sit you ever in the middle of the high board, that your visage and cheer be showed to all men' (quoted in Girouard 1978: 30), while Dame Alice de Bryene offered generous hospitality to her household and visitors to her hall in fifteenth-century Suffolk (Redstone 1931).

In death, the female body was displayed, even paraded, freely. From the later thirteenth century, effigies of men and women were placed in churches to commemorate the dead. That of Eleanor of Castile (d. 1290) showed the queen at the moment of her coronation, her hair loose to her shoulders, wearing a simple tunic and flowing robe, with crown and sceptre. More remarkable was the journey taken by her corpse from

Figure 6.11 The Luttrell Psalter, dated to the early fourteenth century, showing a travelling carriage for royal women.

Source: British Library Additional MS 42130 (f. 181).

Lincoln to London, her body visibly exposed along the route, adorned in full royal regalia (Parsons 1997: 323–5): a funeral cortège marked subsequently by a series of stational monuments, the Eleanor Crosses. This exposure of the body of the queen, and monumental commemoration of the event, may have been intended to display her incorruptibility, signalling both the integrity of the kingdom, and her triumph over the organic processes of the female body (after Bynum 1995).

Conclusion: the contested garden

In medieval England, spatial segregation of the sexes was a formal device used to represent gender difference and social order. Such distancing cannot be equated with simple notions of differential prestige, but was bound closely with moral and medical perceptions of the gendered body, with particular emphasis on segregation in the sacred and public contexts of churches, hospitals and religious houses. Our own concepts of public and private break down when applied to the medieval case: gender domains were reasonably fluid even among the peasantry, fragmented by seasonal practices and patterns in the lifecourse. Prohibitions on the mobility and visibility of women were not carried into later life: widows were *femmes soles*, and could preside in the great hall or travel widely, evidenced in extreme by Chaucer's bawdy 'Wife of Bath', a pilgrim of the *Canterbury Tales*. Spatial seclusion of women was emphasised especially in ceremonial settings: church services, feasts, tournaments, pageants, funerals – but notably not in burial and commemoration. The public could be enveloped in the private spaces of women, when strangers from outside the household were received in the female chamber or garden. Spatial boundaries emphasised gender amongst other social differences, but, like the female body, these membranes were understood as liquid and changeable.

There seems little doubt that noble and royal women were spatially secluded for at least part of their lives, with female chastity and fidelity essential to patrimony. But did such seclusion result in loss of autonomy, limited communication or lower prestige, as cross-cultural studies have suggested? Did the inner spaces that medieval noble women occupied equate with a devalued, domestic domain? It should be recalled that spatial seclusion was used also to designate the sacred body of the king (above, p. 122), and his ultimate status in the realm. Seclusion was used in addition to denote the special status of monks and nuns, the elect, whose prayers were closest to God. The sanctity of their bodies was stressed by the early twelfth-century chronicler Orderic Vitalis: 'True monks are enclosed in royal cloisters as if they were king's daughters, for fear that if they should wander abroad, they may be shamefully defiled' (Chibnall 1969–80 III: 144–5). To medieval women, their seclusion in separate households, chapel 'closets' and gardens was a mark of high prestige. From this vista, they exercised considerable social and economic power, managing estates, maintaining social networks, and, for the queen's part, influencing matters of state through her intercession.

The actual and metaphoric spaces of the castle enclosed both the female and male body. Indeed, its inner spaces were reserved for the man and woman of the highest status, with the chambers of the lord and lady, or king and queen, usually joined. Their social roles differed, as reflected in patterns of access: his leading more easily to the great hall, hers opening onto a private garden. The body of the king represented the sanctity of kingship, while that of the queen symbolised the integrity of the kingdom. This complementarity extended to the cultural symbolism of the castle, both the masculine symbol of lordship and domination, and the feminine symbol of chastity and enclosure. Medieval ambivalence towards the female body is betrayed by the conflicting symbolism of the castle garden: the revered *hortus conclusus* and the satirised Garden of Love; woman chaste and woman treacherous.

Masculine and feminine were embodied through the castle. Its inner, feminine spaces were embellished by vivid colours, textures and scents; the opulent furnishings of private chambers and the sweet smell of gardens contrasted with the drab, pungent world of masculinity. These were not exclusive male and female domains, or simple binary oppositions: perceptions of masculine and feminine were mercurial. The interior spaces of the castle were feminised by courtly etiquette, and although women may have been resident here more regularly, these visceral territories were cohabited by men and women, just as the male domain of nearby parks and forests was sometimes pierced by a female presence hunting and hawking. Medieval concepts of social order, morality and physiology created distinct embodiments and perceptions of masculinity and femininity, but these were not absolute categories. At times the oppositions of public/private, culture/nature, male/female were collapsed, inverted or shared, as gendered metaphors more symbolic than real.

Through the corporeality of the medieval castle and the female body we glimpse the complexities of gender. In certain discourses both the castle and the female body came to represent the wholeness of the body, and its indivisibility from the soul; both were bounded spaces that maintained the completeness of patrimony – fiefdom, kingdom and feudal order. Gender was embodied through the tastes, smells, sounds, colours and textures of medieval masculinity and femininity. Medieval gender was a truly contested garden. Boundaries were mutable: meanings at once overlapping and conflicting, constructed doubly according to secular and religious ideologies, contingent upon personal status and place in the lifecourse.

Chapter 7

Coda

The borders of sex, gender and knowledge

> feminist debate is a radical one to the extent that it must share with other radicalisms the premise that completion is undesirable.
>
> (Marilyn Strathern 1988: 22)

This book has not set out to provide a template or exemplar for how to *do* gender archaeology. From its feminist origins, the subject has inherited a scepticism that will continue to question the construction of archaeological knowledge, and an optimism which relishes the challenge of elucidating the complex nature of gender in past societies. This legacy has endowed gender archaeology with the pluralism, tolerance and eclectism of the feminist third wave: there is no single method or means of doing gender archaeology, and the interrogation of gender in antiquity will never be complete. There are lessons to be learned, however, from the subject's development over the last fifteen years. While there is no desire to *do* gender archaeology in one particular way, the imperative exists to do gender archaeology well.

The concerns of gender archaeology have matured from the feminist critique of androcentrism, to making women 'visible', to a more holistic study of the meaning and experience of sexual difference and gender identity in the past (Chapters 1 and 3). Recent years have witnessed a paradigm shift that rejects universals, including explanations for inequality, cross-cultural models for the sexual division of labour, and 'essentialist' definitions of what it means to be a man or woman. The study of gender as sexual asymmetry, hierarchy or prestige, is being replaced by the concept of gender as difference (Moore 1994). Gender is explored as metaphor, the symbolism that creates the complementarity between men and women that is necessary for the functioning of their society (Strathern 1988).

The empirical nature of archaeological evidence continues to prioritise the issue of gender visibility. Approaches of 'gender attribution' now vie with more abstract considerations, however, such as gender as it is embedded in the social relations of technology (e.g. Dobres 1995), or as it is conveyed visually through representations of the individual (Knapp and Meskell 1997). Is it crucial to make gender visible? To illustrate the detail of men's and women's lives in the past (Costin 1996: 116)? To create visages for the 'faceless blobs' of prehistory (Tringham 1991: 94)? In keeping with the broad aims of our 'materialist' discipline, the answer must surely be yes. But the scope of this visibility must project beyond the conventional approach to the sexual division of labour (Chapter 3), to embrace the embodiment of gender through the perceptual experience of men and women in the past (Chapter 4 and 5).

The social constructionist view of gender, so long favoured by feminists, has been questioned increasingly from the contrasting perspectives of cognitive science, medical history, and queer theory. The extreme positions adopted by feminists *versus* sociobiologists – that gender is fully constructed by either society or biology – need to be reconsidered in light of evidence for cognitive differences in the ways in which men and women use language, space, and bodily gestures (pp. 11–13). Continuing the tradition of the feminist critique of science (Chapter 2) requires an engagement with science, rather than a retreat from it. The contribution of queer theory has been the questioning of predetermined categories of sex, gender and sexuality. Individuals *live* in a gendered body and create the appearance of sex through *performance*, the repeated stylisation of the body (Butler 1990) that constructs identity through everyday acts, gestures, postures, language, dress, and so on.

The collapse of binary categories has been portentous for the empirical discipline of archaeology (Chapter 4). Even the classification of biological sex can be shown to be insecure, more a spectrum than a duality (Fausto-Sterling 1995; Nordbladh and Yates 1990), and perceived historically according to medico-religious models of physiology (Laqueur 1990). From history and ethnography we have come to recognise that gender is not always binary in its expression: multiple genders exist in a diversity of cultural contexts, defined variously by sexual identity, personal mentality, or social role (Herdt 1994). Study of the historical creation of sexuality – the social practices and classifications of bodily pleasure – has been prompted as much by feminist and queer theorists as by the influential work of Michel Foucault (1981, 1985, 1986). Sexuality must be understood as an historical construction, rather than a natural category of experience. Inevitably, projection of the concept of sexuality on to the premodern past risks anachronism. The aim is to identify difference and contradiction, influenced by the project of 'queering'. On no account should queer studies aim to make gays or lesbians 'visible' in antiquity. Instead, they should strive to challenge and disrupt, to 'seek out ... dissonances, gaps, and excesses of meaning that signal heteronormative protocols of representation and that enable a disruption of those same protocols' (Lochrie 1997: 180).

In common with queer theory, masculinist studies attack the complacency of essentialism in readings of gender. While there is a danger that masculine perspectives in archaeology could represent a backlash against feminism, one which reprioritises visibility of the male, a truly masculinist enquiry challenges stereotyping of both males and females. Masculinity is considered as a concept that may be selectively adopted by men and sometimes women (Cornwall and Lindisfarne 1994), in each culture comprising hegemonic and counter-hegemonic values. Gender archaeology must re-examine the metonyms that we have placed on masculinity and femininity, particularly the trappings of warriorhood and the adornments of beauty. Our readings of the past should be open to the possibilities of masculine women and feminine men (Chapter 4).

Increasingly it is clear that categories of gender, the body and sexuality are transcient not just between cultures and through time, but within the course of a single lifetime (Chapter 5). Gender is frequently perceived as cumulative: expanding, receding, transforming with the ageing body. Consequently, men and women may experience time differently, and lead syncopated lives. Through the cultural definition of the lifecourse, the metaphor of gender engages with those of space and time, to reveal cycles and meanings invested in the gendered body. Here it is not sufficient to make particular age groups *visible* archaeologically, such as children or the elderly, but rather to address the embodiment of ageing (Turner 1995), the social values placed on gendered age, and the connections and tensions created between generations.

While gender archaeology may revel in its pluralism, it seldom advocates relativism, and regularly emphasises rigour and innovation in theory and method (Wylie 1992a, 1992b) (Chapter 2). A feminist epistemology seems to have developed in some branches of gender archaeology, that concentrates on the small-scale, on everyday occurrences and relationships between people, on subtle shifts in power and relations of production. This might be seen as the cultivation of 'standpoint feminist knowledge', which, like queer theory, advocates thinking from contradictory positions outside the mainstream (Harding 1993). Wherever interpretative inspiration is found, the creation of gendered knowledge requires precision in the definition and application of terms such as gender, sex, and sexuality; suspicion is called for of essentialist and cross-cultural stereotypes; and care is needed in the critical use of analogy, whether ethnographic or historical (Chapter 3). The most sophisticated readings of gender have been developed from multiple lines of evidence, combining, for example, the use of spatial, iconographic, and environmental data, together with analogic sources. This deployment of parallel lines of evidence allows the discernment of ambiguity and contradiction. Further, the diachronic study of gender should be emphasised, encouraging readings of gender through lives and time.

The major lesson that has been learned is that gender never stands still: boundaries and categories are transient, identity contingent, knowledge incomplete. Gender archaeology is no longer content with cross-cultural definitions of prestige, binary categories and the sexual division of labour, but seeks gender as difference, the private experiences and sensations of being a man or woman, their complementarity and competition through the lifecourse. The gendered past is a land of permeable borders, ripe for exploration.

Further reading

Introductory texts on gender archaeology and anthropology

The best introduction to the issues that motivated gender archaeology remains:

Conkey, M. W. and Spector, J. (1984) 'Archaeology and the study of gender', *Archaeological Methods and Theory 7*: 1–38. New York: Academic Press.
This work is reprinted, together with several ground-breaking articles, in: Hays-Gilpin, K. and Whitley, D. S. (eds) *Reader in Gender Archaeology*, London: Routledge.
Introductions and case studies in gender anthropology can be consulted in: di Leonardo, M. (ed.) (1991)*Gender at the Crossroads of Knowledge: Feminist Anthropology in the Post-Modern Era*, Berkeley CA: University of California Press.
Moore, H. L. (1988) *Feminism and Anthropology*, Cambridge: Polity Press.
Ortner, S. (1996) *Making Gender: The Politics and Erotics of Culture*, Boston MA: Beacon Press.
Ortner, S. and Whitehead, H. (eds) (1981)*Sexual Meanings: the Cultural Construction of Gender and Sexuality*, Cambridge: Cambridge University Press.

Recommended case studies in gender archaeology

Two volumes in particular provide a range of good case studies, the first concentrating more on the study of women and female agency in prehistory, the second also including third-wave feminist perspectives, a focus on children, and case studies that include historical periods:

Gero, J. M. and Conkey, M. W. (eds) (1991) *Engendering Archaeology: Women and Prehistory*, Oxford: Blackwell.

Moore, J. and Scott, E. (1997) (eds) *Invisible People and Processes: Writing Gender and Childhood into European Archaeology*, London: Leicester University Press.

Regional studies of gender archaeology

Several edited volumes concentrate on case studies of particular regions (some of which were published after completion of the text of this book), including:

Claassen, C. and Joyce, R. A. (eds) (1997) *Women in Prehistory: North America and Mesoamerica*, Philadelphia PA: University of Pennsylvania Press.

Hudecek-Cuffe, C. R. (1998) *Engendering Northern Plains Paleoindian Archaeology: Decision-making and Gender Roles in Subsistence and Settlement Strategies*, Oxford: British Archaeological Reports International Series 699.

Kent, S. (ed.) (1998) *Gender in African Prehistory*, Walnut Creek CA: AltaMira Press.

Wadley, L. (ed.) (1997) *Our Gendered Past: Archaeological Studies of Gender in Southern Africa*, Johannesburg: Witwatersrand University Press.

Whitehouse, R. D. (ed.) (1998) *Gender and Italian Archaeology: Challenging the Stereotypes*, Accordia Specialist Studies on Italy, vol. 7. London: Accordia Research Institute, University of London.

Chronological studies of gender archaeology

In addition to the edited volumes on prehistory noted above, there are a number of case studies devoted to medieval and historical archaeology:

Gilchrist, R. (1994) *Gender and Material Culture: the Archaeology of Religious Women*, London: Routledge.

Seifert, D. (ed.) (1991) Gender in Historical Archaeology, *Historical Archaeology*, 25.4.

Wall, D. D. (1994) *The Archaeology of Gender: Separating the Spheres in Urban America*, New York: Plenum Press.

Gender and evolution

See below, and articles reprinted in K. Hays-Gilpin and D. S. Whitley (eds) *Reader in Gender Archaeology*, London: Routledge.

Conkey, M. W. with Williams, S. H. (1991) 'Original narratives: the political economy of gender in archaeology', in M. di Leonardo (ed.) *Gender at the Crossroads of Knowledge: Feminist Anthropology in the Postmodern Era*, 102–39. Berkeley CA: University of California Press.

Hager, L. D. (ed.) (1997) *Women in Human Evolution*, London: Routledge.

Gender and the archaeology of the lifecourse

Derevenski, J. Sofaer (1997) 'Engendering children, engendering archaeology', in J. Moore and E. Scott (eds) *Invisible People and Processes*, 192–202. London: Leicester University Press.
Gilchrist, R. (ed.) (forthcoming, 2000) 'Lifecycles', *World Archaeology*, 31.3.
Grauer, A. L. and Stuart-Macadam, P. (eds) (1998) *Sex and Gender in Paleopathological Perspective*, Cambridge: Cambridge University Press.

Iconographic approaches to gender archaeology

Studies more influenced by art-historical and visual approaches include:

Kampen, N. B. (ed.) (1996) *Sexuality in Ancient Art: Near East, Egypt, Greece and Italy*, Cambridge: Cambridge University Press.
Koloski-Ostrow, A. and Lyons, C. L. (eds) (1997) *Naked Truths: Women, Sexuality and Gender in Classical Art and Archaeology*, London: Routledge.

Masculinity

As yet there is no single volume devoted to the archaeology of masculinity, although there are edited volumes offering perspectives from sociology, medieval studies and ancient history, for example:

Cornwall, A. and Lindisfarne, N. (eds) (1994) *Dislocating Masculinity: Comparative Ethnographies*, London: Routledge.
Foxhall, L. and Salmon, J. (eds) (1998) *Thinking Men: Masculinity and its Self-Representation in the Classical Tradition*, London: Routledge.
Lees, C. A. (1994) *Medieval Masculinities: Regarding Men in the Middle Ages*, Minneapolis MN: University of Minnesota Press.

Sexuality and the body

Historical and ethnographic evidence for the contingent nature of sex and sexuality is presented in Herdt and Laqueur, while Meskell critiques archaeological approaches to the body.

Herdt, G. (ed.) (1994) *Third Sex, Third Gender: Beyond Sexual Dimorphism in Culture and History*, 21–81. New York: Zone Books.

Laqueur, T. W. (1990) *Making Sex: Body and Gender from the Greeks to Freud*, Cambridge MA: Harvard University Press.

Meskell, L. (1996) 'The somatisation of archaeology: discourses, institutions, corporeality', *Norwegian Archaeological Review*, 29.1: 1–16.

The Mother Goddess debate

Critiques of the literature on mother goddesses include:

Meskell, L. (1995) 'Goddesses, Gimbutus and the "New Age" Archaeology', *Antiquity*, 69: 74–86.

Talalay, L. E. (1994) 'A feminist boomerang: the great goddess of great prehistory', *Gender and History*, 6.2: 165–83.

Visual representations of gender in archaeology

The devices used by archaeologists in their visual reconstructions are analysed in:

Gifford-Gonzalez, D. (1993) 'You can hide, but you can't run: representation of women's work in illustrations of Palaeolithic life', *Visual Anthropology Review*, 9.1: 21–41.

Hurcombe, L. (1995) 'Our own engendered species', *Antiquity*, 69: 87–100.

Moser, S. (1993) 'Gender stereotyping in pictorial reconstructions of human origins', in L. Smith and H. duCros (eds) *Women in Archaeology*, 75–92. Canberra: Australian National University.

Bibliography

Allen Brown, R., Colvin, H. M. and Taylor, A. J. P. (1963) *History of the King's Works: The Middle Ages. Volumes I and II*, London: HMSO.

Andrén, A. (1998) *Between Artifacts and Texts: Historical Archaeology in Global Perspective*, New York: Plenum Press.

Ariès, P. (1965) *Centuries of Childhood*, New York: Jonathan Cape.

Arnold, B. (1991) 'The deposed princess of Vix: the need for an engendered European prehistory', in D. Walde and N. D. Willows (eds) *The Archaeology of Gender*, 366–74. Calgary: University of Calgary Archaeological Association.

Arnold, D. E. (1985) *Ceramic Theory and Cultural Process*, Cambridge: Cambridge University Press.

Astill, G. (1988) 'Rural settlement: the toft and the croft', in G. Astill and A. Grant (eds) *The Countryside of Medieval England*, 36–61. Oxford: Blackwell.

Aston, M. (1990) 'Segregation in church', in W. J. Shiels and D. Wood (eds) *Women in the Church*, Studies in Church History 27: 237–94. Oxford: Blackwell.

Austen, D. (1984) 'The castle and the landscape', *Landscape History*, 6: 69–81.

Ayre, J. and Wroe-Brown, R. (forthcoming) *Excavations at Thames Court, Upper Thames Street, London, 1990–6*, London: Museum of London Archaeology Service.

Bahn, P. (1992) 'Bores, bluffers and wankas: some thoughts on archaeology and humour', *Archaeological Review from Cambridge*, 11.2: 315–322.

Balme, J. and Beck, W. (eds) (1995) *Gendered Archaeology: Proceedings of the Second Australian Women in Archaeology Conference*, Research Papers in Archaeology and Natural History 26. Canberra: Australian National University.

Barker, P. (1987) 'Hen Domen revisited', in J. R. Kenyon and R. Avent (eds) *Castles in Wales and the Marches: Essays in Honour of D. J. Cathcart King*, 51–4. Cardiff: University of Wales Press.

Barlow, K. (1995) 'Achieving womanhood and the achievements of women in Murik society: cult initiation, gender complementarity, and the prestige of women', in N. C. Lutkehaus and P. B. Roscoe (eds) *Gender Rituals*, 85–112. London: Routledge.

Barrett, J. C. (1987) 'The Glastonbury Lake Village: models and source criticism', *Archaeological Journal*, 144: 409–423.

——(1989) 'Food, gender and metal: questions of social reproduction' in M. L. S. Sørensen and R. Thomas (eds) *The Bronze Age–Iron Age Transition in Europe*, 304–20. Oxford: British Archaeological Report International Series 483.

Barrett, M. and Phillips, A. (eds) (1992) *Stabilizing Theory: Contemporary Feminist Debates*, Cambridge: Polity Press.

Barron, W. J. R. (trans.) (1974) *Sir Gawain and the Green Knight*, Manchester: Manchester University Press.

Beaudry, M. C., Cook, L. J. and Mrozowski, S. A. (1991) 'Artefacts and active voices: material culture as social discourse', in R. H. McGuire and R. Paynter (eds) *The Archaeology of Inequality*, 150–91. Oxford: Blackwell.

Beck, W. (1994) 'Women in archeology: Australia and the United States', in M. C. Nelson, S. M. Nelson and A. Wylie (eds) *Equity Issues for Women in Archeology*, 99–104. Archeological Papers of the American Anthropological Association no. 5.

Bentley, G. (1996) 'How did prehistoric women bear "man the hunter"? Reconstructing fertility from the archaeological record', in R. P. Wright (ed.) *Gender and Archaeology*, 23–51. Philadelphia: University of Pennsylvania Press.

Bertelsen, R. Lillehammer, A. and Naess, J. (eds) (1987) *Were They all Men? An Examination of Sex Roles in Prehistoric Society*, Norway: Stavanger.

Best, S. (1995) 'Sexualizing space', in E. Grosz and E. Probyn (eds) *Sexy Bodies: The Strange Carnalities of Feminism*, 181–94. London: Routledge.

Binford, L. (1985) 'Brand X versus the recommended product', *American Antiquity*, 50: 580–90.

——(1978) *Nunamiut Ethnoarchaeology*, New York: Academic Press.

Binski, P. (1996) *Medieval Death: Ritual and Representation*, London: British Museum Press.

Binstock, R. H. and Shanas, E. (eds) (1985) *Handbook of Aging and the Social Sciences*, New York: Van Nostrand Reinhold.

Birke, L. (1994) *Feminism, Animals and Science*, Milton Keynes: Open University Press.

Blackwood, E. (1984) 'Sexuality and gender in certain Native American tribes: the case of cross-gender females', *Signs: the Journal of Women in Culture and Society*, 10.1: 27–42.

Blake, N. F. (ed.) (1980) *The Canterbury Tales. By Geoffrey Chaucer*, London: Edward Arnold.

Bleier, R. (1984) *Science and Gender: a Critique of Biology and its Theories on Women*, New York: Pergamon Press.

Boderhorn B. (1993) 'Gendered spaces, public places: public and private revisited on the North Slope of Alaska', in B. Bender (ed.) *Landscape: Politics and Perspectives*, 169–203. London: Berg.

Bolen K. (1992) 'Prehistoric construction of mothering', in C. Claassen (ed.) *Exploring Gender through Archaeology*, 49–62. Madison WI: Prehistory Press.

Bolin, A. (1996) 'Traversing gender: cultural context and gender practices', in S. P. Ramet (ed.) *Gender Reversals and Gender Cultures*, 22–51. London: Routledge.

Bourdieu, P. (1970) 'The Berber house or the world reversed', *Social Science Information*, 9: 151–70.

——(1977) *Outline of a Theory of Practice*, Cambridge: Cambridge University Press.

——(1990) *The Logic of Practice*, Cambridge: Polity Press.

Breuil, H. (1949) *Beyond the Bounds of History*, London: Gawthorn Press.

Bridges, P. S. (1989) 'Changes in activities with the shift to agriculture in the southeastern United States', *Current Anthropology*, 30: 385–94.

Brooks, A. (1997) *Postfeminisms: Feminism, Cultural Theory and Cultural Forms*, London: Routledge.

Brown, J. (1970) 'A note on the division of labor by sex', *American Anthropologist*, 72: 1073–78.

——(1982) 'Cross-cultural perspectives on middle-aged women', *Current Anthropology*, 23.2: 143–56.

Brown, K. A. (1998) 'Gender and sex: what can ancient DNA tell us?', *Ancient Biomolecules*, 2: 3–15.

Browne, K. (1998) *Divided Labours: An Evolutionary View of Women at Work*, London: Weidenfeld and Nicholson.

Bumsted, M. P., Booker, J. E., Barnes, R. M., Boutton, T. W., Amelagos, G. J., Lerman J. C. and Brendel, K. (1990) 'Recognizing women in the archeological record', in S. M. Nelson and A. B. Kehoe (eds) *Powers of Observation: Alternative Views in Archaeology*, 89–101. Washington DC: American Anthropological Association.

Brumbach, H. J. and Jarvenpa, R. (1997) 'Woman the hunter: ethnoarchaeological lessons from Chipewyan life-cycle dynamics', in C. Claassen and R. Joyce (eds) *Women in Prehistory*, 17–32. Philadelphia: University of Pennsylvania Press.

Brumfiel, E. M. (1991) 'Weaving and cooking: women's production in Aztec Mexico', in J. M. Gero and M. W. Conkey (eds) *Engendering Archaeology: Women and Prehistory*, 224–51. Oxford: Blackwell.

——(1996) 'Figurines and the Aztec state: testing the effectiveness of ideological domination', in R. P. Wright (ed.) *Gender and Archaeology*, 143–66. Philadelphia: University of Pennsylvania Press.

Burns, E. J. (1997) 'Refashioning courtly love: Lancelot as ladies' man or lady/man', in K. Lochrie, P. McCracken and J. A. Schultz (eds) *Constructing Medieval Sexuality*, 111–34. Minneapolis MN: University of Minnesota Press.

Butler, J. (1990) *Gender Trouble. Feminism and the Subversion of Identity*, London: Routledge.

——(1993) *Bodies that Matter: On the Discursive Limits of 'Sex'*, London: Routledge.

Bynum, C. W. (1987) *Holy Feast and Holy Fast: the Religious Significance of Food to Medieval Women*, Berkeley CA: University of California Press.

——(1995) *The Resurrection of the Body in Western Christianity, 200–1336*, New York: Columbia University Press.

Cadden, J. (1995) [1993] *Meanings of Sex Difference in the Middle Ages: Medicine, Science and Culture*, Cambridge: Cambridge University Press.

Callender, C. and Kochems, L. M. (1983) 'The North American Berdache', *Current Anthropology*, 24.4: 443–70.

Caplan, P. (ed.) (1987) *The Cultural Construction of Sexuality*, London: Routledge.

——(1997) *Food, Health and Identity*, London: Routledge.

Chamberlain, A. T. (1997) 'Commentary: missing stages of life – towards the perception of children in archaeology', in J. Moore and E. Scott (eds) *Invisible People and Processes*, 248–50. London: Leicester University Press.

Chapman, J. (1998) 'The impact of modern invasions and migrations on archaeological explanation. A biographical sketch of Marija Gimbutas', in M. Díaz-Andreu and M. L. S. Sørensen (eds) *Excavating Women: A History of Women in European Archaeology*, 295–314. London: Routledge.

Cherry, J. (1994) *The Middleham Jewel and Ring*, York: The Yorkshire Museum.

Chibnall, M. (ed.) (1969–80) *The Ecclesiastical History of Orderic Vitalis*, 6 vols, Oxford: Clarendon.

Claassen, C. (1997) 'Changing venue: women's lives in prehistoric North America', in C. Claassen and R. A. Joyce (eds) (1997) *Women in Prehistory: North America and Mesoamerica*, 65–87. Philadelphia PA: University of Pennsylvania Press.

Claassen, C. (ed.) (1992) *Exploring Gender in Archaeology: Selected Papers from the 1991 Boone Conference*, Madison WI: Prehistory Press.

——(1994) *Women in Archaeology*, Philadelphia: University of Pennsylvania Press.

Claassen, C. and Joyce, R. A. (1997) 'Women in the Ancient Americas: archaeologists, gender and the making of prehistory', in C. Claassen and R. Joyce (eds) *Women in Prehistory: North America and Mesoamerica*, 1–14. Philadelphia PA: University of Pennsylvania Press.

Claassen, C. and Joyce, R. A. (eds) (1997) *Women in Prehistory: North America and Mesoamerica*, Philadelphia: University of Pennsylvania Press.

Clarke, D. (1972) 'A provisional model of an Iron Age society and its settlement system', in D. Clarke (ed.) *Models in Archaeology*, 801–69. London: Methuen.

Coles, J. and Minnitt, S. (1995) *'Industrial and fairly civilized': The Glastonbury Lake Village*, Taunton: Somerset County Council Museums Service.

Collier, J. and Rosaldo, M. (1981) 'Politics and gender in simple societies', in S. Ortner and H. Whitehead (eds) *Sexual Meanings*, 275–329. Cambridge: Cambridge University Press.

Colomer, E., Gili, S., González-Marcén, P., Monton, S., Picazo, M., Rihuete, C., Ruiz, M., Sanahuja, M. E. and Tenas, M. (1994) 'Género y arqueología: las mujeres en la prehistoria', *Arqrítica*, 6: 5–8.

Conkey, M. W. and Gero, J. M. (1991) 'Tensions, plurality and engendering archaeology', in J. M. Gero and M. W. Conkey (eds)*Engendering Archaeology: Women and Prehistory*, 3–30. Oxford: Blackwell.

Conkey, M. W. and Spector, J. (1984) 'Archaeology and the study of gender', *Archaeological Method and Theory*, 7: 1–38. New York: Academic Press.

Connell, R. W. (1995) *Masculinities*, Cambridge: Polity Press.

Cook, A. M. and Dacre, M.W. (1985) *Excavations at Portway, Andover, 1973–5*, Oxford: Oxford Committee for Archaeology Monograph Series 4.

Cornwall, A. and Lindisfarne, N. (eds) (1994) *Dislocating Masculinity: Comparative Ethnographies*, London: Routledge.

Costin, C. L. (1996) 'Exploring the relationship between gender and craft in complex societies: methodological and theoretical issues of gender attribution', in R. P. Wright (ed.) *Gender and Archaeology*, 111–40. Philadelphia PA: University of Pennsylvania Press.

Coudart, A. (1998) 'Archaeology of French women and French women in Archaeology', in M. Díaz-Andreu and M. L. S. Sørensen (eds) *Excavating Women: A History of Women in European Archaeology*, 61–85. London: Routledge.

Counihan, C. and Van Esterik, P. (eds) (1997) *Food and Culture: A Reader*, London: Routledge.

Counts, D. A. (1982) 'Comment' on Brown, J. 'Cross-cultural perspectives on middle-aged women', *Current Anthropology*, 23.2: 149.

Crown, P. and Fish, S. (1996) 'Gender and status in the Hohokam pre-Classic to Classic tradition', *American Anthropologist*, 98.4: 803–17.

Cunliffe, B. and Munby, J. (1985) *Excavations at Portchester Castle, Volume IV: Medieval, the Inner Bailey*, London: Society of Antiquaries.

Dahlberg, F. (ed.) (1981) *Woman the Gatherer*, New Haven CT: Yale University Press.

Daniell, C. (1997) *Death and Burial in Medieval England, 1066–1550*, London: Routledge.

Darwin, C. (1859) *The Origin of Species*, London: John Murray.

——(1871) *The Descent of Man, and Selection in Relation to Sex*, London: John Murray.

Davis, J. (1991) *Times and Identities: An Inaugural Lecture*, Oxford: Clarendon Press.

Dawkins, R. (1976) *The Selfish Gene*, Oxford: Oxford University Press.

de Beauvoir, S. (1972) [1949] *The Second Sex*, Harmondsworth: Penguin.

De Pisan, C. (1985) [1405] *The Treasure of the City of Ladies or The Book of the Three Virtues*, Harmondsworth: Penguin.

Deckard, B. (1975) *The Women's Movement: Political, Socio-Economic and Psychological Issues*, New York: Harper and Row.

Derevenski, J. Sofaer (1997a) 'Age and gender at the site of Tiszapolgár-Basatanya, Hungary', *Antiquity*, 71: 875–89.

——(1997b) 'Linking age and gender as social variables', *Ethnographische-Archäeologische Zeitschrift*, 38: 485–93.

——(1997c) 'Engendering children, engendering archaeology', in J. Moore and E. Scott (eds) *Invisible People and Processes*, 192–202. London: Leicester University Press.

Díaz-Andreu, M. and Sørensen, M. L. S. (1998) 'Towards an engendered history of archaeology', in M. Díaz-Andreu and M. L. S. Sørensen (eds) *Excavating Women: A History of Women in European Archaeology*, 1–28. London: Routledge.

Dobres, M. C. (1995) 'Gender and prehistoric technology: on the social agency of technical strategies', *World Archaeology*, 27.1: 25–49.

Dommasnes, L. H. (1992) 'Two decades of women in prehistory and in archaeology in Norway: a review', *Norwegian Archaeological Review*, 25.1: 1–14.

Dommasnes, L. H., Kleppe, E. J., Mandt, G. and Naess, J. (1998) 'Women archaeologists in retrospect: the Norwegian case', in M. Díaz-Andreu and M. L. S. Sørensen (eds) *Excavating Women: A History of Women in European Archaeology*, 105–24. London: Routledge.

Donaldson, E. T. (trans.) (1966) *Beowulf: A New Prose Translation*, New York: Norton.

Douglas, M. (1966) *Purity and Danger: An Analysis of Concepts of Pollution and Taboo*, London: Routledge.

——(1970) *Natural Symbols: Explorations in Cosmology*, Harmondsworth: Penguin.

Duby, G. (1997) *Women of the Twelfth Century, Volume One: Eleanor of Aquitaine and Six Others*, Cambridge: Polity Press.

——(1998) *Women of the Twelfth Century, Volume Two: Remembering the Dead*, Cambridge: Polity Press.

du Cros, H. and Smith, L. (eds) (1993) *Women in Archaeology: A Feminist Critique*, Canberra: Australian National University.

Duffy, E. (1990) 'Holy maydens, holy wyfes: the cult of women saints in fifteenth and sixteenth-century England', *Studies in Church History*, 23: 175–96.

Durkheim, E. (1965) *The Elementary Forms of Social Life* (trans. J. W. Swain) New York: The Free Press.

Egan, G. (1997) 'Children's pastimes in past time: medieval toys found in the British Isles', in G. de Boe and F. Verhaeghe (eds) *Material Culture in Medieval Europe: Papers of the Medieval Europe Brugge 1997 Conference*, vol. 7: 413–20. Brugge: Zellik.

Engels, F. (1884) *The Origins of the Family, Private Property and the State*, Stuttgart: Dietz.

Engelstad, E. (1991) 'Images of Power and Contradiction: feminist theory and post-processual archaeology', *Antiquity*, 65: 502–14.

Engelstad, E., Mandt, G. and Naess, J. (1994) 'Equity issues in Norwegian archeology', in M. C. Nelson, S. M. Nelson and A. Wylie (eds) *Equity Issues for Women in Archeology*, 139–45. Archeological Papers of the American Anthropological Association no. 5.

Evison, V. I (1987) *Dover: The Buckland Anglo-Saxon Cemetery*, London: Historic Buildings and Monuments Commission Archaeological Reports 3.

Fairclough, G. (1992) 'Meaningful constructions: spatial and functional analysis of medieval buildings', *Antiquity*, 66: 348–66.

Falk, D. (1993) 'Sex differences in visuo-spatial skills: implications for hominid evolution', in K. R. Gibson and T. Ingold (eds) *Tools, Language and Cognition in Human Evolution*, 216–29. Cambridge: Cambridge University Press.

——(1997) 'Brain evolution in females: an answer to Mr Lovejoy', in L. D. Hager (ed.) *Women in Human Evolution*, 114–36. London: Routledge.

Fausto-Sterling, A. (1995) 'How to build a man', in R. N. Lancaster and M. Di Leonardo (eds) *The Gender/Sexuality Reader*, 244–8. London: Routledge.

Faulkner, P. A. (1963) 'Castle planning in the fourteenth century', *Archaeological Journal*, 120: 150–83.

——(1970) 'Some medieval archiepiscopal palaces', *Archaeological Journal*, 127: 130–46

Featherstone, M. and Wernick, A. (eds) (1995) *Images of Aging: Cultural Representations of Later Life*, London: Routledge.

Fedigan, L. M. (1986) 'The changing role of women in models of human evolution', *Annual Review of Anthropology*, 15: 22–66.

——(1992) *Primate Paradigms: Sex Roles and Social Bonds*, Chicago IL: University of Chicago Press.

——(1997) 'Is primatology a feminist science?' in L. D. Hager (ed.) *Women in Human Evolution*, 56–75. London: Routledge.

Fell, C. (1984) *Women in Anglo-Saxon England*, Oxford: Blackwell.

Finlay, N. (1997) 'Kid knapping: the missing children in lithic analysis', in J. Moore and E. Scott (eds) *Invisible People and Processes*, 203–12. London: Leicester University Press.

Finucane, R. C. (1977) *Miracles and Pilgrims: Popular Beliefs in Medieval England*, London: Dent.

Flannery, K. and Winter, M. (1976) 'Analyzing household activities', in K. V. Flannery (ed.) *The Early Mesoamerican Village*, 810–69. New York: Academic Press.

Foucault, M. (1981) *The History of Sexuality, Volume I: An Introduction*, Harmondsworth: Penguin.

——(1985) *The Use of Pleasure: The History of Sexuality, Volume II*, Harmondsworth: Penguin.

——(1986) *The Care of the Self: The History of Sexuality, Volume III*, Harmondsworth: Penguin.

Foxhall, L. (1994) 'Pandora unbound: a feminist critique of Foucault's *History of Sexuality*', in A. Cornwall and N. Lindisfarne (eds) *Dislocating Masculinity*, 133–146. London: Routledge.

Foxhall, L. and Salmon, J. (eds) (1998) *Thinking Men: Masculinity and its Self-Representation in the Classical Tradition*, London: Routledge.

Fredsjo, Å. (1981) *Hällristningar Kville härad i Bohnslän Kville Socken*, Gothenburg: Studies in Northern European Archaeology 14/15.

Freud, S. (1905) 'Three essays on the theory of sexuality', in *On Sexuality* (1977) Harmondsworth: Penguin.

Fulton, R. and Anderson, S. W. (1992) 'The Amer-Indian "man-woman": gender, liminality and cultural continuity', *Current Anthropology*, 33: 603–10.

Galloway, P. (1997) 'Where have all the menstrual huts gone? The invisibility of menstrual seclusion in the late Prehistoric southeast', in C. Claassen and R. A. Joyce (eds) *Women in Prehistory:*, 47–62. Philadelphia PA: University of Pennsylvania Press.

Gebürh, M. (1997) 'The Holsteinian housewife and the Danish diva: early Germanic female images in Tacitus and cemetery evidence', *Norwegian Archaeological Review*, 30.2: 113–22.

Geertz, C. (1988) *Works and Lives: The Anthropologist as Author*, Cambridge: Polity Press.

Gero, J. M. (1985) 'Socio-politics and the Woman-at-Home ideology', *American Antiquity*, 50: 342–50.

——(1991a) 'Gender divisions of labor in the construction of archaeological knowledge', in D. Walde and N. D. Willows (eds) *The Archaeology of Gender*, 96–102. Calgary: University of Calgary Archaeological Association.

——(1991b) 'Genderlithics', in J. M. Gero and M. W. Conkey (eds) *Engendering Archaeology: Women and Prehistory*, 163–93. Oxford: Blackwell.

——(1992) 'Feasts and females: gender ideology and political meals in the Andes', *Norwegian Archaeological Review*, 25.1: 15–30.

Gero, J. M. and Conkey, M. W. (eds) (1991) *Engendering Archaeology: Women and Prehistory*, Oxford: Blackwell.

Gibb, J. G. and King, J. A. (1991) 'Gender, activity areas and homelots in the 17th-century Chesapeake Region', *Historical Archaeology*, 25.4: 109–131.

Gibbs, L. (1987) 'Identifying gender representation in the archaeological record: a contextual study', in I. Hodder (ed.) *The Archaeology of Contextual Meanings*, 79–89. Cambridge: Cambridge University Press.

Gifford-Gonzalez, D. (1993) 'You can hide, but you can't run: representation of women's work in illustrations of Palaeolithic life', *Visual Anthropology Review*, 9.1: 21–41.

Gilchrist, R. (1991) 'Women's archaeology? Political feminism, gender theory and historical revision', *Antiquity*, 65: 495–501.

——(1994) *Gender and Material Culture: the Archaeology of Religious Women*, London: Routledge.

——(1995) *Contemplation and Action: the Other Monasticism*, London: Leicester University Press.

——(1997) 'Ambivalent bodies: gender and medieval archaeology', in J. Moore and E. Scott (eds) *Invisible People*, 42–58. London: Leicester University Press.

——(1999) 'Landscapes of the middle ages: churches, castles and monasteries', in J. Hunter and I. Ralston (eds) *The Archaeology of Britain*, 228–46. London: Routledge.

Gimbutas, M. (1989) *The Language of the Goddess*, London: Thames and Hudson.

Ginn, J. and Arber, S. (1995) ' "Only connect": gender relations and ageing', in S. Arber and J. Ginn (eds) *Connecting Gender and Ageing: a Sociological Approach*, 1–14. Buckingham: Open University Press.

Girouard, M. (1978) *Life in the English Country House*, London: Yale University Press.

Goldberg, P. J. P. (1992) *Women, Work, and Life Cycle in a Medieval Economy: Women in York and Yorkshire, c. 1300–1520*, Oxford: Clarendon Press.

Golombok, S. and Fivush, R. (1994) *Gender Development*, Cambridge: Cambridge University Press.

González Marcén, P. (1992) 'Cronologia del grupo argárico. Ensayo de fasificación radio-métrica a partir de la curva de calibración de alta precisión', doctoral thesis, Barcelona: Universitat Autónoma de Barcelona.

Gosden, C. (1994) *Social Being and Time*, Oxford: Blackwell.

Gould, R. A. (1980) *Living Archaeology*, Cambridge: Cambridge University Press.

Graves, C. P. (1989) 'Social space in the English medieval parish church', *Economy and Society*, 18.3: 297–322.

Grauer, A. L. and Stuart-Macadam, P. (eds) (1998) *Sex and Gender in Paleopathological Perspective*, Cambridge: Cambridge University Press.

Green, M. (1997) 'Images in opposition: polarity, ambivalence and liminality in cult representation', *Antiquity*, 71: 898–911.

Grémaux, R. (1994) 'Woman becomes man in the Balkans', in G. Herdt (ed.) *Third Sex, Third Gender: Beyond Sexual Dimorphism in Culture and History*, 241–81. New York: Zone Books.

Grössinger, C. (1997) *Picturing Women in Late Medieval and Renaissance Art*, Manchester: Manchester University Press.

Grosz, E. and Probyn, E. (eds) (1995) *Sexy Bodies: The Strange Carnalities of Feminism*, London: Routledge.

Gunew, S. (ed.) (1991) *A Reader in Feminist Knowledge*, London: Routledge.

Haaland, G. and Haaland, R. (1995) 'Who speaks the Goddess' language? Imagination and method in archaeological research', *Norwegian Archaeological Review*, 28.2: 105–21.

Hager, L. (1997) 'Sex and gender in paleoanthropology', in L. D. Hager (ed.) *Women in Human Evolution*, 1–28. London: Routledge.

Hager, L. (ed.) (1997) *Women in Human Evolution*, London: Routledge.

Halpern, D. (1992) *Sex Differences in Cognitive Abilities*, New Jersey: L. Erlbaum.

Hanawalt, B. (1986) *The Ties that Bound: Peasant Families in Medieval England*, Oxford: Oxford University Press.

Hanen, M. and Kelley, J. (1992) 'Gender and archaeological knowledge', in L. Embree (ed.) *Metaarchaeology*, 195–225. The Netherlands: Kluwer Academic Publishers.

Haraway, D. (1989) *Primate Visions: Gender, Race and Nature in the World of Modern Science*, New York: Routledge.

Harding, S. (1983) 'Why has the sex/gender system become visible only now?' in S. Harding and M. B. Hintikka (eds) *Discovering Reality: Feminist Perspectives on Epistemology, Metaphysics, Methodology and Philosophy of Science*, 311–24. Dordrecht: Reidel.

——(1986) *The Science Question in Feminism*, Ithaca NY: Cornell University Press.

——(1991) *Whose Science? Whose Knowledge? Thinking from Women's Lives*, Milton Keynes: Open University Press.

——(1993) 'Reinventing ourselves as other: more new agents of history and knowledge', in L. Kauffman (ed.) *American Feminist Thought at Century's End: A Reader*, Oxford: Blackwell.

Härke, H. (1989) 'Knives in early Saxon burials: blade length and age at death', *Medieval Archaeology*, 33: 144–8.

——(1990) 'Warrior graves? The background of the Anglo-Saxon weapon burial rite', *Past and Present*, 126: 22–43.

Harvey, J. (1981) *Mediaeval Gardens*, London: Batsford.

Hastorf, C. (1991) 'Gender, space and food in prehistory', in J. M. Gero and M. W. Conkey (eds) *Engendering Archaeology: Women and Prehistory*, 132–59. Oxford: Blackwell.

Hawkes, K., O'Connell, J. F. and Blurton, N. G. (1997) 'Hadza women's time allocation, offspring provisioning, and the evolution of long post-menopausal life spans', *Current Anthropology*, 38.4: 551–77.

Hawking, S. W. (1988) *A Brief History of Time*, London: Bantam.

Hays-Gilpin, K. and. Whitley, D. S. (eds) (1998) *Reader in Gender Archaeology*, London: Routledge.

Heidegger, M. (1962) [1927] *Being and Time*, trans. J. Macquarrie and E. Robinson, Oxford: Blackwell.

Herdt, G. (1987) *The Sambia: Ritual and Gender in New Guinea*, New York: Holt, Rinehart and Winston.

——(1994) 'Introduction: third sexes and third genders', in G. Herdt (ed.) *Third Sex, Third Gender: Beyond Sexual Dimorphism in Culture and History*, 21–81. New York: Zone Books.

Heslop, T. A. (1991) 'Orford Castle, nostalgia and sophisticated living', *Architectural History*, 34: 36–58.

——(1994) *Norwich Castle Keep: Romanesque Architecture and Social Context*, Norwich: Centre of East Anglian Studies.

Hill, E. (1998) 'Gender-informed archaeology: the priority of definition, the use of analogy, and the multivariate approach', *Journal of Archaeological Method and Theory*, 5.1: 99–128.

Hingley, R. (1990) 'Domestic organization and gender relations in Iron Age and Romano-British households', in R. Samson (ed.) *The Social Archaeology of Houses*, 125–47. Edinburgh: Edinburgh University Press.

Hinton, D. (1990) *Archaeology, Economy and Society: England from the Fifth to the Fifteenth Century*, London: Seaby.

Hitchcock, L. A. (1997) 'Engendering domination: a structural and contextual analysis of Minoan and Neopalatial bronze figures', in J. Moore and E. Scott (eds) *Invisible People and Processes*, 113–30. London: Leicester University Press.

Hodder, I. (1984) 'Burials, houses, women and men in the European Neolithic, in D. Miller and C. Tilley (eds) *Ideology, Power and Prehistory*, 51–68. Cambridge: Cambridge University Press.

——(1986) *Reading the Past: Current Approaches to Interpretation in Archaeology*, Cambridge: Cambridge University Press.

——(1990) *The Domestication of Europe*, Oxford: Blackwell.

——(1991) 'Gender representation and social reality', in D. Walde and N. D. Willows (ed.) *The Archaeology of Gender*, 11–16. Calgary: University of Calgary Archaeological Association. Reprinted in I. Hodder (1995) *Theory and Practice in Archaeology*, 254–62. London: Routledge.

Hodder, I. (ed.) (1982) *Symbolic and Structural Archaeology*, Cambridge: Cambridge University Press.

——(1987) *The Archaeology of Contextual Meanings*, Cambridge: Cambridge University Press.

Hollimon, S. E. (1992) 'Health consequences of sexual division of labor among prehistoric Native Americans: the Chumash of California and the Arikara of the North Plains', in C. Claassen (ed.) *Exploring Gender in Archaeology*, 81–8. Madison WI: Prehistory Press.

——(1997) 'The third gender in Native California: two-spirit undertakers among the Chumash and their neighbours', in C. Claassen and R. A. Joyce (eds) *Women in Prehistory*, 173–88. Philadelphia PA: University of Pennsylvania Press.

Horgan, F. (1994) *The Romance of the Rose. By Guillaume de Lorris and Jean de Meun*, Oxford: Oxford University Press.

Hudecek-Cuffe, C. R. (1998) *Engendering Northern Plains Paleoindian Archaeology: Decision-making and Gender Roles in Subsistence and Settlement Strategies*, Oxford: British Archaeological Reports International Series 699.

Humm, M. (1995) *The Dictionary of Feminist Theory. Second Edition*, London: Prentice Hall/Harvester Wheatsheaf.

Hurcombe, L. (1995) 'Our own engendered species', *Antiquity*, 69: 87–100.

Irigaray, L. (1985) *The Sex Which is Not One*, Ithaca NY: Cornell University Press.

James, L. (ed.) (1997) *Women, Men and Eunuchs: Gender in Byzantium*, London: Routledge.

James, T. B. (1990) *The Palaces of Medieval England, c. 1050–1550*, London: Seaby.

James, T. B. and Robinson, A. M. (1988) *Clarendon Palace: The History and Archaeology of a Medieval Palace and Hunting Lodge near Salisbury, Wiltshire*, London: Society of Antiquaries Report 45.

Jesch, J. (1991) *Women in the Viking Age*, Woodbridge: Boydell.

Jones, R. (1984) *Carisbrooke Castle: a tour of the castle through the ages*, Carisbrooke: Carisbrooke Castle Museum.

Jones, S. and Pay, S. (1990) 'The legacy of Eve', in P. Gathercole and D. Lowenthal (eds) *The Politics of the Past*, 160–71. London: Unwin Hyman.

Jordanova, L. (1989) *Sexual Visions*, London: Harvester Wheatsheaf.

Joyce, R. A. (1992) 'Images of gender and labor organization in Classic Maya society', in C. Claassen (ed.) *Exploring Gender in Archaeology*, 63–70. Madison WI: Prehistory Press.

——(1996) 'The construction of gender in Classic Maya monuments', in R. P. Wright (ed.) *Gender and Archaeology*, 167–95. Philadelphia PA: University of Pennsylvania Press.

Joyce, R. A. and Claassen, C. (1997) 'Women in the Ancient Americas: archaeologists, gender and the making of prehistory', in C. Claassen and R. A. Joyce (eds) *Women in Prehistory*, 1–14. Philadelphia PA: University of Pennsylvania Press.

Kampen, N. B. (1996) 'Introduction', in *Sexuality in Ancient Art: 1–10*, Cambridge: Cambridge University Press.

Kampen, N. B. (ed.) (1996) *Sexuality in Ancient Art: Near East, Egypt, Greece and Italy*, Cambridge: Cambridge University Press.

Keith, J. (1985) 'Age in anthropological research', in R. H. Binstock and E. Shanas (eds) *Handbook of Aging and the Social Sciences*, 231–63. New York: Van Nostrand Reinhold.

Keller, E. F. (1984)*Reflections on Gender and Science*, New Haven CT: Yale University Press.

Kelly-Gadol, J. (1976) 'The social relations of the sexes: methodological implications of women's history', *Signs: the Journal of Women in Culture and Society*, 1: 809–23.

Kent, S. (1990) 'A cross-cultural study of segmentation, architecture, and the use of space', in S. Kent (ed.) *Domestic Architecture and the Use of Space*, 127–52. Cambridge: Cambridge University Press.

Kent, S. (ed.) (1998) *Gender in African Prehistory*, Walnut Creek CA: AltaMira Press.

Kenyon, J. R. (1990) *Medieval Fortifications*, London: Leicester University Press.

Kinsey, A. C., Pomeroy, W. B. and Martin, C. E. (1948) *Sexual Behavior in the Human Male*, Philadelphia PA: W. B. Saunders.

Kitson, S. (1997) 'Medieval noblewomen and castles', unpublished B.A. dissertation, University of Reading.

Knapp, A. B. (1998) 'Boys will be boys: masculinist approaches to a gendered archaeology', in K. Hays-Gilpin and D. S. Whitley (eds) *Reader in Gender Archaeology*, 365–73. London: Routledge.

Knapp, B. and Meskell, L. (1997) 'Bodies of evidence in Cypriot prehistory', *Cambridge Archaeological Journal*, 7.2: 183–204.

Knight, C. (1991) *Blood Relations: Menstruation and the Origins of Culture*, London: Yale University Press.

Knight, J. K. (1991) *Chepstow Castle*, Cardiff: CADW Welsh Historic Monuments.

Kokkinidou, D. and Nikolaidou, M. (1997) 'Body imagery in the Aegean Neolithic: ideological implications of anthropomorphic figurines' in J. Moore and E. Scott (eds) *Invisible People and Processes*, 88–112. London: Leicester University Press.

Koloski-Ostrow, A. and Lyons, C. L. (eds) (1997) *Naked Truths: Women, Sexuality and Gender in Classical Art and Archaeology*, London: Routledge.

Kuhn, T. (1962) *The Structure of Scientific Revolutions*, Chicago IL: University of Chicago Press.

Labarge, M. W. (1965) *A Baronial Household of the Thirteenth Century*, London: Eyre and Spottiswoode.

La Fontaine, J. S. (1985) *Initiation: Ritual Drama and Secret Knowledge across the World*, Harmondsworth: Penguin.

Landsberg, S. (1998) *The Medieval Garden*, London: British Museum Press.

Laqueur, T. W. (1987) 'Orgasm, generation, and the politics of reproductive biology', in C. Gallagher (ed.) *The Making of the Modern Body*, 1–41. Berkeley CA: University of California Press.

——(1990) *Making Sex: Body and Gender from the Greeks to Freud*, Cambridge MA: Harvard University Press.

Larsen, C. S. (1997) *Bioarchaeology: Interpreting Behavior from the Human Skeleton*, Cambridge: Cambridge University Press.

Laslett, P. (1995) 'Necessary knowledge: age and aging in the societies of the past', in D. I. Kertzer and P. Laslett (eds) *Aging in the Past: Demography, Society and Old Age*, 3–77. Berkeley CA: University of California Press.

Lee, R. B. (1968) 'What hunters do for a living, or how to make out on scarce resources', in R. Lee and I. DeVore (eds) *Man the Hunter*, 30–48. Chicago IL: Aldine.

——(1979) *The !Kung San: Men, Women and Work in a Foraging Society*, Cambridge: Cambridge University Press.

Lee, R. B. and DeVore, I. (eds) (1968) *Man the Hunter*, Chicago IL: Aldine.

Lees, C. A. (1994) *Medieval Masculinities: Regarding Men in the Middle Ages*, Minneapolis MN: University of Minnesota Press.

LeVay, S. (1993) *The Sexual Brain*, Cambridge MA: MIT Press.

Lévi-Strauss, C. (1969) *The Elementary Structures of Kinship*, London: Tavistock.

Lillehammer, G. (1989) 'A child is born: the child's world in an archaeological perspective', *Norwegian Archaeological Review*, 22: 89–105.

Linton, S. (1971) 'Woman the gatherer: male bias in anthropology', in S. E. Jacobs (ed.) *Women in Perspective: A Guide for Cross-Cultural Studies*, 9–21. Urbana IL: University of Illinois Press.

Lochrie, K. (1997) 'Mystical acts, queer tendencies', in K. Lochrie, P. McCracken and J. A. Schultz (eds) *Constructing Medieval Sexuality*, 180–200. Minneapolis MN: University of Minnesota Press.

Lovejoy, C. O. (1981) 'The origin of man', *Science*, 211: 341–50.

Lucy, S. J. (1997) 'Housewives, warriors and slaves? Sex and gender in Anglo-Saxon burials', in J. Moore and E. Scott (eds) *Invisible People and Processes*, 150–68. London: Leicester University Press.

Lutkehaus, N. C. (1995) 'Feminist anthropology and female initiation in Melanesia', in N. C. Lutkehaus and P. B. Roscoe (eds) *Gender Rituals*, 3–29. London: Routledge.

Lutkehaus, N. C. and Roscoe, P. B. (eds) (1995) *Gender Rituals: Female Initiation in Melanesia*, London: Routledge.

Lyons, C. L. and Koloski-Ostrow, A. (1997) 'Naked truths about classical art: an introduction', in A. Koloski-Ostrow and C. L. Lyons (eds) *Naked Truths*, 1–11. London: Routledge.

Lyons, D. (1998) 'Witchcraft, gender, power and intimate relations in Mura compounds in Déla, northern Cameroon', *World Archaeology*, 29.3: 344–62.

McDermott, L. (1996) 'Self-representation in Upper Paleolithic female figurines', *Current Anthropology*, 37.2: 227–48.

McDowell, L. (1996) 'Spatializing feminism: geographical perspectives', in N. Duncan (ed.) *Body Space: Destabilizing Geographies of Gender and Sexuality*, 28–44. London: Routledge.

McElhinny, B. (1994) 'An economy of affect: objectivity, masculinity and the gendering of police work', in A. Cornwall and N. Lindisfarne (eds) *Dislocating Masculinity*, 159–71. London: Routledge.

McEwan, B. G. (1991) 'The archaeology of women in the Spanish New World', *Historical Archaeology*, 25.4: 33–41.

McLean, T. (1981) *Medieval English Gardens*, London: Collins.

McNeill, T. (1992) *Castles*, London: English Heritage/Batsford.

Mandt, G. (1987) 'Female symbolism in rock art', in R. Bertelsen, A. Lillehammer and J. Naess (eds) *Were They all Men?*, 65–77. Norway: Stavanger.

Marcus, M. (1996) 'Sex and the politics of female adornment in pre-Achaemenid Iran', in N. Kampen (ed.) *Sexuality in Ancient Art*, 41–54. Cambridge: Cambridge University Press.

Mayes, P. and Butler, L. (1983) *Sandal Castle Excavations 1964–73: A Detailed Archaeological Report*, Wakefield: Wakefield Historical Publications.

Meaney, A. L. (1981) *Anglo-Saxon Amulets and Curing Stones*, Oxford: British Archaeological Report 96.

Meillassoux, C. (1981) *Maidens, Meal and Money*, Cambridge: Cambridge University Press.

Merleau-Ponty, M. (1962) [1945] *The Phenomenology of Perception*, London: Routledge.

Mertes, K. (1988) *The English Noble Household 1250–1600: Good Governance and Political Rule*, Oxford: Blackwell.

Meskell, L. (1995) 'Goddesses, Gimbutus and the "New Age" Archaeology', *Antiquity*, 69: 74–86.

——(1996) 'The somatisation of archaeology: discourses, institutions, corporeality', *Norwegian Archaeological Review*, 29.1: 1–16.

——(1998a) 'An archaeology of social relations in an Egyptian village', *Journal of Archaeological Method and Theory*, 5.3: 209–43.

——(1998b) 'The irresistible body and the seduction of archaeology', in D. Montserrat (ed.) *Changing Bodies, Changing Meanings: Studies on the Human Body in Antiquity*, 139–61. London: Routledge.

——(1999) *Archaeologies of Social Life: Age, Sex, Class, etc. in Ancient Egypt*, Oxford: Blackwell.

Millett, B. (1982) *Hali Meidhad*, Early English Text Society 284. Oxford: Oxford University Press.

Millett, B. and Wogan-Browne, J. (eds) (1990) *Medieval English Prose for Women: Selections from the Katherine Group and Ancrene Wisse*, Oxford: Clarendon.

Moi, T. (ed.) (1987) *French Feminist Thought: A Reader*, Oxford: Blackwell.

Molleson, T. (1994) 'The eloquent bones of Abu Hureyra', *Scientific American*, 271.2: 60–65.

Moore, H. L. (1986) *Space, Text and Gender: An Anthropological Study of the Marakwet of Kenya*, Cambridge: Cambridge University Press.

——(1988) *Feminism and Anthropology*, Cambridge: Polity Press.

——(1993) 'The differences within and the differences between', in T. Del Valle (ed.) *Gendered Anthropology*, 193–204. London: Routledge.

——(1994) *A Passion for Difference*, Cambridge: Polity Press.

Moore, J. and Scott, E. (1997) (eds) *Invisible People and Processes: Writing Gender and Childhood into European Archaeology*, London: Leicester University Press.

Moorhouse, S. (1991) 'Ceramics in the medieval garden', in A. E. Brown (ed.) *Garden Archaeology*, 100–17. London: Council for British Archaeology.

Montserrat, D. (ed.) (1998) *Changing Bodies, Changing Meanings: Studies on the Human Body in Antiquity*, London: Routledge.

Morley, B. and Gurney, D. (1997) *Castle Rising Castle, Norfolk*, East Anglian Archaeology 81. Dereham: Norfolk Museums Service.

Morris, E. (1994) 'Extracts from *Women in British Archaeology*', in M. C. Nelson, S. M. Nelson and A. Wylie (eds) *Equity Issues for Women in Archeology*, 203–12. Archeological Papers of the American Anthropological Association no. 5.

Mortet, V. (1911) 'Chronique de Lambert d'Ardres', in *Recueil des Texts Relatifs a l'Histoire de l'Architecture en France*, I, Paris.

Moser, S. (1993) 'Gender stereotyping in pictorial reconstructions of human origins', in L. Smith and H. duCros (eds) *Women in Archaeology*, 75–92. Canberra: Australian National University.

Mulvey, L. (1975) 'Visual pleasure and narrative cinema', *Screen*, 16.3: 6–19.

Murdock, G. P. (1937) 'Comparative data on the division of labor by sex', *Social Forces*, 15: 551–53.

Murdock, G. P. and Provost, C. (1973) 'Factors in the division of labor by sex: a cross-cultural analysis', *Ethnology*, 12: 203–25.

Nanda, S. (1994) 'Hijras: an alternative sex and gender role in India', in G. Herdt (ed.) *Third Sex, Third Gender: Beyond Sexual Dimorphism in Culture and History*, 373–417. New York: Zone Books.

Nelson, S. (1997) *Gender in Archaeology: Analyzing Power and Prestige*, Walnut Creek CA: AltaMira Press.

Nelson, M. C., Nelson, S. M. and Wylie, A. (eds) (1994) 'Equity issues for women in archeology', *Archeological Papers of the American Anthropological Association*, no. 5.

Nevett, L. (1994) 'Separation or seclusion? Towards an archaeological approach to investigating women in the Greek household in the fifth to third centuries BC', in M. Parker Pearson and C. Richards (eds) *Architecture and Order: Approaches to Social Space*, 98–112. London: Routledge.

Nikolaidou, M. and Kokkinidou, D. (1998) 'Greek women in archaeology', in M. Díaz-Andreu and M. L. S. Sørensen (eds) *Excavating Women: A History of Women in European Archaeology*, 266–94. London: Routledge.

Nordbladh, J. and Yates, T. (1990) 'This perfect body, this virgin text: between sex and gender in archaeology', in I. Bapty and T. Yates (eds) *Archaeology after Structuralism*, 222–37. London: Routledge.

Ortner, S. (1974) 'Is female to male as nature is to culture?' in M. Rosaldo and L. Lamphere (eds) *Woman, Culture and Society*, 67–88. Stanford CA: Stanford University Press.

——(1978) 'The virgin and the state', *Feminist Studies*, 4.3: 19–35.

——(1996) *Making Gender: The Politics and Erotics of Culture*, Boston MA: Beacon Press.

Ortner, S. and Whitehead, H. (eds) (1981) 'Introduction: accounting for sexual meanings', in S. Ortner and H. Whitehead (eds) *Sexual Meanings*, 1–27. Cambridge: Cambridge University Press.

——*Sexual Meanings: the Cultural Construction of Gender and Sexuality*, Cambridge: Cambridge University Press.

Owens, D. and Hayden, B. (1997) 'Prehistoric rites of passage: a comparative study of transegalitarian hunter-gatherers', *Journal of Anthropological Archaeology*, 16: 121–61.

Pader, E. J. (1982) *Symbolism, Social Relations and the Interpretation of Mortuary Remains*, Oxford: British Archaeological Report International Series 130.

Park, R. W. (1998) 'Size counts: the miniature archaeology of childhood in Inuit societies', *Antiquity*, 72: 269–81.

Parsons, J. Carmi (1994a) 'Family, sex and power: the rhythms of medieval queenship', in J. Carmi Parsons (ed.) *Medieval Queenship*, 1–11. Stroud: Sutton.

——(1994b) 'Mothers, daughters, marriage, power: some Plantagenet evidence, 1150–1500', in J. Carmi Parsons (ed.) *Medieval Queenship*, 63–92. Stroud: Sutton.

——(1997) ' "Never was a body buried in England with such solemnity and honour": the burials and posthumous commemoration of English queens to 1500', in A. J. Duggan (ed.) *Queens and Queenship in Medieval Europe*, 317–37. Woodbridge: Boydell.

Peacock, N. R. (1991) 'Rethinking the sexual division of labour: reproduction and women's work among the Efe', in M. di Leonardo (ed.) *Gender at the Crossroads of Knowledge: Feminist Anthropology in the Post-Modern Era*, 339–60. Berkeley CA: University of California Press.

Picazo, M. (1997) 'Hearth and home: the timing of maintenance activities', in J. Moore and E. Scott (eds) *Invisible People and Processes: Writing Gender and Childhood into European Archaeology*, 59–67. London: Leicester University Press.

——(1998) 'Fieldwork is not the proper preserve of a lady: the first women archaeologists in Crete', in M. Díaz-Andreu and M. L. S. Sørensen (eds) *Excavating Women: A History of Women in European Archaeology*, 198–213. London: Routledge.

Pouchelle, M. (1990) *The Body and Surgery in the Middle Ages*, Cambridge: Polity Press.

Pounds, N. J. G. (1990) *The Medieval Castle in England and Wales: a Social and Political History*, Cambridge: University Press.

Power, C. and Aiello, L. (1997) 'Female proto-symbolic strategies', in L. D. Hager (ed.) *Women in Human Evolution*, 153–71. London: Routledge.

Power, E. (ed.) (1928) *The Goodman of Paris*, c. *1393*, London: Routledge.

Pratt, K. (1997) 'The image of the queen in Old French literature', in A. J. Duggan (ed.) *Queens and Queenship in Medieval Europe*, 236–59. Woodbridge: Boydell.

Prentice, G. (1986) 'Origins of plant domestication in the Eastern United States: promoting the individual in archaeological theory', *Southeastern Archaeology*, 5: 103–19.

Pritchard, F. (1996) 'The textile industry AD 500–1500', in A. Devonshire and B. Wood (eds) *Women in Industry and Technology from Prehistory to the Present Day*, 111–24. London: Museum of London.

Ramet, S. P. (1996) 'Gender reversals and gender cultures: an introduction', in S. P. Ramet (ed.) *Gender Reversals and Gender Cultures: Anthropological and Historical Perspectives*, 1–21. London: Routledge.

Ramet, S. P. (ed.) (1996) *Gender Reversals and Gender Cultures: Anthropological and Historical Perspectives*, London: Routledge.

Rawcliffe, C. (1995) *Medicine and Society in Later Medieval England*, Stroud: Alan Sutton.

Redstone, V. B. (ed.) (1931) *The Household Book of Dame Alice de Bryene*, Ipswich: Suffolk Institute of Archaeology and Natural History.

Rega, E. (1997) 'Age, gender and biological reality in the Early Bronze Age cemetery at Mokrin', in J. Moore and E. Scott (eds) *Invisible People and Processes*, 229–47. London: Leicester University Press.

Reilly, J. (1997) 'Naked and limbless: learning about the feminine body in Ancient Athens', in A. Koloski-Ostrow and C. L. Lyons (eds) *Naked Truths*, 154–73. London: Routledge.

Rice, P. C. (1981) 'Prehistoric Venuses: symbols of motherhood or womanhood?', *Journal of Anthropological Research*, 37.4: 402–14.

Richardson, N. (1998) 'A new approach to the study of queens' apartments in medieval palaces', unpublished B.A. dissertation, King Alfred's University College, Winchester.

Ricoeur, P. (1988) *Time and Narrative. Volume 3*, Chicago IL: Chicago University Press.

Ringrose, K. M. (1994) 'Living in the shadows: eunuchs and gender in Byzantium', in G. Herdt (ed.) *Third Sex, Third Gender: Beyond Sexual Dimorphism in Culture and History*, 85–109. New York: Zone Books.

Robb, J. (1994) 'Gender contradictions, moral coalitions and inequality in Prehistoric Italy', *Journal of European Archaeology*, 2.1: 20–49.

——(1997) 'Female beauty and male violence in early Italian society', in A. Koloski-Ostrow, and C. L. Lyons (eds) *Naked Truths*, 43–65. London: Routledge.

Rodgers, R. (1995) 'Woman underfoot in life and art: female representations in fourth-century Romano-British mosaics', *Journal of European Archaeology*, 3.1: 177–87.

Rolle, R. (1989) *The World of the Scythians*, London: Batsford.

Rosaldo, M. Z. (1974) 'Woman, culture and society: a theoretical overview,' in M. Z. Rosaldo and L. Lamphere (eds) *Woman, Culture and Society*, 14–42. Stanford CA: Stanford University Press.

——(1980) 'The use and abuse of anthropology: reflections on feminism and cross-cultural understanding', *Signs: Journal of Women in Culture and Society*, 5.3: 389–417.

Rosaldo, M. Z. and Lamphere, L. (eds) (1974) *Woman, Culture and Society*, Stanford CA: Stanford University Press.

Roscoe, P. B. (1995) 'Initiation in cross-cultural perspective', in N. C. Lutkehaus and P. B. Roscoe (eds) *Gender Rituals*, 219–38. London: Routledge.

Roscoe, W. (1994) 'How to become a berdache: toward a unified analysis of gender diversity', in G. Herdt (ed.) *Third Sex, Third Gender: Beyond Sexual Dimorphism in Culture and History*, 329–72. New York: Zone Books.

Rubin, G. (1975) 'The traffic in women: notes on the "political economy" of sex', in R. Reiter (ed.) *Toward an Anthropology of Women*, 157–210. New York: Monthly Review Press.

Saladin, B. D'Anglure (1988) 'Penses le feminin chamanique ou le tiers-sex des chamanes Inuit', *Recherches Amérindiennes au Québec*, 18: 19–50.

Sanday, P. (1981) *Female Power and Male Dominance: on the Origins of Sexual Inequality*, Cambridge: Cambridge University Press.

Sassaman, K. E. (1992) 'Lithic technology and the hunter-gatherer sexual division of labor', *North American Archeologist*, 13.3: 249–62.

Scott, E. (1992) 'Images and contexts of infants and infant burials: some thoughts on some cross-cultural evidence', *Archaeological Review from Cambridge*, 11.1: 77–92.

Scott, E. M. (1991) 'A feminist approach to historical archaeology: eighteenth-century fur trade society at Michilimackinac', *Historical Archaeology*, 25.4: 42–53.

Schulting, R. (1996) 'Antlers, bone pins and flint blades: the mesolithic cemeteries of Téviec and Hoëdic, Brittany', *Antiquity*, 70: 335–50.

Segal, L. (1990) *Slow Motion: Changing Masculinities, Changing Men*, London: Virago.

Sekules, V. (1987) 'Women and art in England in the thirteenth and fourteenth centuries', in J. Alexander and P. Binski (eds) *Art in Plantagenet England 1200–1400*, 41–8. London: Weidenfeld and Nicholson.

Shahar, S. (1990) *Childhood in the Middle Ages*, London: Routledge.

——(1997) *Growing Old in the Middle Ages*, London: Routledge.

Shanks, M. and Tilley, C. (1987a) *Reconstructing Archaeology: Theory and Practice*, Cambridge: Cambridge University Press.

——(1987b) *Social Theory and Archaeology*, Cambridge: Polity Press.

Shilling, C. (1993) *The Body and Social Theory*, London: Sage.

Silverblatt, I. (1988) 'Women in states', *Annual Review of Anthropology*, 17: 427–60.

Silverman, I. and Eals, M. (1992) 'Sex differences in spatial abilities: evolutionary theory and data', in J. H. Barkow, L. Cosmides and J. Tooby (eds) *The Adapted Mind: Evolutionary Psychology and the Generation of Culture*, 533–49. Oxford: Oxford University Press.

Small, D. B. (1991) 'Initial study of the structure of women's seclusion in the archaeological past', in D. Walde and N. D. Willows (eds) *The Archaeology of Gender*, 336–42. Calgary: University of Calgary Archaeological Association.

Smyser, H. M. (1956) 'The domestic background to Troilus and Criseyde', *Speculum*, 31: 297–315.

Sørensen, M. L. S. (1988) 'Is there a feminist contribution to archaeology?', *Archaeological Review from Cambridge*, 7.1: 9–20.

——(1991) 'The construction of gender through appearance', in D. Walde and N. D. Willows (eds) *The Archaeology of Gender*, 121–29. Calgary: University of Calgary Archaeological Association.

——(1992) 'Gender archaeology and Scandinavian Bronze Age studies', *Norwegian Archaeological Review*, 25.1: 31–49.

Spector, J. (1983) 'Male/female task differentiation among the Hidatsa: toward the development of an archaeological approach to the study of gender', in P. Albers and B. Medicine (eds) *The Hidden Half*, 77–99. Washington DC: University Press of America.

Sperling, S. and Beyene, Y. (1997) 'A pound of biology and a pinch of culture or a pinch of biology and a pound of culture? The necessity of integrating biology and culture in reproductive studies', in L. D. Hager (ed.) *Women in Human Evolution*, 137–52. London: Routledge.

Stein, E. (ed.) (1990) *Forms of Desire: Sexual Orientation and the Social Constructionist Controversy*, London: Routledge.

Strasser, S. and Kronsteiner, R. (1993) 'Women in the field: reflections on a never-ending journey', in T. del Valle (ed.) *Gendered Anthropology*, 162–76. London: Routledge.

Stalsberg, A. (1991) 'Women as actors in North European Viking age trade', in R. Samson (ed.) *Social Approaches to Viking Studies*, 75–86. Glasgow: Cruithne.

Strathern, M. (1988) *The Gender of the Gift: Problems with Women and Problems with Society in Melanesia*, Berkeley CA: University of California Press.

——(1992) *Reproducing the Future: Anthropology, Kinship and the New Reproductive Technologies*, London: Routledge.

Talalay, L. E. (1994) 'A feminist boomerang: the great goddess of great prehistory', *Gender and History*, 6.2: 165–83.

Taylor, C. (1991) 'Garden archaeology: an introduction', in A. E. Brown (ed.) *Garden Archaeology*, 1–5. London: Council for British Archaeology.

Taylor, C., Everson, P. and Wilson-North, R. (1990) 'Bodiam Castle, Sussex', *Medieval Archaeology*, 34: 155–7.

Taylor, T. (1996) *The Prehistory of Sex: Four Million Years of Human Sexual Culture*, London: Fourth Estate.

Tcherkezoff, S. (1993) 'The illusion of dualism in Samoa: "Brothers-and-sisters" are not "men-and women"', in T. Del Valle (ed.) *Gendered Anthropology*, 54–87. London: Routledge.

Thomas, J. (1996) *Time, Culture and Identity: An Interpretive Archaeology*, London: Routledge.

Thompson, M. W. (1985) *Pickering Castle, Yorkshire*, London: English Heritage.

Tilley, C. (1994) *A Phenomenology of Landscape: Places, Paths and Monuments*, Oxford: Berg.

Tong, R. (1989) *Feminist Thought: a Comprehensive Introduction*, London: Routledge.

Townsend, P. K. (1995) 'The washed and the unwashed: women's life-cycle rituals among the Saniyo-Hiyowe of East Sepik Province, Papua New Guinea', in N. C. Lutkehaus and P. B. Roscoe (eds) *Gender Rituals*, 165–82. London: Routledge.

Treherne, P. (1995) 'The warrior's beauty: the masculine body and self-identity in Bronze-Age Europe', *Journal of European Archaeology*, 3.1: 105–44.

Trigger, B. G. (1989) *A History of Archaeological Thought*, Cambridge: Cambridge University Press.

Tringham, R. (1991) 'Households with faces: the challenge of gender in prehistoric architectural remains', in J. M. Gero and M. W. Conkey (eds) *Engendering Archaeology*, 93–131. Oxford: Blackwell.

Turner, B. S. (1995) 'Aging and identity: some reflections on the somatization of the self', in M. Featherstone and A. Wernick (eds) *Images of Aging: Cultural Representations of Later Life*, 227–60. London: Routledge.

——(1996) *The Body and Society*, London: Sage.

Turner, V. (1969) *The Ritual Process: Structure and Anti-Structure*, Ithaca NY: Cornell University Press.

Van Gennep, A. (1960) [1908] *The Rites of Passage*, trans. M. B. Vizedom and G. L. Caffee, Chicago IL: University of Chicago Press.

Vida, M. C. (1998) 'The Italian scene: approaches to the study of gender', in R. Whitehouse (ed.) *Gender and Italian Archaeology. Challenging the Stereotypes*, 15–22. London: Accordia Specialist Studies on Italy, Volume 7.

Vida Navarro, M. C. (1992) 'Warriors and weavers: sex and gender in early Iron Age graves from Pontecagnano', *The Accordia Research Papers*, 3: 67–99.

Wadley, L. (ed.) (1997) *Our Gendered Past: Archaeological Studies of Gender in Southern Africa*, Johannesburg: Witwatersrand University Press.

Walde, D. and Willows, N. D. (eds) (1991) *The Archaeology of Gender: Proceedings of the 22nd Annual Chacmool Conference*, Calgary: Archaeological Association of the University of Calgary.

Wall, D. D. (1994) *The Archaeology of Gender: Separating the Spheres in Urban America*, New York: Plenum Press.

Ward, J. C. (1992) *English Noblewomen in the Later Middle Ages*, London: Longman.

Washburn, S. L. and Lancaster, C. S. (1968) 'The evolution of hunting', in R. Lee and I. DeVore (eds) *Man the Hunter*, 293–303. Chicago IL: Aldine.

Watson, P. J. and Kennedy, M. C. (1991) 'The development of horticulture in the Eastern Woodlands of North America: women's role', in J. M. Gero and M. W. Conkey (eds) *Engendering Archaeology*, 255–75. Oxford: Blackwell.

Weedon, C. (1987) *Feminist Practice and Post-structuralist Theory*, Oxford: Blackwell.

Whelan, M. K. (1991) 'Gender and historical archaeology: Eastern Dakota patterns in the 19th century', *Historical Archaeology*, 25.4: 17–32.

Whitehead, H. (1981) 'The bow and the burden strap: a new look at institutionalized homosexuality in Native North America', in S. B. Ortner and H. Whitehead (eds) *Sexual Meanings: the Cultural Construction of Gender and Sexuality*, 80–115. Cambridge: Cambridge University Press.

Wilson, M. (1951) *Good Company: a Study of Nyakyusa Age Villages*, Oxford: Oxford University Press.

Wittig, M. (1982) 'The category of sex', *Feminist Issues*, 2.2: 63–8.

Wright, R. P. (1991) 'Women's labor and pottery production in prehistory', in J. M. Gero and M. W. Conkey (eds) *Engendering Archaeology*, 194–223. Oxford: Blackwell.

——(1996a) 'Gendered ways of knowing in archaeology', in R. P. Wright (ed.) *Gender and Archaeology*, 1–19. Philadelphia PA: University of Pennsylvania Press.

——(1996b) 'Technology, gender and class: worlds of difference in Ur III Mesopotamia', in R. P. Wright (ed.) *Gender and Archaeology*, 79–110. Philadelphia PA: University of Pennsylvania Press.

Wright, R. P. (ed.) (1996) *Gender and Archaeology*, Philadelphia PA: University of Pennsylvania Press.

Wylie, A. (1985) 'The reaction against analogy', *Advances in Archaeological Method and Theory*, 63–111.

——(1991a) 'Feminist critiques and archaeological challenges', in D. Walde and N. D. Willows (eds) *The Archaeology of Gender*, 17–23. Calgary: University of Calgary Archaeological Association.

——(1991b) 'Gender theory and the archaeological record: why is there no archaeology of gender?' in J. M. Gero and M. W. Conkey (eds) *Engendering Archaeology*, 31–54. Oxford: Blackwell.

——(1992a) 'Feminist theories of social power: some implications for a processual archaeology', *Norwegian Archaeological Review*, 25.1: 51–68.

——(1992b) 'The interplay of evidential constraints and political interests: recent archaeological research on gender', *American Antiquity*, 59: 15–35.

Yates, T. (1993) 'Frameworks for an archaeology of the body', in C. Tilley (ed.) *Interpretative Archaeology*, 31–72. Oxford: Berg.

Yentsch, A. (1991) 'Engendering visible and invisible ceramic artifacts, especially dairy vessels', *Historical Archaeology*, 25.4: 132–55.

Zihlman, A. L. (1978) 'Women in evolution. Part II: subsistence and social organisation among early hominids', *Signs: Journal of Women in Culture and Society*, 4.1: 4–20.

——(1997) 'The paleolithic glass ceiling: women in human evolution', in L. D. Hager (ed.) *Women in Human Evolution*, 91–113. London: Routledge.

Name index

Subject index

Printed in the United States
94880LV00002B/658/A

9 780415 216005